ROMANCE MONOGRAPHS, INC.
Number 25

STÉPHANE MALLARMÉ
TWENTIETH-CENTURY CRITICISM
(1901-1971)

ROMANCE MONOGRAPHS, INC.
Number 25

STÉPHANE MALLARMÉ
TWENTIETH-CENTURY CRITICISM
(1901-1971)

BY

D. HAMPTON MORRIS

UNIVERSITY, MISSISSIPPI
ROMANCE MONOGRAPHS, INC.
1 9 7 7

PRINTED IN SPAIN

IMPRESO EN ESPAÑA

I.S.B.N. 84-399-6423-4

DEPÓSITO LEGAL: V. 942 - 1977

ARTES GRÁFICAS SOLER, S. A. - JÁVEA, 28 - VALENCIA (8) - 1977

Library of Congress Cataloging in Publication Data

Morris, Drewry Hampton, 1945-
    Stéphane Mallarmé, twentieth-century criticism, 1901-1971.

    (Romance monographs; no. 25)
    Includes indexes.

    1. Mallarmé, Stéphane, 1842-1898—Bibliography. I. Title.

Z8545.M76   1977   [PQ2344]   016.841'8   77-708

ACKNOWLEDGEMENTS

I would like to offer here my appreciation to the Smith Fund Committee, University of North Carolina at Chapel Hill, and the Grant-in-Aid Committee, Auburn University, for enabling me to obtain necessary research materials; to Pattie B. McIntyre and her staff, Humanities Reference Department, Louis Round Wilson Library, University of North Carolina at Chapel Hill, and Ruth G. Fourier and her staff, Humanities Division, Ralph Brown Draughon Library, Auburn University, for helping me to find many an elusive item; to the Interlibrary Loan Services of the Wilson and Draughon Libraries, particularly Frances M. Honour and David N. King of the latter institution, for obtaining books and articles from often distant shelves; and to Alfred G. Engstrom, Alumni Distinguished Professor of French, University of North Carolina at Chapel Hill, and Dorothy M. DiOrio, Associate Professor and Head, Department of Foreign Languages, Auburn University, for providing me with their constant wise counsel and inspiration.

Familiae meae

CONTENTS

PREFACE

THE PRESENT STUDY is an attempt to provide scholars with a convenient reference to twentieth-century Mallarmé criticism (1901-1971). It does not claim to be exhaustive. Such a work would involve literally thousands of items, many of which would concern only occasional references to Mallarmé or purely biographical and bibliographical data.

This bibliography offers a listing of books and articles containing significant criticism of Stéphane Mallarmé and his work. With a few exceptions, daily and weekly periodicals have been omitted, but major journals and reviews containing articles on Mallarmé are included. Most items are followed by commentaries as to the nature, subject, scope, and approach of the book or article in question, including references to reviews where appropriate. Generally, exegesis of individual poems is not annotated, since overall indications on this type of criticism can be misleading.

Preceding the bibliography, the reader will find an introduction considering the general development of twentieth-century Mallarmé studies: basic trends, areas of interest, changes in attitude, critical approaches, etc. The following points outline further details concerning the method of bibliographical presentation:

a. Except in direct quotations, Mallarmé is referred to as M.

b. References are in chronological order according to dates of publication, arranged alphabetically by author within the year. In every case an attempt was made to consult the original edition of books, and where this was not possible, the entry gives bibliographical data on the first and later editions.

c.   Those items that could not be located and verified *de visu* have been marked with an asterisk (*). Some of these references may represent incomplete or inaccurate bibliographical information furnished by other bibliographies consulted.

d.   The bibliography is concluded by 1) an alphabetical index of authors, editors of critical editions, and translators and 2) a cross-reference subject index of entries.

I. INTRODUCTION

TODAY STÉPHANE MALLARMÉ is regarded as one of the greatest French poets, a precursor of modern poetry whose theories of language and literature were well ahead of his time. But this was not always so. During the last years of the nineteenth century, unfavorable critics often ridiculed Mallarmé as either a "clever hoaxer" or as a "madman." In spite of the efforts of "Mallarmistes" to counter these charges, notably Albert Mockel's *Stéphane Mallarmé: un héros* (Paris: Mercure de France, 1899), this negative attitude prevailed well into the twentieth century. In fact, it was not until 1945 that Henri Mondor, Mallarmé's biographer, could state with assurance that, after years of mockery and derision, "la gloire de Stéphane Mallarmé est l'une des plus pures" and that the poet could at last take his place "de premier rang, avec Baudelaire et Rimbaud" (349). [1] Thereafter, critical appreciation of Mallarmé and his works grew steadily year by year. This introductory essay reviews the development of Mallarmé criticism in the twentieth century, taking into consideration changes in attitude, critical approaches, highlights, and special areas of interest.

Twentieth-century Mallarmé scholarship can be divided into seven periods corresponding roughly with the decades: 1901-1911, 1912-1921, 1922-1931, 1932-1941, 1942-1951, 1952-1961 and 1962-1971. The reason for beginning the second period with 1912 instead of 1911 will be made apparent later.

---

[1] Throughout the Introduction numerical references to the bibliographical entries in Part II are given in parentheses.

1. *1901-1911*

Twentieth-century criticism of Mallarmé began where nineteenth century criticism ended — in an unresolved battle between "Mallarmistes" and "anti-Mallarmistes." In the first year of the century the most serious criticism of Mallarmé came from outside France. In *Zeitgenössische Franzozen* (4), the German critic Max Nordau called Mallarmé a "lamentable eunuch" with a "weak mind" who only had "moments of versification." In 1903, a French critic, Adolphe Retté, supported Nordau's opinion by stating that "si Mallarmé avait été réellement un des ces esprits exceptionnels qui marquent à leur empreinte toute une génération, on nous eût révélé en quoi consistaient ses leçons" (12). The most serious criticism came from Jean-Marc Bernard, who attacked Mallarmé for his "literary sterility" and his obscurity, stating that he was actually incapable of poetry and was only a "dilettante épris de toute beauté" (18). Léon Bocquet published a brief article seconding Bernard's opinions (23).

But Mallarmé was not without his champions. In *Le Problème du style* (7), Remy de Gourmont openly defended him against the most serious charge of his captious critics that his poetry was "obscure" and could not be understood. Gourmont, believing that the "hermetic" aspect of Mallarmé's works had been inordinately exaggerated, replied: "...il est le poète de la grâce et de la limpidité matinale." In 1909, Gourmont again sought to mitigate the criticism of obscurity, proclaiming that Mallarmé's "œuvre contient plus d'une page difficile, soit... mais les vers limpides ou opalins, les poèmes doucement lumineux et parfois rouges d'un incendie rapide sont les plus nombreux." And further, Gourmont went so far as to state that *Le Tombeau de Charles Baudelaire* "est aussi clair pour moi que *le Lac,* et beaucoup plus que *la Tristesse d'Olympio*" (28).

However, all of these protestations of "clarity" in Mallarmé's works were to no avail. The fact that many of Mallarmé's poems and prose writings were literary enigmas upon first and subsequent readings did not disappear. Critics soon began to realize that there was much more to Mallarmé that only careful study and exegesis could illuminate. André Gide, for example, readily accepted Mallarmé's obscurity as a necessary element of *poésie pure* and stated that, to be understood, Mallarmé's works require "une très lente et progressive initiation" (9).

After Bernard published an article attacking Mallarmé in the *Société Nouvelle* (22), it was Gide who accepted the challenge and counter-attacked Bernard with an article in the *Nouvelle Revue Française* (27). This was perhaps the most serious confrontation between detractors and supporters of Mallarmé; however, all of this verbal battle did little to establish any critical value of Mallarmé's poetry. Rather, it degenerated quickly into an *argumentum ad hominem*.

Other significant items in this period are Pierre Jaudon's article in *La Plume* (8) considering similarities between Mallarmé and Victor Hugo — the first of many such studies comparing Mallarmé with another author; Catulle Mendès' brief essay in *Le Mouvement poétique français de 1867 à 1900* (11), in which Mendès states that he was among the first to recognize Mallarmé's poetic genius; Henry Roujon's commentary in which he calls Mallarmé "un saint" (25); the first thematic study of Mallarmé's poetry, Paul Delior's "La Femme et le sentiment de l'amour chez Stéphane Mallarmé" (30); and André Barre's quite perceptive and appreciative essay discussing in detail Mallarmé's poetic method (32).

2. *1912-1921*

The year 1912 is the most momentous in the history of Mallarmé studies, for this was the year that Albert Thibaudet published *La Poésie de Stéphane Mallarmé* (40), marking the beginning of serious criticism of Mallarmé and his work. Opposition to Mallarmé was still strong at this period, particularly by "university scholarship." Thibaudet's thesis on Mallarmé was rejected by the Sorbonne as "une plaisanterie de mauvais goût"; and, when the publishers refused his manuscript, Thibaudet had to publish his text at his own expense (see 122).

It was fortunate for Mallarmé scholars that Thibaudet did so, for his book did much to establish Mallarmé as a respected French poet. Thibaudet's sober, meticulous scholarship and criticism demonstrated that standard critical methods could be applied to Mallarmé's works as well as to those by Jean Racine or other "classical" authors. Leaving aside biographical consideration, Thibaudet discussed in detail the poetical forms and elements of Mallarmé's poetry and offered intelligent explications of many of his poems (particularly *Hérodiade, L'Après-midi d'un faune, Prose pour des Esseintes,* and *Un Coup de dés*).

In spite of the admirable efforts of Thibaudet, the Mallarmiste and anti-Mallarmiste conflict raged on. In 1913, Jean-Marc Bernard published another unfavorable article in which he stated that Mallarmé "n'a point créé une œuvre littéraire véritable, ni ne pouvait le faire" (41). Gustave Lanson's *Histoire de la littérature française* (53) included only three references to Mallarmé, and the poet is characterized therein as "un artiste incomplet, inférieur, qui n'est pas arrivé à s'exprimer." And Henri Ghéon, reviving the charge that Mallarmé was no more than a "hoaxer," stated in an article in *Ecrits Nouveaux*: "En somme, on se demande s'il a jamais pris au sérieux une seule idée pour elle-même et s'il a cessé un moment de se moquer de soi et des autres . . ." (66).

Remy de Gourmont remained one of Mallarmé's faithful supporters. In the fourth volume of his *Promenades littéraires* (38), published in 1912, Gourmont again defended Mallarmé's obscurity: "On lui reprocha comme un crime l'obscurité de quelques-uns de ses vers, sans tenir compte de toute la partie limpide de son œuvre. . . ." And comparing Mallarmé's poetic technique to that of the Impressionist painters, Gourmont calls Mallarmé the "Claude Monet of poetry." Likewise, Henri de Régnier protested that although "les vers de Stéphane Mallarmé sont souvent obscurs . . . ils ne sont jamais inintelligibles" (47). In *Princes de l'esprit* (62), Camile Mauclair went even further in defending Mallarmé against the charge of obscurity: "L'obscurité de Mallarmé ne provient donc que du degré d'inattention qu'on apporterait à le lire."

It is of interest that, after years of proclaiming clarity in Mallarmé's works, in a complete about-face, Gourmont finally admitted in the fifth volume of his *Promenades littéraires* (45) that most of Mallarmé's poems are definitely obscure and cannot be easily understood by merely considering his poetic procedure. But Gourmont did not stop here. Now representing the school that appreciated Mallarmé's compositions only for the "pure sensations of poetry" that they afford, Gourmont rejected any explication of Mallarmé's works, stating his belief that "il n'y a pas grand profit ni esthétique ni intellectuel, à analyser de trop près un langage, quand il s'est voulu hermétique. La valeur d'une pensée est dans son expression."

Other important items within this period were Jean Dornis' critical appreciation of Mallarmé's rôle in the development of modern poetry (37); Jean de Cours' study of elements of synesthesia in his verse (51); a thematic study by Paul Escoube discussing women and expressions of love in his poetry (43); another comparative study, "Gongora et Mallarmé," by Zdislas Milner (67); and A. Zerega-Fombona's consideration of Mallarmé's influence upon Spanish poetry (60). All of these studies indicated that Mallarmé was slowly, but surely, becoming recognized as an outstanding poet worthy of more than casual critical attention.

3. *1922-1931*

This period showed a remarkable increase in critical activity. A principal reason for this was the commemoration of the twenty-fifth anniversary of Mallarmé's death in 1923, which inspired numerous laudatory articles published mainly in periodicals devoted entirely or in part to Mallarmé (see 76, 86, 94, and 117). Also, it was during this decade that Mallarmé's poetry began to appear in translation. In England, Roger Fry (72) and Arthur Ellis were notable translators; in Italy, Angelo Marasca (132); and in Germany, Franz Julius Nobiling.

Another important achievement for Mallarmé studies was René Lalou's very favorable treatment of Mallarmé in his *Histoire de la littérature française contemporaine* (98), in which, indicating that Mallarmé was at last formally recognized for his contributions to the development of French poetry, Lalou stated that Mallarmé's influence "sur l'évolution symboliste fut grande. Elle ne tint pas seulement à son œuvre.... Parmi les poètes de la fin du XIXe siècle, Mallarmé est apparu revêtu d'un prestige héroïque."

The publication of *Igitur, ou la Folie d'Elbehnon* (110) in 1925 by Edmond Bonniot, Mallarmé's son-in-law, from manuscripts left by the poet was another impetus for Mallarmé studies. This was the first of several posthumous publications of Mallarmé's works which were often no more than a confused mass of papers and notes intelligible only to Mallarmé himself. However, years of painstaking analysis and research have enabled scholars to reconstitute as nearly as possible Mallarmé's original intentions and ideas behind these compositions.

Ironically, the publication of these volumes was contrary to the wishes of Mallarmé, who had instructed his wife and daughter to burn all of his manuscripts and notes immediately after his death:

"Brûlez, par conséquent: il n'y a pas là d'héritage littéraire, mes pauvres enfants. Ne soumettez même pas à l'appréciation de quelqu'un: ou refusez toute ingérence curieuse ou amicale... croyez que ce devait être très beau." It is indeed fortunate for Mallarmistes that the poet's last wishes were not carried out to the letter and that these papers were preserved from what would otherwise have been a tragic loss.

The republication of Thibaudet's *La Poésie de Stéphane Mallarmé* (122) in 1926 indicated a growing acceptance of Mallarmé as a significant French poet; and, with his reputation's becoming more or less established, Mallarmé studies began to abandon polemics and branch out in different directions. This period saw the real beginning of Mallarméan exegesis: the detailed analysis of Mallarmé's texts. In 1926, Camille Soula published the first of these studies, which were little more than "literal explications" or paraphrases of Mallarmé's works, often as enigmatic as the originals (see 119, 120, 159, 171). Soon others, notably the German scholars Victor Klemperer and Franz Julius Nobiling, pursued this area of interest (see 129, 153, 154, 167).

Scholars also began to investigate thoroughly the various influences of other authors upon Mallarmé, especially those of Charles Baudelaire (81), Edgar Allan Poe (93, 150), and Richard Wagner (78, 168, 172). André Levinson wrote the first study treating Mallarmé's conception of the other arts, "Stéphane Mallarmé, métaphysicien du ballet" (99). Charles Mauron's article on Mallarmé and Taoism (102) initiated another direction in Mallarmé criticism: the examination of Mallarmé's personal philosophy and its connection with both Western and Oriental thought. Denis Saurat's article on *Don du poème* continued this approach by suggesting the influence of Kabbalistic philosophy upon Mallarmé (170).

It is important to point out that, in spite of the apparent victory of the Mallarmistes, anti-Mallarméan sentiment had not completely disappeared and indeed would not for years to come. As late as 1930, Francis Jammes advanced in his *Leçons poétiques* (166) that "Stéphane Mallarmé n'est qu'un faune qui, tour à tour, se déguise en professeur d'anglais et en yachtman, jamais en poète." In the same year, Edmond Bonniot felt called upon to defend his father-in-law from the criticism that he was an "ivory-tower" poet, entirely withdrawn form life: "Mallarmé n'était pas le poète irréel, détaché du sol, vivant dans l'abstraction que l'on pourrait supposer" (162).

4. *1932-1941*

This decade saw a greatly accelerated development in all the branches of Mallarmé studies previously mentioned, but especially in comparative studies, which ceased to be mere parallels or indications of similarities and became investigations into the direct influence of other authors upon Mallarmé and into the possible sources for many of the themes found in his poetry. In 1932, André Fontainas pointed out Hugo's influence on Mallarmé's works including *Un Coup de dés* (174). The following year Thibaudet signaled Hugo's influence on Mallarmé's *juvenilia* (197). Other authors considered in this context were Poe (177, 255), Samuel Taylor Coleridge (200), Leconte de Lisle (234), John Keats (235, 267), Théodore de Banville (267), Chateaubriand (267), and Racine (287). In this same general category was a study concerning Wagner's influence upon Mallarmé's aesthetics by Isabelle de Wyzéwa (201).

There were only two thematic studies during this period: Charles E. Rietmann's catalogue and analysis of images of rest and movement in Mallarmé's writings (182) and Kurt Wais's investigation of Mallarmé's use of the "sea" as a poetic theme (254).

During this decade a new type of Mallarmé criticism appeared with the advent of stylistic studies. In 1936, Walter Naumann published the first such investigation, *Der Sprachgebrauch Mallarmés* (225), which treated in detail Mallarmé's word usage in his poetry. This was soon followed by Deborah A. K. Aish's meticulous examination of the Mallarméan metaphor, its themes, forms, and the rôle it plays within the entire structure of Mallarmé's poetic system (237).

In Spain, Alfonso Reyes published translations of much of Mallarmé's poetry (181, 249); in Germany, the *Mallarmé Gedichte* of Nobiling offered German versions of his *Poésies* (247); in England, Roger Fry's translations of thirty-six poems with commentaries by Charles Mauron were published in 1936 (223); and in Italy, C. Paladini presented translations of poems and prose writings which he called *Interpretazione di Mallarmé* (233).

Until 1940, German scholarship continued to dominate the field of exegesis with analyses such as those of Nobiling and Theophil Spoerri (see 179, 180, 194, 210). But with the publication of Emilie Noulet's *L'Œuvre poétique de Stéphane Mallarmé* (271) in 1940, French-language exegesis finally came of age. The second part of Noulet's work is devoted to detailed explications of Mallarmé's poems taken in chronological order. These studies showed quite an advance over Soula's "paraphrases" (see p. 18).

Investigation of Mallarmé's personal philosophy flourished within this period. In 1933, Hasye Cooperman's *The Aesthetics of Stéphane Mallarmé* (187) offered a meticulous study of Mallarmé's aesthetic principles based upon the thesis that "the aesthetics of Stéphane Mallarmé was not an innovation; at its least it was an adaptation of the doctrines of Richard Wagner, — ideas borrowed and assimilated." [2] In *L'Expérience poétique* (250), André Rolland de Renéville considered the relationship between Mallarmé's thought and Oriental philosophy, including the Kabbalah; and André Bernard found definite parallels between Mallarmé's philosophy and Hindu thought (285).

As noted above, anti-Mallarméan sentiment died a slow death, vestiges of it remaining until 1952. In this period, its most outspoken representative was Léon Levrault, who stated in 1933 that Mallarmé was "le mystificateur — ou le demi-fou — qui amena des poètes bien doués à écrire tant de poèmes ridicules" (192).

As for the Mallarmistes, Paul Valéry remained a true champion of his former master. In his article, "Je disais quelquefois à Stéphane Mallarmé" (184), he boldly defended Mallarmé's obscurity by proclaiming that an absolute, objective "explication" of Mallarmé's work is impossible and is indeed contrary to Mallarmé's aesthetic principles: "L'œuvre de Mallarmé exigeant de chacun une interprétation assez personnelle, n'appelait, n'attachait à soi que des intelligences séparées, conquises une à une, et de celles qui fuient vivement l'unanimité." General French criticism was also beginning to accept Mallarmé wholeheartedly for his contributions to the development of poetry. For example, in his *De Baudelaire au surréalisme* (196), Marcel Raymond saw the poet's major contribution to poetry as consisting "surtout à avoir porté la lumière de la conscience sur un instinct

---

[2] For an opposing viewpoint, see 684.

auquel s'abandonnaient spontanément, avant lui, la plupart des grands poètes."

Other critics began to recognize Mallarmé's salutary influence on other national literatures. Alfonso Reyes discussed Mallarmé's influence in Spain (181), and Alan Rowland Chisholm investigated Mallarmé's influence upon Australian poetry, particularly that of Christopher Brennan (241). It must be noted here also that, although Benedetto Croce admired Mallarmé and his work, he advised against the application of Mallarmé's poetical theories to Italian poetry (188); however, this admonition did not prevent such a development, as we shall see later.

The most momentous achievement of this period occurred near its end: the publication of Kurt Wais's *Mallarmé* (256) in 1938, Charles Mauron's *Mallarmé l'obscur* (282), and the definitive biography of Mallarmé by Henri Mondor (284) in 1941. Wais's *Mallarmé* marked another milestone in the history of Mallarmé criticism. Whereas Thibaudet's treatment of Mallarmé was synchronic, taking all of Mallarmé's writings as a whole, with little consideration of evolution, Wais's study was diachronic, taking into account as much of the biographical data on Mallarmé as was known at the time and correlating these facts with their effects upon the genesis and composition of individual works. Wais was also the first critic to signal the importance of the death of Mallarmé's American friend Harriet Smyth in the thematic development of his poetry.

Mauron's work was the first in a series of his psychocritical studies in which he insisted upon the importance of Mallarmé's traumatic losses of his mother and sister upon the genesis of his poetry. Mauron interpreted Mallarmé's poetry from this critical standpoint by a comparative examination of the texts, investigating the significance of recurring interrelated metaphors and poetical themes.

Until the appearance of Mondor's *Vie de Mallarmé* in 1941, biographical knowledge about the poet was incomplete and furnished only in piecemeal fashion by his *Autobiographie* (100), his daughter (117), and friends who knew him well, especially the "Mardistes" who attended his Tuesday *soirées*. Henri Mondor was a physician by profession who became interested in collecting Mallarmé's manuscripts, letters, and other *Mallarméana* as a pastime. Mondor's fascination with the poet grew until he finally decided to devote a major portion of his life to the publication of numerous articles, essays, and books concerning Mallarmé and his work. These include the supplemental volumes to his biography in which Mondor offered quite detailed information about the poet's early years, family life and social life (see 333, 574, and 747). The *Vie de Mallarmé* gave a crucial impetus to the development of Mallarmé criticism. Its new data inspired many scholars to approach Mallarmé who had not done so previously, and several critics, notably Wais, later revised their studies in order to incorporate the new material from Mondor's biography (see 256).

5. *1942-1951*

This decade was an especially memorable period for Mallarmé studies, for it includes the commemoration of two important dates: the centenary of Mallarmé's birth in 1942 and the fiftieth anniversary of his death in 1948. Throughout the decade numerous commemorative studies were published, particularly in reviews and special volumes devoted to an "Hommage à Mallarmé": *Stéphane Mallarmé: essais et témoignages* (299), Grange Woolley's *Stéphane Mallarmé* (311), *Le Point* (337), *Cahiers du Nord* (402), *Empreintes* (407), *L'Immagine* (417), and *Les Lettres* (419). [3]

As has been mentioned, it was at the midpoint of this period that Mondor was able to write with certainty that Mallarmé had at last achieved the glory he deserved (see p. 13). This is not to say, however, that anti-Mallarmé criticism had vanished. It held on persistently throughout the decade. In 1945, Julien Benda stated that Mallarmé was an excellent representative of *pure littérature* "devoid of any intelligence" (339). The year following, Denis Saurat included an unfavorable essay in his *Modern French Literature* (365), in which, although he recognized the genius of Mallarmé's literary vision, he proclaimed that "Mallarmé's great handicap is that he cannot write, either in prose or in poetry." Finally, Yvor Winters criticized Mallarmé severely in his *Defense of Reason* (400), published in 1947. [4]

In spite of this opposition, this was the decade of the Mallarmistes, and all areas of Mallarmé research received careful consideration. Well-known critics began to turn their attention to Mallarmé.

---

[3] It should be noted that the Second World War undoubtedly prevented the publication of even more items commemorating the poet's birth.

[4] For a recent refutation of Winters' critical remarks, see 947.

Albert-Marie Schmidt called Mallarmé "un saint laïque dont la gloire exemplaire ... ne cesse de s'accroître (308). In 1943, Maurice Blanchot began a series of essays devoted to Mallarmé (see 313, 354, and 447) in which he recognized Mallarmé's genius and originality, particularly in his extraordinary use of language: "Nul poète n'a plus fortement senti que tout poème, si mince qu'en fût le prétexte, était nécessairement engagé dans la création du langage poétique et peut-être de tout langage" (447). Others began to view Mallarmé as a "founder of a new national religion" (419), a "sorcerer" (419), a "grand prêtre et martyr du langage" (438), and a "ritualist," combining the rôles of poet, professor, and magician (510).

But perhaps the most significant indicator of Mallarmé's acceptance as an important figure in French literature is the considerable attention that he began to receive in the "manuals" and histories of French literature. The most noteworthy of mention here are Philippe Van Tieghem's *Les Grandes Doctrines littéraires en France* (371), Anna Balakian's *Literary Origins of Surrealism* (374), C. M. Bowra's *The Heritage of Symbolism* (376), and René Jasinski's *Histoire de la Littérature française* (390).

There were six notable general studies of Mallarmé within this period: Pierre Beausire's *Essai sur la poésie et la poétique de Mallarmé* (288), in which the author insists upon Mallarmé's uniqueness in the history of letters; Jean Fretet's psychoanalytical study (356), which presented the thesis that Mallarmé was a "manic-depressive schizophrenic";[5] Francis de Miomandre's *Mallarmé* (248), in which Miomandre continues the counter-attack of the Mallarmistes by attempting to dispel completely the legend of the poet's "literary impotency"; Jacques Gengoux's *Le Symbolisme de Mallarmé* (478), which offered analysis of most of Mallarmé's poetry; Charles Mauron's *Introduction à la psychanalyse de Mallarmé* (486), which investigated in more detail the thesis that he had presented in *Mallarmé l'obscur* (see p. 21); and, for the first time, a considerable Italian study on Mallarmé, Carlo Bo's *Mallarmé* (340).

Exegesis was the area of Mallarmé scholarship which received the most attention during this period. There were over thirty separate studies on individual poems, with *Un Coup de dés* being the favorite topic of discussion (see Subject Index under titles of individual poems

---

[5] For a refutation of this thesis, see 397.

for specific references). It was in this decade that French exegesis at
last caught up with German scholarship, and several Italian- and
English-language critics joined these ranks as well. Noteworthy exegetes of this period were: Antoine Adam, Charles Chassé, Robert
Greer Cohn, Gardner Davies, Jacques Duchesne-Guillemin, Wallace
Fowlie, Mario Luiz, Renato Mucci, and Emilie Noulet (see Author
Index for specific references). In this context, it is of interest that
several critics perceived that exegesis was getting somewhat "out of
hand." In his survey of Mallarmé criticism published in 1947 (383),
Gardner Davies reminded Mallarmé scholars that "whilst the few are
patiently pursuing this programme of research in the best traditions
of scholarship, others are busily confusing the issues...." And a few
years later, A. R. Chisholm warned against the danger of reading
too much into Mallarmé's poetry (see 505).

Other areas of critical interest which also made strides were the
stylistic studies, of which the most noteworthy was Jacques Schérer's
L'Expression littéraire dans l'œuvre de Mallarmé (395),[6] and the
thematic studies, of which the most extensive and perceptive was
Georges Poulet's article, "Espace et temps mallarméens" (488), the
first in a series of several essays concerning Mallarmé's conception
of space and time and its literary expression in his works.

Studies comparing Mallarmé with certain authors and attempts
to isolate specific sources continued throughout the decade. Mallarmé
was compared with Marcel Proust (294), Brennan (451), Pietro Bembo
(472), and Góngora (489). And sources were suggested from the works
of Théodore Aubanel and Frédéric Mistral (351); classical antiquity,
Keats, and Shelley (367); Louis Bouilhet, Thalès Bernard, and
Charles Nodier (372); Ovid, Virgil, Dante, and Hugo (424); William
Cullen Bryant (388); and Goethe (511). More general influences on
Mallarmé were also investigated: Villiers de l'Isle-Adam (325), Poe
(331, 469), and Wagner (496).

Additional essays considered Mallarmé's influence upon other
authors and literatures: Stefan George (338), Wallace Stevens (368),
Eugenio de Castro (379), Spanish literature (306, 419), English
literature (419), German literature (419), Portuguese literature (419),
and Italian literature (487).

---

[6] See also 330 and 344.

Consideration of Mallarmé's personal philosophy continued to attract the critics. There were studies concerning Mallarmé's relationship to Platonism (328); Edmund Husserl (342); Oriental philosophers, mystics, Kant, Hegel, Berkeley, and others (436); Oriental philosophy (481), and Schopenhauer (483). Guy Delfel's *L'Esthétique de Stéphane Mallarmé* (508) investigated Mallarmé's aesthetic principles, concluding that Mallarmé actually had no systematic aesthetic thought: "Plus qu'une 'esthétique', la pensée mallarméenne aboutit à une vue complète du monde strictement unifiée."

Another extremely important date for Mallarmé studies is the publication of the *Œuvres complètes* (346) by Mondor and G. Jean-Aubry in 1945. Before the appearance of this text, anyone desirous of studying Mallarmé's works as an *ensemble* had to gather together several volumes, many not readily available or *épuisés*, and locate rather obscure reviews and journals for variant versions of poems and prose works. In addition, the *Œuvres complètes* included previously unpublished material. However, as Jean-Pierre Richard points out in his *Univers imaginaire de Stéphane Mallarmé*, the title of this edition of Mallarmé's works is actually unjustified, as it does not in fact present the *complete* works. In his extensive bibliography, Richard offers a list of writings not included in the *Œuvres complètes* and their location in other publications (see 752). The *Œuvres complètes* were preceded and followed by many editions of Mallarmé's works with introductions and critical commentaries by Mallarmé scholars (see Author Index under "Mallarmé, Stéphane"), but the Mondor and Jean-Aubry edition remains today the most solid basis for all modern Mallarmé scholarship.

6. *1952-1961*

The beginning of this period saw the end of unfavorable criticism. Its last vestige appeared in 1952 in Romain Rolland's *Le Cloître de la rue d'Ulm* (541), which contained several seriously critical remarks concerning Mallarmé. From this point on, however, acceptance of Mallarmé as a great French poet was no longer challenged, at least in publication. An interesting indicator of this change in attitude was Paul Tuffrau's major revision of Lanson's treatment of Mallarmé in the *Histoire de la littérature française* (532). In the revised edition, Mallarmé is credited with having affirmed, "plus vigoureusement que

Baudelaire, la nécessité d'éliminer toutes les scories et de rechercher l'essence propre de la Poésie. . . ." And in 1960, Maurice Rat wrote an extremely laudatory essay on Mallarmé stating that "son incomparable mérite, c'est dans les poèmes les plus *liés* qu'on ait écrits en France, et qui n'ont d'égal dans la littérature latine et grecque que les odes d'Horace et de Callimaque, d'avoir *lié* ses rimes aux vertus du contexte, musical, sensoriel, idéal et symbolique, de l'œuvre" (727).

Almost every area of Mallarmé scholarship advanced considerably during the decade. Essays indicated the possible influence of Banville (524), Hugo (544), Louis Desnoyers (617), Poe (618 and 664), Gustave Flaubert (625), and Chateaubriand (630) upon the composition of Mallarmé's works. Mallarmé was compared with André Gide (554), Poe (586), Joubert (685), Voltaire (696), and Hofmannsthal (705). Mallarmé's influence on James Joyce was thoroughly investigated in 1956 by David Hayman (626) and in 1958 in a dissertation by J. D. Brickwood (661). In 1957, Olga Ragusa (657) published an excellent comprehensive study on Mallarmé's influence in Italy.

Mallarmé's personal philosophy was examined by Claude Ernoult (526), Georges Poulet (539), Robert Champigny (615), and John Senior (706); and several critics continued to consider Mallarmé's relationship to the other arts: the dance (537, 616), painting (531), music (538, 684, 710, 728), and the theater (718).

Thematic studies included examinations of Mallarmé's use of the following themes: sterility and virginity (546), "man's weakness for woman" (560), Hamlet (569, 590, 593), mirrors (687, 697), death (689), the sun (694), and, as an example of the extremes to which psychocriticism can be taken, Jean-Paul Weber presented the thesis that the numerous images of birds, wings, feathers, flight, etc., found in Mallarmé's poetry are the result of the poet's feelings of guilt for having participated as a young boy in the killing of small birds in their nests (see 731).

Curiously, stylistic studies *per se* all but disappeared during this period. There is only one notable study of this sort: Mallarmé's use of nautical vocabulary (640). Perhaps the principal reason for this *lacuna* is the consideration of this aspect of Mallarmé studies within the field of exegesis, which again attracted more and more critics each year.

Over fifty separate studies on Mallarmé's works were published during this period. In 1961, the periodical *L'Esprit Créateur* (736) devoted an issue to Mallarmé which contained several quite valuable essays, particularly interpretations of individual works. *Un Coup de dés* was still the favorite topic of discussion, followed by *L'Après-midi d'un faune* and *Hérodiade*; but the *Prose pour des Esseintes* also received special attention. Many new exegetes began to make themselves known, and again English-language critics made very significant contributions in this field: Lloyd James Austin, Alan Rowland Chisholm, Austin Gill, James R. Lawler, and Richard R. Miller.

Significant general studies of Mallarmé published in this period were those by Fowlie (550); Michaud (555); Chassé (565), who presented the thesis that the "key" to Mallarmé's poetry is Littré's dictionary;[7] Adile Ayda (588); Robert Goffin (623); Daniel Boulay (711); and Jean-Pierre Richard (752). English translations of Mallarmé's works were continued by Bradford Cook (619), Daisy Aldan (628), and C. F. MacIntyre (650).

Perhaps the most significant achievements of the entire decade were the publications of Mallarmé's *juvenilia* in Mondor's *Mallarmé lycéen* (574); Jacques Schérer's edition of *Le "Livre" de Mallarmé* (658), which presents drafts and notes for Mallarmé's grandiose literary project, to which the poet often referred as "the Book";[8] Gardner Davies' edition of *Les Noces d'Hérodiade* (701), the unfinished manuscript that Mallarmé intended for a long dramatic poem; and Jean-Pierre Richard's edition of *Pour un tombeau d'Anatole* (745), which consists of incomplete texts that Mallarmé began after the death of his eight-year-old son.

In 1959, Henri Mondor began the publication of Mallarmé's *Correspondance*. He had published extracts of letters by Mallarmé in *Propos sur la poésie* (348) in 1946, but the *Correspondance* began to offer the complete texts of Mallarmé's letters. The first volume (700) covered the period 1862-1871 and was co-edited by Jean-Pierre Richard. Subsequent volumes, edited by Mondor and L. J. Austin, covered the periods 1871-1885 (855) and 1886-1889 (993).

---

[7] For a challenge to this thesis, see 612.

[8] For an opposing viewpoint concerning Mallarmé's conception of the "Grand Œuvre," see 764.

7. 1962-1971

This was the first period entirely free of negative Mallarmé criticism. Mallarmé was internationally acclaimed as having made a major contribution to the development of not only French, but world literature. His influence was seen in the works of Brennan (763, 967), George (835), Walter Benjamin (996), and William Butler Yeats (1031), as well as in the writings of Alain Robbe-Grillet, Michel Butor, and other authors of the *nouveau roman* (836, 838), Claudel (892), the French symbolists (982), Valéry (988, 1036), and Aldous Huxley (1004).

On the other hand, the influence of others on Mallarmé continued to be investigated in detail: Poe (755, 800), Banville (784, 790, 818, 879), Wagner (791, 845, 962), Thomas De Quincey (809), Baudelaire (850, 906), Lamartine (858), Keats (1026), and Vigny (1043). And Mallarmé was compared with Novalis (802), Rainer Maria Rilke (898), Baudelaire (952), Jules Laforgue (975), Gottfried Benn (981), Théophile Gautier (1009), Proust (1027), Husserl (1066), and James Joyce (1075). Other scholars turned their interest to Mallarmé's opinions and influence on the theater (782, 815), music (882, 914), and the novel (1011).

Significant general studies in this period were those by Edward A. Bird (757), Alan Rowland Chisholm (764), Pierre Olivier Walzer (803), and Frederic Chase St. Aubyn (1005). There was only one edition of translations: Anthony Hartley's *Mallarmé* (852).

Thematic studies concerned themselves with the following themes and images: Hamlet (820), the *monstre d'or* (822), clowns (902), windows (925), *ennui* (1003), sterility (1013), and absence (1050). Stylistic and vocabulary studies were numerous (806, 811, 817, 828, 829, 830, 841, 876, 881, 957), and the most detailed of these was Pierre Missac's study (828) of Mallarmé's use of the preposition *à*.

Interpretations of Mallarmé's personal philosophy also continued to interest scholars. There were five general studies on this subject (819, 888, 889, 1015, 1033), and others treating specific areas of consideration: Orphism (807, 1017, 1073), Hinduism (905), alchemy (968), anarchism (983), occultism (995, 1048), Christianity (997), aesthetics (999), and mysticism (1048).

Exponents of contemporary approaches to criticism have not neglected Mallarmé. Jacques Derrida's "La double séance" (1029) is a "nouvelle critique" analysis of Mallarmé; Jean-Paul Sartre has offered an existentialist interpretation of the poet (1006); and, after announcing that almost every other possible critical approach had been attempted, Guy Michaud did not hesitate to present an astrological consideration of Mallarmé's personality (955).

In this decade another periodical, *Synthèses* (963), devoted an issue to Mallarmé studies with eighteen essays collected and edited by Emilie Noulet.

As in the last two periods, exegesis was the branch of Mallarmé scholarship that made the most advances. In this ten-year interval there were over a hundred separate studies on Mallarmé's works. *Un Coup de dés* still maintained its position as the favorite exegetical subject; but, surprisingly, *Autre Eventail de Mademoiselle Mallarmé,* which had passed practically unnoticed until this time, received the attention of seven scholars. In this period English-language exegesis began to dominate the field, particularly through the admirable efforts of the Australian Alan Rowland Chisholm, who has published over twenty exegetical studies.

The latest arrival on the scene of Mallarmé studies is the series *Documents Stéphane Mallarmé,* edited by Carl Paul Barbier (see 939, 1019, and 1051). This collection has published manuscripts, variant versions of poems, letters, little-known texts, and other valuable *Mallarméana* welcomed by Mallarmistes everywhere.

An especially interesting aspect of Mallarmé criticism is the unusually large number of non-native French critics who have been attracted to Mallarmé, particularly English-language scholars, grouped into what Professor Léon Cellier has called "l'Internationale des Mallarmistes." The following table presents the most notable members of this group and their national affiliations:

1) *Australia*
Lloyd James Austin
Alan Rowland Chisholm
Gardner Davies
James R. Lawler

2) *Belgium*
Robert Goffin
Emilie Noulet
Georges Poulet

3) *England*
Charles Chadwick
Austin Gill

4) *France*
Léon Cellier
Charles Chassé
Henri Mondor
Jean-Pierre Richard
Jacques Schérer

5) *Germany*   7) *Switzerland*
Walter Naumann   Claude Roulet
Franz Julius Nobiling   Pierre-Olivier Walzer
Kurt Wais
                                       8) *Turkey*
6) *Italy*   Adile Ayda
Mario Luzi
Renato Mucci   9) *United States*
Luigi di Nardis   Robert Greer Cohn
                                       Wallace Fowlie

Many reasons have been advanced for Mallarmé's international popularity. His attraction for numerous English language critics has been attributed to Mallarmé's interest in English as evidenced by his linguistic texts (*Les Mots anglais* and *Les Thèmes anglais*) and his translations of English writings, the most significant of which are, of course, the poems of Edgar Allan Poe. A quite plausible explanation for the world-wide interest in Mallarmé is that the difficulty of Mallarmé's texts tends to place all critics on a more or less equal level. It is almost as if Mallarmé's works were written in an "international language" and were thus a legitimate patrimony for all, regardless of language background.

This international congregation of Mallarmé critics reminds one of the society of poets that Mallarmé wanted to initiate and organize. Mallarmé wrote in a letter to Mistral, dated 1 November 1873: "L'Angleterre abonde dans notre visée. L'Italie de même. Mon cher ami, c'est tout simplement une franc-maçonnerie ou un compagnonnage. Nous sommes un certain nombre qui aimons une chose honnie [poetry]: il est bon qu'on se compte, voilà tout, et qu'on se connaisse, que les associés se lisent et que les voyageurs se voient. Tout cela, indépendamment de mille points de vue différents, qui ne le sont plus, du reste, après qu'on s'est étudié ou qu'on a causé." Although it is made up of critics, and not poets, the world-wide group of Mallarmistes is at least a partial fulfillment of Mallarmé's dream.

II. CRITICAL BIBLIOGRAPHY

1901

1. Brandes, Georg. *Samlede Skrifter*. Vol. 7. Copenhagen: Gyldendalske Boghandels Forlag, 1901.

    Essay entitled "Fransk Lyrik" includes a discussion of M. (pp. 264-268).

★2. Mauclair, Camille. *L'Art en silence*. Paris: Ollendorff, 1901. vii, 340p.

3. ———. "L'Esthétique de Stéphane Mallarmé." *Chronique des Livres*, 2 (1901), 7-13, 38-46, 89-95.

    Article defending M. against recent criticism.

4. Nordau, Max. *Zeitgenössische Franzozen: litteraturgeschichtliche Essays*. Berlin: Ernst Hoffmann, 1901. 357p.

    French edition: *Vus du dehors: essai de critique scientifique et philosophique sur quelques auteurs français contemporains*. Translated by Auguste Dietrich. Paris: Félix Alcan, Editeur, 1903. ii, 332p.
    Unfavorable criticism of M. Calling M. a "lamentable eunuque," Nordau says, "Stéphane Mallarmé en lui-même est très peu intéressant. Quand on commence à le lire, on s'étonne; puis on s'irrite. Ensuite on sourit, et plus tard on reste tout à fait indifférent.... Mallarmé était un débile d'esprit qui avait des moments de versification."

5. Régnier, Henri de. *Figures et caractères*. Paris: Mercure de France, 1901. 351p.

    Contains a general essay on M. (pp. 115-137). Believes that M. "fut, en nos temps, la représentation exacte et parfaite du

Poète, si son caractére consiste à la recherche exclusive de la Beauté et de la Vérité." Régnier admits that M. is an obscure author, but states that "il y a dans une page ou dans un vers de Stéphane Mallarmé tous les éléments nécessaires à sa clarté; seulement ils s'y trouvent épars, situés au lieu exact de leur utilité pour l'élégance graphique de la phrase."

1902

6. Calmettes, Fernand. *Un Demi-siècle littéraire: Leconte de Lisle et ses amis.* Paris: Motteroz, 1902. ii, 345p.

   Chapter 13 concerns M. and Leconte de Lisle's opinion of the younger poet.

7. Gourmont, Remy de. *Le Problème du style.* Paris: Société du Mercure de France, 1902. 328p.

   Contains several references to M. and says of the poet: "... il est le poète de la grâce et de la limpidité matinales; les idées ordinaires retrouvent par lui une fraîcheur qu'on ne croyait plus possible." Gourmont calls *Hérodiade* "le poème le plus pur, le plus transparent de la langue française."

8. Jaudon, Pierre. "Hugoliens et Mallarméens." *La Plume,* 1 (1902), 417-420.

   A comparative study of Hugo and M.

1903

9. Gide, André. *Prétextes: réflexions critiques sur quelques points de littérature et de morale.* Paris: Mercure de France, 1903.

   Later edition: 1947. 254p.
   Contains an essay *in memoriam* of M. (written in 1898). Gide foresees M.'s future glory in spite of contemporary derision and ridicule of the poet's writings. Calls for an edition of M.'s complete works (not published until 1945; see 346). States that "à part quelques poèmes admirables isolément... l'œuvre de Mallarmé demande, pour être comprise, une trés lente et progressive initiation."

10. Grierson, Francis. "Stéphane Mallarmé." *Atlantic Monthly,* 92 (1903), 839-843.

    Personal notes on Grierson's visits with M.

11. Mendès, Catulle. *Le Mouvement poétique français de 1867 à 1900*. Paris: Imprimerie Nationale, 1903. 340p.

> Contains a section on M. (pp. 135-141), whom Mendès calls "le plus délicieux des esprits, le plus aimable des âmes." Mendès states that he recognized early M.'s poetic genius. Indicates disapproval of *Igitur*, but concerning M.'s other works, says that "même les parties les plus obscures, les plus hermétiques de l'œuvre de Mallarmé réservent des surprises de charmes et de clarté; il y est, presque souvent, le délicieux génie en qui nous avions eu foi les premiers." M. is also included in the "Dictionnaire bibliographique et critique," which quotes various opinions on M.

12. Retté, Adolphe. *Le Symbolisme: anecdotes et souvenirs*. Paris: A. Messein, 1903. 277p.

> Contains a chapter entitled "Les Mardis de Mallarmé" in which Retté severely criticizes M., especially for his obscure style in both writing and speech, stating that "si Mallarmé avait été réellement un de ces esprits exceptionnels qui marquent à leur empreinte toute une génération, on nous eût révélé en quoi consistaient ses leçons."

1905

13. Le Cardonnel, Georges, and Charles Vellay. *La Littérature contemporaine (1905): opinions des écrivains de ce temps*. Paris: Mercure de France, 1905. 331p.

> Contains numerous references to M.

14. Longhaye, Georges. *Dix-neuvième siècle: esquisses littéraires et morales*. 4 vols. Paris: Victor Rétaux, 1901-1906.

> Vol. 3 (1905), pp. 356-360, contains quite unfavorable criticism of M. Insinuates that M.'s poetry "n'est plus un langage humain; ce n'est plus même un balbutiement; c'est un hoquet."

1906

15. Des Essarts, Emmanuel. "S. Mallarmé, professeur d'anglais." *Intermédiaire des Chercheurs et Curieux*, 54 (1906), 583-585.

> A personal note on M.

16. Gourmont, Remy de. *Promenades littéraires*. Second series. Paris: Mercure de France, 1906. 346p.

> Contains "La *Dernière Mode* de Stéphane Mallarmé."

17. Rimestad, Christian. *Fransk Poesi i det nittende aarhunrede*. Copenhagen: Det Schubotheske Forlag, 1906. 200p.

1907

18. Bernard, Jean-Marc. "Stéphane Mallarmé et l'idée d'impuissance." *Occident*, No. 66 (1907), pp. 242-247.

> An unfavorable essay. Calls M. a "dilettante épris de toute beauté."

19. Myrick, Arthur B. "A Note on a Sonnet of Stéphane Mallarmé." *Modern Language Notes*, 22 (1907), 127.

> Concerns "Ses purs ongles...."

*20. Van Hamel, Anton Gerard. *Het letterkundig leven van Frankrijk: III*. Amsterdam: Van Kampen en Zoon, 1907.

21. Vielé-Griffin, Francis. "La Discipline mallarméenne." *La Phalange*, 2 (1907), 949-954.

> Concerns M.'s influence upon the development of symbolism: "La discipline mallarméenne, par un procédé tant soit peu socratique, créa le Symbolisme: Mallarmé fut un accoucheur d'esprits."

1908

22. Bernard, Jean-Marc. "L'idée d'impuissance chez Mallarmé." *Société Nouvelle*, 14, No. 1 (1908), 177-195.

> See 23 and 26.

23. Bocquet, Léon. "Contre Mallarmé." *Nouvelle Revue Française*, No. 1 (1908), pp. 77-81.

> Supports Jean-Marc Bernard's article (18), which attacks M. severely, particularly on account of his "literary impotence" and his obscurity. See 26.

*24. Moréas, Jean. *Esquisses et souvenirs*. Paris: Mercure de France, 1908.

25. Roujon, Henry. *La Galerie des bustes*. Paris: J. Rueff, 1908. 325p.

> Offers general commentary and personal notes on M. States that M. "fut un saint."

1909

*26. Bernard, Jean-Marc. "Contre Mallarmé: réponse à l'entrefilet d'André Gide dans la *Nouvelle Revue Française* de février 1909." *Nouvelle Revue Française*, March 1909.

27. Gide, André. "Contre Mallarmé." *Nouvelle Revue Française*, 1 (1909), 96-98.

> Attacks Jean-Marc Bernard who had severely criticized M.'s poetry. See 22.

28. Gourmont, Remy de. *Promenades littéraires*. Third series. Paris: Mercure de France, 1909. 432p.

> Contains "Stéphane Mallarmé devant la chronique," an essay defending M. against criticism of his obscurity: "Son œuvre contient plus d'une page difficile, soit; quelques autres peuvent passer pour impossibles, c'est encore vrai; mais les vers limpides ou opalins, les poèmes doucement lumineux et parfois rouges d'un incendie rapide sont les plus nombreux." Gourmont states further that *Le Tombeau de Charles Baudelaire* "est aussi clair pour moi que *le Lac*, et beaucoup plus que *la Tristesse d'Olympio*."

*29. Seillière, Ernest. "Stéphane Mallarmé." *Pan*, March 1909.

1910

30. Delior, Paul. "La Femme et le sentiment de l'amour chez Stéphane Mallarmé." *Mercure de France*, 86 (1910), 193-206.

> Concerns M.'s poetic representation of women and love in his works.

31. Thibaudet, Albert. "La Poésie de Stéphane Mallarmé." *La Phalange*, 5, No. 54 (1910), 481-506.

An extract from 40.

1911

32. Barre, André. *Le Symbolisme: essai historique sur le mouvement symboliste en France de 1885 à 1900.* Paris: Jouve, 1911. 295p.

Contains one of the earliest perceptive essays on M. Discusses in detail M.'s poetic method and cites as the poet's general aesthetic principle: "L'art en effet consiste moins à communiquer ou à suggérer aux autres ce qu'on ressent soi-même qu'à créer pour autrui des motifs de pensées, de suggestions ou de rêves." Includes an extensive bibliography concerning Symbolist poetry.

33. Thibaudet, Albert. "La Poésie de Stéphane Mallarmé." *La Phalange*, 6, No. 55 (1911), 20-47.

An extract from 40.

1912

34. Chassé, Charles. "Mallarmé universitaire." *Mercure de France*, 99 (1912). 449-464.

Concerns M.'s years as a teacher of English.

*35. Dauphin, Léopold. *Quatre articles sur Stéphane Mallarmé.* Paris: Béziers, 1912. 47p.

*36. "Des Pages oubliées de Mallarmé." *L'Œil de Veau*, Feb. 1912.

37. Dornis, Jean. *La Sensibilité dans la poésie française contemporaine (1885-1912).* Paris: Arthème Fayard, Editeur, 1912. 357p.

Contains numerous references to M. as "chef de l'école symboliste" and as an influential figure in the development of the literature of the period studied. For example, author states that "c'est encore Stéphane Mallarmé qui a proposé la composition de la poétique nouvelle, orchestrée comme de la musique."

38. Gourmont, Remy de. *Promenades littéraires.* Fourth series. Paris: Mercure de France, 1912. 348p.

> Contains a study on M. in which the author defends the poet's obscurity. For example, Gourmont states, "On lui reprocha comme un crime l'obscurité de quelques-uns de ses vers, sans tenir compte de toute la partie limpide de son œuvre et sans essayer de chercher comment la logique même de son esthétique symboliste l'avait amené à ne plus exprimer que le second terme de la comparaison.... Aussi ne faut-il pas analyser la phrase selon la méthode logique ordinaire, de même qu'il ne faut pas regarder de trop près les tableaux impressionnistes...." Also calls M. the "Claude Monet of poetry."

*39. Roinard, Paul-Napoléon. *Hommage à Mallarmé.* Paris: E. Figuière, 1912.

40. Thibaudet, Albert. *La Poésie de Stéphane Mallarmé: étude littéraire.* Paris: Editions de la Nouvelle Revue Française, 1912. ix, 384p.

> Later edition: Gallimard, 1926. 470p.
> The publication of this admirable volume marks the beginning of serious M. criticism. Completely leaving aside biographical considerations, Thibaudet applies standard critical techniques to M.'s poetry, discussing its poetical elements and forms and offers intelligent interpretations of many of the poems (particularly *Hérodiade, L'Après-midi d'un faune, Prose pour des Esseintes,* and *Un Coup de dés*) which have rarely been surpassed. Concluding chapters consider M.'s influence and place in French literature.

1913

41. Bernard, Jean-Marc. "L'Echec de Mallarmé." *Revue Critique des Idées et des Livres,* 21 (1913), 144-159.

> Unfavorable criticism of M. States that M. "n'a point créé une œuvre littéraire véritable, ni ne pouvait le faire."

*42. Davidescu, N. "Note pe volumel tin Stephane Mallarme." *Nova Revista Romano,* 5 May 1913.

43. Escoube, Paul. *Préférences: Charles Guérin, Rémy de Gourmont, Stéphane Mallarmé, Jules Laforgue, Paul Verlaine.* Paris: Mercure de France, 1913. 359p.

Contains an essay, "La Femme et le sentiment de l'amour chez Mallarmé," which presents the thesis that, although women and expressions of love are found throughout M.'s poetry, "Mallarmé n'est pas un poète de l'amour.... La poésie de Stéphane Mallarmé porte en elle, effroyable et consciente — et sans regrets, — cette impuissance d'aimer...."

44. Gosse, Edmund Wilson. *French Profiles*. Revised edition. London: William Heinemann, 1913. xiv, 383p.

First edition: 1905.
A collection of articles previously published in various journals. The original edition (1905) contains a personal view of M. on the occasion of his death. The revised edition includes an augmented essay in which the author says of M.'s poetical technique: "His desire was to use his words in such harmonious combinations as will induce in the reader a mood or a condition which is not mentioned in the text, but was nevertheless paramount in the poet's mind at the moment of composition."

45. Gourmont, Remy de. *Promenades littéraires*. Fifth series. Paris: Mercure de France, 1913. 287p.

In an essay concerning Thibaudet's *La Poésie de Stéphane Mallarmé* (40), Gourmont revises somewhat his previous position that most of M.'s poetry is not obscure and can be understood if one considers carefully M.'s poetic procedure: "...je crois qu'il n'y a pas grand profit ni esthétique, ni intellectuel, à analyser de trop près un langage, quand il s'est voulu hermétique. La valeur d'une pensée est dans son expression." Gourmont gives as the major reason for M.'s hermeticism the poet's desire for complete originality in his poetry: "De bonne heure, il a voulu faire des vers qui ne ressembleraient à ceux de personne, surtout pas aux vers de Baudelaire...."

46. Haas, Albert. "Pariser Bohemezeitschriften." *Neue Rundschau*, 24 (1913), vol. 2, 1130-1143.

General commentary on M., including a discussion of his "Mardis" and his influence upon the young poets of the period.

47. Régnier, Henri de. *Portraits et souvenirs*. Paris: Mercure de France, 1913. 334p.

Contains "A propos de Mallarmé" offering general commentary on M. States that "les vers de Stéphane Mallarmé sont souvent obscurs... mais ils ne sont jamais inintelligibles."

1914

48. Gide, André. "Verlaine et Mallarmé." *La Vie des Lettres,* April 1914, pp. 1-23.

> Text of a speech delivered 22 Nov. 1913 at the Théâtre du Vieux-Colombier.

*49. Tilgher, Adriano. *Studi di poetica.* Rome: Libreria di Science e Lettere, 1914.

1915

50. Borgese, Giuseppe Antonio. *Studi di letterature moderne.* Milan: Fratelli Treves, 1915. vii, 383p.

> Contains a general essay, "Mallarmé svelato" (pp. 128-135).

1916

51. Cours, Jean de. "L'audition colorée et la sensation du poème." *Mercure de France,* 114 (1916), 649-661.

> Includes a discussion of elements of synesthesia in M.'s poetry.

1918

52. Casella, Georges. *Pèlerinages.* Paris: Payot, 1918. 301p.

> The chapter on M. (pp. 11-24) contains personal notes on the poet and his "Mardis."

53. Lanson, Gustave. *Histoire de la littérature française.* Paris: Librairie Hachette, 1918. xviii, 1204p.

> Contains only three references to M.: (1) mentions his "vers énigmatiques"; (2) characterizes the poet unfavorably as "un artiste incomplet, inférieur, qui n'est pas arrivé à s'exprimer"; (3) in a note, lists several editions of M.'s works.

54. Poizat, Alfred. "Stéphane Mallarmé." *Revue de Paris,* 4 (1918), 171-202.

> A general study of M. and his poetry including personal notes.

1919

55. Dujardin, Edouard. *De Stéphane Mallarmé au prophète Ezéchiel et essai d'une théorie de réalisme symbolique.* Paris: Mercure de France, 1919. 85p.

a) J. de Gourmont, *Mercure de France*, 139 (1920), 160-162.

56. Mauclair, Camille. *L'Art indépendant français sous la Troisième République.* Paris: Renaissance du Livre, 1919. xv, 170p.

Includes a section discussing M.'s thought and its influence on Symbolism (pp. 91-100).

★57. ————. *Les Héros de l'orchestre.* Paris: Fischbacher, 1919.

58. Moore, George. *Avowals.* London: Private Printing, 1919. 310p.

Later edition: New York: Boni and Liveright, 1926. 308p.

Tells of a visit to one of M.'s "Mardis" (pp. 269-272).

59. Poizat, Alfred. *Le Symbolisme: de Baudelaire à Claudel.* Paris: Renaissance du Livre, 1919.

Revised edition: Librairie Bloud et Gay, 1924. 269p.

A personal view of M. by one of the "Mardistes." Contains interesting descriptions of the Tuesday *soirées*, particularly M.'s "monologues" of which Poizat says, ". . . comme un grand oiseau planeur, il retrouvait, pour exprimer les vues les plus originales et les plus profondes, cette phrase si sûre, qui dans la pureté de son cristal laissait voir la course vive et lumineuse, la montée et la descente de mots, qui étaient des idées." Also includes a brief discussion of M.'s poetry.

60. Zerega-Fombona, A. *Le Symbolisme français et la poésie espagnole moderne.* Paris: Mercure de France, 1919. 84p.

Contains a discussion of M.'s influence on Spanish poetry. States that "pour la poésie espagnole son effet fut bienfaisant, même avec les exagérations des poètes de second ordre."

1920

61. Divoire, Fernand. "L'Exemple Mallarmé." *L'Encrier,* No. 11 (1920), unpaged.

> An interesting brief note stating that "il est certain que les Mallarméens ont empêché Mallarmé d'évoluer."

62. Mauclair, Camille. *Princes de l'esprit.* Paris: Librairie Paul Ollendorff, 1920. 317p.

> Contains "Les recherches de Mallarmé," in which Mauclair discusses M.'s poetic principles and defends M. against the charge of obscurity. "L'obscurité de Mallarmé ne provient donc que du degré d'inattention qu'on apporterait à le lire . . ."; and "Le souvenir de Mallarmé," personal notes.

63. Raynaud, Ernest. *La Mêlée symboliste (1870-1890).* 3 vols. Paris: La Renaissance du Livre, 1920.

> A recollection, rich in personal insights, of the vicissitudes of the Symbolist movement. Second volume contains a chapter on M. which offers a biographical sketch, considers M.'s poetical principles, and surveys the reaction of M.'s contemporaries and critics to his poetry.

64. Royère, Jean. *La Poésie de Mallarmé.* Paris: Emile-Paul, 1920. 24p.

> Text of a speech delivered 14 Nov. 1919 at the Théâtre de la Renaissance.
>
> a) J. de Gourmont, *Mercure de France,* 145 (1921), 166.

65. Valéry, Paul, and Guy Lavaud. "Controverse sur un poème de Mallarmé." *Les Marges,* 18 (1920), 68-77.

> Letters by Valéry and Lavaud stating their basic disagreement concerning the interpretation of *Un Coup de dés.*

1921

66. Ghéon, Henri. "La Poésie." *Ecrits Nouveaux,* 7, No. 4 (1921), 59-70.

> Contains unfavorable critical comments on M.: "En somme, on se demande s'il a jamais pris au sérieux une seule idée pour

elle-même et s'il a cessé un moment de se moquer de soi et
des autres. ..."

67. Milner, Zdislas. "Gongora et Mallarmé: la connaissance de
l'absolu par les mots." *Esprit Nouveau*, No. 3 (1921), pp. 285-
296.

> A comparative study of Góngora and M.: "...ce qui est iden-
> tique chez les deux, c'est la source idéale de l'exécution poé-
> tique, l'état psychologique de l'artiste au moment où, l'inspira-
> tion étant mûre, la réalisation commence." States that M.'s
> obscurity, like Góngora's is "le résultat de l'évolution intérieure
> de l'artiste, de l'effort continuel vers des formes d'expression
> plus parfaites."

68. Montesquiou, Robert de. *Diptyque de Flandre, triptyque de
France.* Paris: E. Sansot, 1921. 293p.

> Essay entitled "La Porte ouverte au jardin fermé du Roi" offers
> personal notes on M. as well as commentary on much of M.'s
> work.

69. Trombly, Albert Edmund. "Un traducteur de Poe." *Nouvelle
Revue*, 51 (1921), 26-36.

> Concerns M.'s translations of Poe's poetry. Says of M.'s ver-
> sions, "J'y trouve un vocabulaire trop recherché, un style dif-
> ficile et tourmenté. En un mot, c'est du Mallarmé que j'y trouve
> plutôt que du Poe."

1922

*70. Angioletti, G. B. "La Technique de Mallarmé." *Trifalco*,
Feb. 1922.

71. Duhamel, Georges. *Les Poètes et la poésie, 1912-1914.* Paris:
Mercure de France, 1922. 281p.

> Contains a brief section on M. (pp. 115-121). States that M.
> "est parmi les rares poètes dont l'œuvre est si curieusement
> parfaite qu'elle en fait mieux, par ses faiblesses, sentir l'im-
> puissance de l'âme humaine à s'identifier au divin."

72. Fry, Roger. "Mallarmé's *Hérodiade*." *Criterion*, 1, No. 1
(1922), 119-126.

English translations of *Don du poème,* *Hérodiade* (Scène) and *Cantique de Saint Jean,* with brief commentary.

73. Lièvre, Pierre. "L'Evolution de la langue et du style." In *Vingt-cinq ans de littérature française: tableau de la vie littéraire de 1885 à 1920.* Edited by Eugène Montfort. 2 vols. Paris: Librairie de France, 1922.

> Concerns M.'s influence on the development of French style in both poetry and prose: "Mallarmé... complique la syntaxe et sait en même temps se satisfaire d'un lexique relativement simple."

74. Mauclair, Camille. *Servitude et grandeur littéraires.* Paris: Librairie Ollendorff, 1922. xii, 256p.

> Includes notes on the "Mardis."

75. Thibaudet, Albert. "Réflexions sur la littérature: Mallarmé et Rimbaud." *Nouvelle Revue Française,* 18 (1922), vol. 1, 199-206.

> Concerns M.'s and Rimbaud's influence upon contemporary literature. States that "l'influence essentielle exercée par Mallarmé a été celle de son exemple."

1923

76. *Belles-Lettres,* Sept. 1923, pp. 246-283.

> Issue devoted to M. on the occasion of the twenty-fifth anniversary of his death. Contains: Maurice Landeau, "Stéphane Mallarmé"; "Au 25ᵉ anniversaire de la mort de Stéphane Mallarmé," a collection of brief critical judgments on M. by friends, disciples, and admirers; Henry Charpentier, "Réflexions sur l'œuvre de Mallarmé"; Robert-Sigl, "Le Parnasse et Mallarmé," concerning Parnassian elements in M.'s poetry; Edouard Dujardin, "Elle dit le mot: Anastase!" in which Dujardin goes so far as to compare M. to Socrates and Jesus; André Fontainas, "Un portrait et une appréciation"; André Delacour, "L'influence de Mallarmé," discussing M.'s influence on younger poets, particularly Paul Valéry and Jean Royère.

★77. Bocquet, Léon. "Autour de Stéphane Mallarmé." *Renaissance d'Occident,* Sept.-Oct. 1923.

78. Dujardin, Edouard. "La Revue Wagnérienne." *Revue Musicale*, 4 (1923), 141-160.

> Mentions M. as a collaborator of the *Revue Wagnérienne*. Author relates that he introduced M. to Wagner's music by taking him to a Lamoureux concert on Good Friday, 1885: "La soirée fut décisive pour Mallarmé, qui reconnut dans la musique et surtout dans la musique wagnérienne, une des voix du mystère qui chantait en sa grande âme, et qui ne cessa plus dès lors de fréquenter les concerts du dimanche."
>
> Reprinted with minor changes in author's *Mallarmé par un des siens* (218).

79. Fontainas, André. "Le Culte de Verlaine et de Mallarmé." *Le Flambeau*, 6 (1923), vol. 1, 307-325.

> Personal notes on the adoration of Verlaine and M. by younger poets of Fontainas' generation.

80. Ghil, René. *Les Dates et les œuvres: symbolisme et poésie scientifique*. Paris: Editions G. Crès, 1923. 338p.

> Contains numerous references to M. as well as one chapter devoted to the poet in which the author considers M.'s work in three periods: 1) early poems influenced by Baudelaire, 2) *Hérodiade* and *L'Après-midi d'un faune* in which M. first showed a unique poetic style, and 3) M.'s conception of "the Book."

81. Lemonnier, Léon. "Baudelaire et Mallarmé." *Grande Revue*, 112 (1923), 16-32.

> Discusses Baudelaire's influence on M.

*82. Massot, Pierre de. *De Mallarmé à 391*. Saint-Raphael: "Au Bel Exemplaire," 1923.

83. Maurras, Charles. *Poètes*. Paris: Le Divan, 1923. 111p.

> Contains "La poésie de Mallarmé." States that "Mallarmé vécut et mourut Parnassien...."

84. Monda, Maurice. "Stéphane Mallarmé." *Maîtres de la Plume*, 1, No. 5 (1923), 7-9.

> General article.

85. Montesquiou, Robert de. *Les Pas effacés: mémoires.* 3 vols. Paris: Emile-Paul Frères, 1923.

   Includes personal notes on M.

86. *Nouvelles Littéraires,* 13 Oct. 1923.

   Issue which includes an "Hommage à Stéphane Mallarmé" on the twenty-fifth anniversary of his death. Contains: Paul Valéry, "Stéphane Mallarmé"; Edouard Dujardin, "L'Œuvre rêvée"; André Fontainas, "Les Fiers Mardis de la rue de Rome"; Gabriel Mourey, "Souvenirs sur Mallarmé"; Maurice Betz, "Mallarmé et la poésie allemande"; Albert Mockel, "Stéphane Mallarmé, le maître et l'ami"; Grillot de Givry, "La Classe d'anglais de Stéphane Mallarmé," in which author states that the Gothic Bible of Bishop Ulfilas, which M. greatly admired and cited in his English classes, influenced the poet's unusual style.

   a) *Chronique des Lettres Françaises,* 1 (1923), 770-773.

87. Poizat, Alfred. "Mallarmé et son école." *Le Correspondant,* 292 (1923), 696-712.

   Personal notes on M.

*88. Prado, Jacques. "Le Tombeau de Mallarmé." *Manuscrit Autographe,* Sept.-Oct. 1923, p. 48.

89. Régnier, Henri de. "Par Valéry vers Mallarmé." *Revue de France,* 4 (1923), 642-649.

   Personal notes.

90. ———. "Sur Mallarmé." *Revue de France,* 4 (1923), 853-859.

   Personal notes.

*91. Royère, J. "La Vie mystique de Mallarmé." *Monde Nouveau,* Aug.-Sept. 1923.

92. ———. "Stéphane Mallarmé." *Le Flambeau,* 6 (1923), vol. 3, 483-490.

   Text of a speech delivered at Valvins in October 1923. General commentary.

93. Seylaz, Louis. *Edgar Poe et les premiers symbolistes*. Lausanne: La Concorde, 1923. 184p.

> Chapter 6 contains a section concerning Poe's influence on M.

1924

94. *Cahiers Idéalistes*, No. 9 (1924), unpaged.

> Issue devoted to "une commémoration de Mallarmé." Contains: "La Commémoration de Stéphane Mallarmé," concerning the ceremony in memory of the poet held at Valvins, 14 Oct. 1923; Robert de Souza, "Une dernière visite à Stéphane Mallarmé"; "Une lettre de Maurice Barrès," which tells of Barrès' refusal to take part in the ceremony; personal notes on M. by Joseph Caillaux, Charles Vildrac, André Salmon, and Georges Pillement; "Une lettre d'André Breton," which states why Breton refused to contribute to this issue; Jean Royère, "Stéphane Mallarmé" (see 92); and Edouard Dujardin, "A ceux qui sont venus et à ceux dont le cœur était là," the text of a short speech delivered during the ceremony.

95. Clouard, Henri. *La Poésie française moderne: des romantiques à nos jours*. Paris: Gauthier-Villars, 1924. vi, 398p.

> Contains a section on M. (pp. 84-95) in which author briefly treats the poet, his work, and poetical doctrine, concluding that "en s'évadant définitivement du discours, en affinant à sa manière aiguë, même après Baudelaire, le sens de la beauté des mots dans leurs ensembles rythmiques, en marchant enfin vers le mirage d'une perfection de tour d'ivoire, Mallarmé retint sa part dans la nouveauté symboliste."

96. Faure, Gabriel. *Mallarmé à Tournon: lettres de Mallarmé à Aubanel et à Mistral*. Saint-Félicien-en-Vivarais: Au Pigeonnier, 1924. 43p.

> A presentation of M.'s correspondence with Aubanel and Mistral during the poet's stay in Tournon. Republished in a later expanded edition (278).

97. Gaultier, Jules de. *La Vie mystique de la nature*. Paris: G. Crès, 1924. 254p.

> Includes a reference to *Hérodiade* (pp. 207-208) which author says contains "les plus beaux vers de la langue française."

98. Lalou, René. *Histoire de la littérature française contemporaine (1870 à nos jours)*. Revised edition. Paris: Editions G. Crès, 1924. xi, 755p.

> Contains a good overall view of the poet and his work and indicates that M.'s influence "sur l'évolution symboliste fut grande. Elle ne tint pas seulement à son œuvre.... Parmi les poètes de la fin du XIXe siècle, Mallarmé est apparu revêtu d'un prestige héroïque."

99. Levinson, André. "Stéphane Mallarmé, métaphysicien du ballet." *Revue Musicale*, 5 (1923-24), 21-33.

> Discusses M.'s unusual conception of the dance as "une écriture corporelle."

100. Mallarmé, Stéphane. *Autobiographie: lettre à Verlaine*. Preface by Edmond Bonniot. Paris: Albert Messein, 1924. 24p.

101. ———. *Lettres à Aubanel et à Mistral*. Saint-Félicien-en-Vivarais: Au Pigeonnier, 1924. 43p.

> See 96.

102. Mauron, Charles. "Mallarmé et le 'Tao.'" *Cahiers du Sud*, May 1924, pp. 351-366.

> See 486.

103. Rodenbach, Georges. *Evocations*. Paris: Renaissance du Livre, 1924. 319p.

> Includes a brief discussion of M.'s poetry (pp. 248-252).

*104. Thibaudet, Albert. "Le Triptyque de la poésie moderne: Verlaine, Rimbaud, Mallarmé." *Causeries Françaises*, 15 Feb. 1924, pp. 19-29.

1925

*105. Brulé, André. "Une page de Mallarmé sur Hamlet et Fortinbras." *Revue Franco-Allemande-Américaine*, 2 (1925), 330-332.

106. Dujardin, Edouard. "Die französische Literatur der Gegenwart: Die Verherrlichung von Mallarmé." *Deutsche Rundschau*, 204 (1925), 69-73.

> A general study of M.

107. Faure, Gabriel. *Ames et décors romanesques.* Paris: Eugène Fasquelle, 1925. 207p.

> Contains "Mallarmé à Tournon."

108. Faÿ, Bernard. *Panorama de la littérature contemporaine.* Paris: Simon Kra, 1925. 217p.

> Contains "Stéphane Mallarmé: technicien du symbolisme intellectuel."

109. Kahn, Gustave. *Silhouettes littéraires.* Paris: Editions Montaigne, 1925. 123p.

> Contains "Stéphane Mallarmé avant la gloire" (pp. 11-18).

110. Mallarmé, Stéphane. *Igitur, ou la Folie d'Elbehnon.* Preface by Edmond Bonniot. Paris: Libraire Gallimard, 1925. 81p.

111. Régnier, Henri de. *Proses datées.* Paris: Mercure de France, 1925. 267p.

> Includes "Sur Mallarmé" and "Par Valéry vers Mallarmé."

★112. Revaitour, Jean-Michel. *Mes coups de griffes.* ... Paris: Editions de "La Griffe," 1925.

113. Royère, Jean. *Clartés sur la poésie.* Paris: Albert Messein, 1925. 224p.

> Contains "La poésie de Mallarmé" and "Mallarmé et la Poésie actuelle."

★114. Thomas, Jean. "De Stéphane Mallarmé." *Revue Nouvelle,* 15 Nov. 1925.

1926

★115. Ermini, Filippo. *La Lirica domestica nella letteratura contemporanea.* Pocca S. Casciano: Capelli, 1926.

116. Fort, Paul, and Louis Mandin. *Histoire de la poésie française depuis 1850.* Paris: Ernest Flammarion-Henri Didier, 1926. vi, 392p.

Includes an essay on M. entitled "Le Maître du Symbolisme: Stéphane Mallarmé."

117. *La Nouvelle Revue Française*, 27 (1926), 513-646.

Issue published 1 Nov. 1926 devoted in part to "Hommage à Mallarmé." Contains several articles, mainly of a biographical or general nature: Geneviève Bonniot-Mallarmé, "Mallarmé par sa fille"; T. S. Eliot, "Note sur Mallarmé et Poe"; Giuseppe Ungaretti, "Innocence et mémoire"; Paul Claudel, "La Catastrophe d'Igitur," discussing this particular work by M., which Claudel calls "un drame, le plus beau, le plus émouvant, que le XIXᵉ siècle ait produit..."; Henry Charpentier, "De Stéphane Mallarmé"; Francis Ponge, "Notes d'un poème"; Henri Rambaud, "Poétique de Mallarmé"; Albert Thibaudet, "Réflexions sur la littérature: épilogue à la *Poésie de Stéphane Mallarmé*," concerning the republication of his *Poésie de Stéphane Mallarmé*.

118. Rauhut, Franz. *Das Romantische und Musikalische in der Lyrik Mallarmés*. Marburg: Neueren Sprachen, 1926. 55p.

a) F. Nobiling, *Neueren Sprachen*, 35 (1927), 636-639.

119. Soula, Camille. *La Poésie et la pensée de Stéphane Mallarmé: essai sur l'hermétisme mallarméen*. Paris: Edouard Champion, 1926. 103p.

"Literal explications" of *Prose pour des Esseintes, Hommage* (à Wagner), *Sainte*, "Tout orgueil fume-t-il du soir," "Surgi de la croupe et du bond," "Une dentelle s'abolit," and *Hommage* (à Puvis de Chavannes). Soula defines "literal explication" as "une méthode scientifique me permettant de remonter de la manifestation poétique à la connaissance des fonctions du langage de l'auteur."

a) D. Mornet, *Revue d'Histoire Littéraire de la France*, 34 (1927), 619-620.

120. ———. *La Poésie et la pensée de Mallarmé: essai sur le symbole de la chevelure*. Paris: Edouard Champion, 1926. 61p.

Explication of six sonnets linked by the symbol *chevelure*: "Dame sans trop d'ardeur," "Victorieusement fui le suicide...," "Ses purs ongles très haut...," "La chevelure vol d'une flamme...," "Quelle soie aux baumes de temps...," and "M'introduire dans ton histoire...." Soula says of this image, "Tout ce qu'a dit de personnel Stéphane Mallarmé sur l'amour évolue autour d'une chevelure...."

121. Suarès, André. *Présences*. Paris: Emile-Paul Frères, 1926. 303p.

> Includes an essay on M.

122. Thibaudet, Albert. "Epilogue à la *Poésie de Stéphane Mallarmé*." *Nouvelle Revue Française*, 27 (1926), 553-561.

> Discusses the publication of a new edition of Thibaudet's *La Poésie de Stéphane Mallarmé* (40). Thibaudet contrasts the present period, when M. is better appreciated as a poet, with the time when he first wrote his study, which was rejected by the publishers and was published only at his own expense. Also includes general commentary on M.

123. ————. "Poésie." *Nouvelle Revue Française*, 26 (1926), 104-113.

> A comparison of the poetry of Poe, M., and Valéry.

1927

124. André, Marius. "Gongora et Mallarmé." *Revue Fédéraliste*, 10 (1927), 441-452.

> Considers parallels between the two poets' styles.

125. Charpentier, John. *Le Symbolisme*. Paris: Les Arts et le Livre, 1927. 321p.

> Contains a section on M. (pp. 195-219) which discusses the English influences on the development of M.'s poetry, particularly the aesthetics of the Pre-Raphaelite artists: "Mallarmé crée une optique spéciale qui requiert simultanément le concours de la vue et de l'ouïe... Il cultive les intervalles irréguliers, et rompt sa ligne comme il recherche la dissonance. On reconnaît là l'esthétique même des préraphaélites...." (This section is reprinted in the author's *L'Evolution de la poésie lyrique*: 163.)

126. Chassé, Charles. "Les Influences anglaises sur Mallarmé." Dissertation. Paris, 1927.

127. Ellis, Arthur, translator. *Stéphane Mallarmé in English Verse*. Introduction by G. Turquet-Milnes. London: Jonathan Cape, Ltd., 1927. 159p.

Verse translations of fifty-one of M.'s poems. Introduction is a critical study by Turquet-Milnes, who believes M. to be "a pupil of the great group of English nineteenth-century poets — Keats, Shelley, Coleridge." In a concluding note, states that the "ideal biography of Mallarmé is Valéry's *La soirée avec M. Teste*."

128. Fontainas, André. "De Mallarmé à Valéry." *Revue de France* 5 (1927), 327-344.

Extracts from Fontainas' journal in which he noted conversations during the "Mardis."

129. Klemperer, Victor. " 'Victorieusement fui' (Zur Bewertung Mallarmés)." *Germanisch-Romanische Monatsschrift*, 15 (1927), 286-302.

*130. Latourette, Louis. "Sur la tombe de Mallarmé." *Nouvelle Revue Critique*, 15 March 1927, pp. 65-74.

131. Mallarmé, Stéphane. *Contes indiens*. Preface by Edmond Bonniot. Paris: L. Carteret, 1927. viii, 101p.

132. Marasca, Angelo. *Stéphane Mallarmé, poeta simbolista*. Rome: Tipografia del Littorio, 1927. 118p.

A general study of M. and his works followed by Marasca's Italian translations of several poems.

a) *Revue de Littérature Comparée*, 8 (1928), 399.

133. Planhol, René de. "La Grande Aventure de la poésie française." *Nouvelle Lanterne*, No. 6 (1927), pp. 9-20.

Contains several unfavorable comments on M.'s style: "... en Mallarmé revit la pire tradition de la littérature précieuse. Et l'obscurité de principe, dont il l'aggrave, est des plus malfaisantes."

134. Poizat, Alfred. *La Poésie contemporaine de Mallarmé à M. Paul Valéry*. Monaco: Imprimerie de Monaco, 1927. 35p.

Text of a speech delivered 10 Jan. 1927.

135. Royère, Jean. *Stéphane Mallarmé*. Paris: Simon Kra, 1927. xxxi, 141p.

Later edition: Albert Messein, Editeur, 1931. 191p.

A general study of M. and his poetry which investigates "la mystique de Mallarmé," the belief in the "totale réalisation du poète dont le *moi* personnel disparaît quand elle s'accomplit dans une sorte de transsubstantiation de l'homme en héros: c'est alors que le poète devient vraiment... le prêtre de l'Art...."

This study is preceded by Valéry's "Lettre sur Mallarmé" in which he discusses M.'s contribution to French letters: "Mallarmé créait donc en France la notion d'*auteur difficile*. Il introduisit dans l'art l'obligation de l'effort intellectuel."

a) P. Loewel, *Avenir*, 30 June 1927.

b) S. A. Rhodes, *Romanic Review*, 23 (1932), 164-165.

136. Thérive, André. *Du siècle romantique*. Paris: Editions de la Nouvelle Revue Critique, 1927. 219p.

Includes a discussion (pp. 167-176) of M. and his poetry. Sees M.'s influence on poetry as much greater than that of Verlaine "parce qu'il créa une doctrine et un mode d'expression."

137. Valéry, Paul. "Lettre sur Mallarmé." *Revue de Paris*, 2 (1927), 481-491.

Preface to Royère's *Mallarmé* (see 135).

138. Varlet, Théo. "Mallarmé." *Manuscrit Autographe*, No. 11 (1927), pp. 109-114.

Concerns 135.

1928

139. Chassé, Charles. *Styles et physiologie: petite histoire naturelle des écrivains*. Paris: Albin Michel, 1928. 316p.

A section on M. (pp. 80-88) classifies the poet as a "cinétique": "Je crois... qu'on peut facilement démontrer que, malgré certaines apparences, les sensations visuelles prenaient le pas chez lui sur les sensations auditives.... Il fut donc visuel mais d'une vision très limitée et qui se satisfait dans les teintes grises."

140. Claudel, Paul. *Positions et propositions*. Vol. 1. Paris: Gallimard, 1928. 253p.

Includes "La Catastrophe d'Igitur" (see 117).

*141. Fernandat, René. *Mallarmé et Paul Valéry*. Paris: Cahiers d'Occident, 1928.

142. Fontainas, André. *De Stéphane Mallarmé à Paul Valéry: notes d'un témoin (1894-1922)*. Preface by Paul Valéry. Paris: Edmond Bernard, Editions du Trèfle, 1928. 60p.

> Offers, in journal form, an intimate view of M. by André Fontainas, a Mardiste and good friend. Especially interesting for its reporting of M.'s conversations during the Mardis and elsewhere.

143. ———. *Mes Souvenirs du symbolisme*. Paris: Nouvelle Revue Critique, 1928. 220p.

> Contains numerous references to M. Chapter 9 answers the charge that the Symbolists divorced themselves from life and reality: "Stéphane Mallarmé... son esthétique, quoi qu'en allègue une 'croyance sombre' ne s'est jamais abstraite d'un concept certain de la vie." Also offers personal recollections of the "Mardis."

144. Gosse, Edmund. "Mallarmé en Angleterre." *Manuscrit Autographe*, No. 15 (1928), pp. 94-96.

> Discusses M.'s influence in England, which, author says, "n'a pas été considérable."

*145. Maurras, Charles, and Raymond de La Tailhède. *Un Débat sur le romantisme*. Paris: Flammarion, 1928.

146. Nobiling, Franz. "Mallarmés *Prose pour des Esseintes*." *Zeitschrift für Neufranzösische Sprache und Literatur*, 51 (1928), 419-436.

147. Thibaudet, Albert. "Mallarmé en Angleterre et en Allemagne." *Nouvelle Revue Française*, 30 (1928), 95-101.

> Concerns recent M. criticism in England and Germany.

1929

148. Ayrault, Roger. "Sur un sonnet de Mallarmé." *Le Mail*, No. 11 (1929), pp. 23-30.

> Concerns "Ses purs ongles...."

149. Bonniot, Edmond. "La genèse poétique de Mallarmé d'après ses corrections." *Revue de France*, 9 (1929), 631-644.

> A study of M.'s poetic creation comparing previous versions of poems and M.'s emendations of these texts: *Le Sonneur, Le Pitre châtié*, and "Victorieusement fui le suicide beau...."

150. Lemonnier, Léon. "Influence d'Edgar Poe sur Mallarmé." *Revue Mondiale*, 188 (1929), 361-371.

> States that "l'influence d'Edgar Poe constitue certainement l'un des facteurs importants du mouvement symboliste, et c'est grâce à Mallarmé qu'elle s'est surtout exercée."

151. Louÿs, Pierre. *Journal intime: 1882-1891*. Paris: Editions Montaigne, 1929. 377p.

> Includes personal notes on M. and the "Mardis."

152. Mallarmé, Stéphane. *Dix-neuf lettres de Stéphane Mallarmé à Emile Zola*. Introduction by Léon Deffoux. Commentary by Jean Royère. Paris: Jacques Bernard, 1929. 74p.

153. Nobiling, F. "Die erste Fassung der *Hérodiade*." *Deutsche-Französische Rundschau*, 2 (1929), 91-103.

> Concerns the first version of *Hérodiade*.

154. ———. "Mallarmés *Dame sans trop d'ardeur*." *Neophilologus*, 14 (1928-29), 172-181.

155. Quennell, Peter. *Baudelaire and the Symbolists*. London: Chatto and Windus, 1929. xii, 221p.

> A series of essays on Baudelaire, Nerval, Villiers de l'Isle-Adam, Laforgue, Corbière, Rimbaud, and Mallarmé. Believes that our heritage from M. is "not so much the dogmatic trend of his weekly *causeries*, their matter, as the accomplished and persuasive manner in which they were delivered."

156. Rauhut, Franz. *Das französische Prosagedicht*. Hamburg: Friederischen, de Gruyter and Co., 1929. 121p.

> Chapter 11 discusses M.'s prose poems, including *Un Coup de dés*.

157. Reynaud, Louis. *La Crise de notre littérature des romantiques à Proust, Gide et Valéry.* Paris: Librairie Hachette, 1929. 256p.

> Contains a rather unfavorable appraisal of M. in the chapter entitled "L'orientation délibérée vers l' 'artificiel.' " Deplores M.'s influence upon Symbolism, preferring that of Verlaine.

158. Taupin, René. *L'Influence du symbolisme français sur la poésie américaine (de 1910 à 1920).* Paris: Champion, 1929. 302p.

> Contains numerous references to M.

159. Soula, Camille. *La Poésie et la pensée de Stéphane Mallarmé: notes sur le "Toast funèbre."* Paris: Edouard Champion, 1929. 31p.

> An exegetical study of *Toast funèbre.*

160. Souriau, Maurice. *Histoire du Parnasse.* Paris: Editions Spes, 1929. liv, 466p.

> Includes a discussion of M.'s relationship with *Le Parnasse contemporain* (pp. 400-407).

161. Varlet, Théo. "Au soleil de Mallarmé." *Manuscrit Autographe,* No. 19 (1929), pp. 96-100.

> Indicates M.'s influence on Jean Royère.

1930

162. Bonniot, Edmond. "Mallarmé et la vie." *Revue de France,* 10 (Jan.-Feb. 1930), 59-72.

> Defends M. from the criticism that he was an "ivory-tower" poet entirely separated from life: "Mallarmé n'était pas le poète irréel, détaché du sol, vivant dans l'abstraction, que l'on pourrait supposer." Indicates M.'s social consciousness in two previously unpublished poems, *Haine du pauvre* and *Galanterie macabre,* and in other works.

163. Charpentier, John. *L'Evolution de la poésie lyrique de Joseph Delorme à Paul Claudel.* Paris: Les Œuvres Representatives, 1930. 305p.

> See 125.

164. Fontainas, André. *Dans la lignée de Baudelaire*. Paris: Editions de la Nouvelle Revue Critique, 1930. 251p.

> Includes a general essay on M. entitled "L'initiateur: Stéphane Mallarmé."

*165. Philipon, René. *Médailles*. Paris: A. Vertcœur, 1930.

166. Jammes, Francis. *Leçons poétiques*. Paris: Mercure de France, 1930. 287p.

> Contains quite unfavorable criticism of M. States that "Stéphane Mallarmé n'est qu'un faune qui, tour à tour, se déguise en professeur d'anglais et en yachtman, jamais en poète."

167. Nobiling, Franz. "Die *Hérodiade* Mallarmés." *Zeitschrift für Neufranzösische Sprache und Literatur*, 53 (1929-30), 218-242.

1931

168. Jäckel, Kurt. *Richard Wagner in der französischen Literatur*. Vol. 1. Breslau: Priebatsch's Buchhandlung, 1931. 284p.

> Contains an essay concerning Wagner's influence on M. (pp. 112-128).

*169. Mallarmé, Stéphane. *Poésies*. Preface by Paul Valéry. Paris: "Les Cent Une," 1931.

170. Saurat, Denis. "La Nuit d'Idumée: Mallarmé et la cabale." *Nouvelle Revue Française*, 37 (1931), 920-922.

> Presents possible Kabbalistic sources for *Don du poème*.

171. Soula, Camille. *La Poésie et la pensée de Stéphane Mallarmé: Un Coup de dés*. Paris: Edouard Champion, 1931. 45p.

> An exegetical study of *Un Coup de dés*.
> a) S. A. Rhodes, *Romanic Review*, 23 (1932), 256-258.

172. Woolley, Grange. *Richard Wagner et le symbolisme français: les rapports principaux entre le wagnérisme et l'évolution de l'idée symboliste.* Paris: P.U.F., 1931. 176p.

> Contains numerous references to M.

1932

173. Des Granges, Charles-Marc. *Les Poètes français: 1820-1920.* Paris: Librairie A. Hatier, 1932. 510p.

> Contains *L'Azur, Le Tombeau d'Edgar Poe,* "Le vierge, le vivace et le bel aujourd'hui," with notes and commentary, and *Les Fenêtres* accompanied by an *explication de texte.*

174. Fontainas, André. "Mallarmé et Victor Hugo." *Mercure de France,* 238 (1932), 63-78.

> Indicates Hugo's influence on M.'s works, including *Un Coup de dés.*

175. Halévy, Daniel. *Pays parisiens.* Paris: Bernard Grasset, 1932. 289p.

> Includes personal notes on M. by one of his students.

*176. Jobbé-Duval, Emile. *Le XIX*ᵉ *siècle et la littérature contemporaine.* Namur: A. Wemael-Chartier, 1932.

177. Lemonnier, Léon. *Edgar Poe et les poètes français.* Paris: Editions de la Nouvelle Revue Critique, 1932. 256p.

> Devotes a section to Poe's influence on M., which Lemonnier believes was superficial: "Il est possible que l'influence de Poe se soit exercée plus sur la vie de Mallarmé que sur son œuvre; car les traces précises que l'on en trouve dans ses poèmes ne sont point nombreuses, et elles sont toutes superficielles."

178. MacCarthy, Desmond. *Criticism.* London: Putnam, 1932. xii, 311p.

> Contains a brief treatment of M.'s basic poetic principles (pp. 145-146).

179. Nobiling, Franz Julius. "Mallarmés *Le Pitre châtié.*" *Zeitschrift für Neufranzösische Sprache und Literatur,* 55 (1931-32), 325-329.

180. ———. "Mallarmés *Le Sonneur.*" *Neophilologus,* 17 (1931-32), 5-8.

181. Reyes, Alfonso. "Mallarmé en espagnol." *Revue de Littérature Comparée,* 12 (1932), 546-568.

     Contains Spanish translations of M.'s works. Includes author's translations of several texts with commentaries.

182. Rietmann, Charles E. *Vision et mouvement chez Stéphane Mallarmé.* Paris: Les Presses Modernes, 1932. xxvii, 51p.

     A thematic study of M.'s poetry. Catalogues and analyzes images of rest (visual) and images of movement (dynamic).

183. Royère, Jean. *Frontons.* First series. Paris: Editions Seheur, 1932. 223p.

     Contains "Le sens et le son chez Mallarmé" (pp. 43-49).

184. Valéry, Paul. "Je disais quelquefois à Stéphane Mallarmé." *Nouvelle Revue Française,* 38 (1932), 824-843.

     A significant article in which Valéry gives his personal view concerning M. and what he attempted to accomplish in his poetry. Valéry defends M.'s obscurity and states that an absolute, objective "explication" of M.'s works is impossible and is indeed contrary to M.'s aesthetic principles: "L'œuvre de Mallarmé, exigeant de chacun une interprétation assez personnelle, n'appelait, n'attachait à soi que des intelligences séparées, conquises une à une, et de celles qui fuient vivement l'unanimité."

1933

*185. Alcanter de Brahm. *Cent ans de poésie: 1830-1930.* Paris: Ecrivains Indépendants, F. Piton, 1933.

186. Auriant. "Sur des vers retrouvés de Stéphane Mallarmé." *Nouvelle Revue Française,* 40 (1933), 836-839.

     Concerns *Contre un poète parisien* and *Soleil d'hiver.*

187. Cooperman, Hasye. *The Aesthetics of Stéphane Mallarmé.*
New York: Koffern Press, 1933. 301p.

> An investigation of M.'s aesthetic principles based upon the
> thesis that "the aesthetics of Stéphane Mallarmé was not an
> innovation; at its least it was an adaptation of the doctrines of
> Richard Wagner, — ideas borrowed and assimilated." (For an
> opposing viewpoint, see 684.) Special consideration is given to
> *Igitur* and *Coup de dés* which the author believes to be "virtual-
> ly the key" to M.'s poetry and to have "their original source
> in Shakespeare's *Hamlet*."

188. Croce, Benedetto. "Intorno al Mallarmé." *Critica* 31 (1933),
241-250.

> Critical commentary on M. Advises against the application of
> M.'s poetical theories to Italian poetry.

189. Duthie, Enid Lowry. *L'Influence du Symbolisme français dans
le renouveau poétique de l'Allemagne.* Paris: Honoré Champion, 1933. viii, 571p.

> Contains numerous references to M. concerning his influence
> on German poetry.

190. Fabureau, Hubert. *Stéphane Mallarmé: son œuvre.* Paris:
Nouvelle Revue Critique, 1933. 94p.

> A general study of M. and his work. Criticizes commentators
> who read too much into M.'s poems. Refusing to explicate,
> Fabureau offers only "notions simples" concerning M.'s hermetic
> poems.
>
> a) G. Brunet, *Mercure de France,* 251 (1934), 575-576.

191. Gavelle, Robert. "Callot, Aloysius Bertrand, Baudelaire, Mallarmé et Valéry." *Revue d'Histoire Littéraire de la France,* 40
(1933), 101-102.

> A note on the indirect influence on M. through Baudelaire of
> Callot's engraving, "Les Bohémiens."

192. Levrault, Léon. *La Poésie lyrique des origines à nos jours.*
Paris: Mellottée, 1933. 221p.

> Levrault criticizes M. severely and calls him "le mystificateur
> — ou le demi-fou — qui amena des poètes bien doués à écrire
> tant de poèmes ridicules."

193.   Mallarmé, Stéphane. *La Dernière mode.* Introduction by S. A. Rhodes. New York: Publications of the Institute of French Studies, Inc., 1933. 107p.

194.   Nobiling, Franz Julius. "Die Künstler-huldigungen Mallarmés." *Neophilologus,* 18 (1932-33), 92-100.

> Exegesis of *Le Tombeau d'Edgar Poe.*

195.   ———. "Mallarmé-Studien in Anschluss an Mallarmé-Übersetzungen." *Archiv für das Studium der Neueren Sprachen und Literaturen,* 163 (1933), 90-100.

> Discusses various translations of M.'s poetry, particularly those by Arthur Ellis.

196.   Raymond, Marcel. *De Baudelaire au surréalisme: essai sur le mouvement poétique contemporain.* Paris: Editions R.-A. Corrêa, 1933. 413p.

> Introduction devotes a section to M. (pp. 30-38) offering a general study of his poetics. Sees the poet's major contribution to poetry as consisting "surtout à avoir porté la lumière de la conscience sur un instinct auquel s'abandonnaient spontanément, avant lui, la plupart des grands poètes." Contains numerous additional references to M.

197.   Thibaudet, Albert. "A l'ombre des 'Contemplations': Baudelaire et Mallarmé." *Nouvelle Revue Française,* 40 (1933), 865-880.

> Indicates Baudelaire's *Voyage à Cythère* as a source for Hugo's *Cerigo* and discusses Hugo's influence on the composition of *Sa Fosse est creusée!* ... and *Sa Tombe est fermée.*

198.   Valéry, Paul. "Stéphane Mallarmé." *Conferencia,* 27 (1932-33), vol. 1, 441-453.

> Text of a lecture presented on 17 Jan. 1933.

1934

199.   Chisholm, Alan Rowland. *Towards Herodiade: A Literary Genealogy.* Melbourne: Melbourne University Press, 1934. 174p.

A study of nineteenth-century poetry which investigates "how, as a result of various influences, partly Germanic and Hindoo, partly French, the most representative poets from Leconte de Lisle to Mallarmé attempted to break down the plastic structure of the universe and found behind phenomena, first, an immense and incessant flux, and then a sheer void." The last chapter, "The Mallarmean Synthesis," is an essay on M.'s poetical "condensation" into classical form of various influences of his era: "Dionysism, musicalisation, occultism, romanticism." Particular consideration from this point of view is given to *Hérodiade*, which Chisholm regards as the "greatest and most beautiful of Mallarmé's works."

200. Hughes, Randolph. "Mallarmé: A Study in Esoteric Symbolism." *Nineteenth Century and After*, 116 (1934), 114-128.

> Offers a brief discussion of M.'s literary doctrine and compares M. to Coleridge, who is called "a precursor of Mallarmé in his most developed stages."

201. Wyzéwa, Isabelle de. *La "Revue Wagnérienne": essai sur l'interprétation esthétique de Wagner en France.* Paris: Librairie Académique Perrin, 1934. 219p.

> The first chapter (pp. 28-41) discusses briefly M.'s aesthetic principles and their influence upon the Symbolist doctrine as presented in the *Revue Wagnérienne*. States that M.'s and Wagner's ideas were far from convergent, but that these two men shared one significant belief: "... c'est le caractère sacré, le rôle religieux de l'art."

1935

202. Ambrière, Francis. "Deux ouvrages inconnus de Stéphane Mallarmé." *Bulletin du Bibliophile*, 14 (1935), 506-513.

> Concerns *Le Carrefour des Demoiselles*, a pamphlet of verse written in collaboration with Emmanuel des Essarts, and M.'s edition with annotations of J. Stephen's *Favourite Tales for Very Young Children*, intended for use in English classes.

203. Charpentier, Henry. "*La Dernière Mode* de Stéphane Mallarmé." *Minotaure*, No. 6 (1935), pp. 25-28.

> A brief discussion of *La Dernière Mode* followed by selected texts from the periodical and several reproductions of engravings.

204. Dérieux, Henry. *La Poésie française contemporaine: 1885-1935*. Paris: Mercure de France, 1935. 293p.

   Contains numerous references to M.

205. Duval, Maurice. *La Poésie et le principe de transcendance: essai sur la création poétique*. Paris: Librairie Félix Alcan, 1935. 430p.

   Includes a section on M. (pp. 197-204). Interprets *Le Guignon*.

★206. Lachèvre, Frédéric. *Une Tentative d'initiation à la poésie mallarméenne et valéryenne*. Paris (?): Private Printing, 1935.

207. Le Sidaner, Louis. "Stéphane Mallarmé." *Nouvelle Revue Critique*, 19, No. 79 (1935), 256-261.

   Concerns 190 and 280.

208. Mauclair, Camille. *Mallarmé chez lui*. Paris: Bernard Grasset, 1935. 190p.

   A personal view of M. Mauclair met the poet in 1890 and became one of his most devoted "Mardistes." Includes photographic reproductions of several letters by M.

209. Planhol, René de. "Le Souvenir et l'exemple de Mallarmé." *Nouvelle Lanterne*, No. 82 (1935), pp. 113-128.

   Concerns 208.

210. Spoerri, Theophil. "Über ein Sonnett Mallarmés." In *Festschrift für Ernst Tappolet*. Basel: Benno Schwabe, 1935. xv, 278p.

   Concerns "Victorieusement fui le suicide beau...."

★211. Thelliez, Charles. "Stéphane Mallarmé et l'occultisme." *Paris-Cité*, 5 May 1935.

212. Winkel, J. "Mallarmé — Wagner — Wagnerismus." Dissertation. Münster, 1935.

1936

213. Beaume, Georges. "Mallarmé inédit." *Revue Bleue,* 74 (1936), 483-488.

> Biographical notes on M.

214. Bonniot, Edmond. "Notes sur les Mardis." *Les Marges,* 57, No. 224 (1936), 11-18.

> Notes which Edmond Bonniot, M.'s future son-in-law, took on M.'s conversations during the "Mardis" (1892-93).

215. Carcassonne, E. "Wagner et Mallarmé." *Revue de Littérature Comparée,* 16 (1936), 347-366.

> A comparison of Wagner's and M.'s aesthetic theories.

216. Charpentier, Henry. "Mardi soir, rue de Rome." *Les Marges,* 57, No. 224 (1936), 7-10.

> Presents Bonniot's "Notes sur les Mardis" (see 214).

217. Daudet, Léon. "Mallarmé par un des siens." *Revue Universelle,* 66 (1936), 89-92.

> Concerns 218.

218. Dujardin, Edouard. *Mallarmé par un des siens.* Paris: Albert Messein, Editeur, 1936. 234p.

> Contains a personal view of M. by one of the "Mardistes." Discusses various aspects of M.'s poetic doctrine, or "Mallarmism." States that much of the poet's obscurity is based upon the following principle: "Des deux termes de la comparaison, Mallarmé ne décrit dans le premier que le second." Also includes a chapter on "the Book," which Dujardin sees as "l'œuvre rêvée... qu'il ébaucha dans *Igitur,* qu'il commenta dans ses conversations et dans maintes pages de *Divagations,* et dont il réalisa un aspect dans le *Coup de dés.*"
> a) A. Thérive, *Temps,* 25 June 1936.

219. Dumesnil, René. *Le Réalisme.* Paris: J. de Gigord, 1936.

> Later edition: *Le Réalisme et le naturalisme.* 1955. 454p.

Later published as Vol. 9 of *Histoire de la littérature française.*
Edited by J. Calvet. Paris: Del Duca, Editeurs, 1956. 452p.
Contains a biographical and critical sketch of M. in which
Dumesnil sees *Igitur* as the "key" to the poet's obscurity: "On
trouve dans ce conte... le germe des idées que Mallarmé
développera tant dans ses poèmes que dans ses écrits en prose."

220. Fontainas, André. *Confession d'un poète.* Paris: Mercure de
France, 1936. 219p.

> Includes personal notes on M.

221. Hess, Gerhard. "Stéphane Mallarmé's *L'Après-midi d'un
Faune.*" *Neophilologische Monatsschrift,* 1936, pp. 398-407.

222. Kahn, Gustave. *Les Origines du symbolisme.* Paris: Albert
Messein, 1936. 71p.

> Includes numerous references to M. concerning his influence
> upon the development of Symbolism.

223. Mallarmé, Stéphane. *Poems.* Translated by Roger Fry. Introduction and commentary by Charles Mauron. London: Chatto
and Windus, 1936. xii, 307p.

> Later edition: New York: New Directions, 1951. viii, 312p.
> Translations of twenty-nine poems by M. with commentaries
> by Mauron (translated into English).

224. Marie, Aristide. *La Forêt symboliste: esprits et visages.* Paris:
Firmin-Didot, 1936. 296p.

> Contains "Valvins et Stéphane Mallarmé," biographical notes
> on M.

225. Naumann, Walter. *Der Sprachgebrauch Mallarmés.* Marburg:
Lahn, 1936.

> Later edition: Darmstadt: Wissenschaftliche Buchgesellschaft,
> 1970. 25cp.
> An extensive stylistic investigation concerned primarily with
> M.'s word usage in his poetry. Appendix includes a useful
> catalogue of M.'s poems indicating first publications, variant
> versions, translation, exegesis, and discussions.

226. Raynaud, Ernest. *En Marge de la mêlée symboliste.* Paris: Mercure de France, 1936. 287p.

> Supplements author's *Mêlée symboliste* (63). Contains "La Triple Evolution de Mallarmé," offering a personal view of M. by one of the "Mardistes" and telling of Raynaud's first meeting with the poet. Divides M.'s literary production into three periods: 1) before and during M.'s stay in London when he was greatly influenced by Baudelaire; 2) after his return to France when he began to write *Hérodiade* and *L'Après-midi d'un faune*; and 3) after the poet became somewhat well known when "il cède la place au prosateur et au théoricien." Believes M.'s originality to be his consideration for the poem as "une formule magique."

227. ———. *La Triple Evolution de Mallarmé.* Paris: Mercure de France, 1936.

> See 226.

228. Thibaudet, Albert. *L'Histoire de la littérature française de 1789 à nos jours.* Paris: Librairie Stock, 1936. xi, 587p.

> Contains a brief, perceptive section on M. in which he is classified, together with Verlaine, Rimbaud, Corbière, and Lautréamont, as a "dissident." States that in M.'s pure poetry "l'initiative est cédée aux mots comme, dans la mystique du pur amour, l'initiative est laissée à Dieu."

229. Weidlé, Wladimir. *Les Abeilles d'Aristée: essai sur le destin actuel des lettres et des arts.* Paris: Desclée De Brouwer, 1936. 285p.

> Contains numerous references to M. in the chapter entitled "La poésie pure."

1937

230. Béguin, Albert. *L'Ame romantique et le rêve: essai sur le romantisme allemand et la poésie française.* Marseilles: Editions des Cahiers du Sud, 1937. xvii, 413p.

> Contains a section on M. and Rimbaud in which Béguin defines M.'s "rêve" as "cet univers des essences, qui séduit irrésistiblement le poète et qui s'oppose à la vie méprisée. Dans cette étrange mystique, la vision spirituelle favorisée par un savant emploi irrégulier du langage, sollicite le dévouement entier de l'existence éphémère."

231.   Faure, Gabriel. "Mallarmé à Tournon." *Revue des Deux Mondes*, 2 (1937), 106-115.

A study of M.'s stay at Tournon. Concerns the genesis of *Hérodiade* and *L'Après-midi d'un faune*.

232.   Mallarmé, Stéphane. *Thèmes anglais pour toutes les grammaires*. Preface by Paul Valéry. Paris: Gallimard, 1937. 298p.

233.   Paladini, C. *Interpretazione di Mallarmé: poesie e prose*. Ancona: La Lucerna, 1937. 130p.

Italian translation of thirty-four poems and prose writings including a prefatory essay by the translator.

234.   Schinz, A. "D'où sort *L'Aprés-midi d'un faune* de Mallarmé?" *Modern Language Notes*, 52 (1937), 485-487.

Suggests Leconte de Lisle's *Pan* as a source.

235.   Wais, Kurt. "Mallarmés Neuschöpfung eines Gedichtes von Keats." *Zeitschrift für Neufranzösische Sprache und Literatur*, 60 (1935-37), 183-196.

Discusses possible influences of Keats's poetry on M.

236.   ———. "Psychologie des dichterischen Wortschatzes: am Beispiel Mallarmés." *Archiv für das Studium der Neuren Sprachen und Literaturen*, 172 (1937), 188-198.

Concerns 225.

1938

237.   Aish, Deborah A. K. *La Métaphore dans l'œuvre de Stéphane Mallarmé*. Paris: Librairie E. Droz, 1938. 211p.

A detailed examination of the Mallarméan metaphor, its themes, forms, and the rôle it plays within the structure of M.'s poetic symbolism. Aish emphasizes the poet's unique use of metaphor: "La métaphore chez lui est fort originale; elle part des choses les plus ordinaires pour s'élever d'un seul trait à la pensée la plus pure — la pensée qui dirige l'univers." (Publication of the author's thesis presented in Paris in 1938.)

a) J. Schérer, *Modern Language Notes*, 54 (1939), 225-228.

b) G. Turquet-Milnes, *Modern Language Review,* 35 (1940), 110-111.

238. Ajalbert, Jean. "Mémoires à rebours, fragments." *Mercure de France,* 281 (1938), 259-289.

> Includes personal notes on M. by Ajalbert, who was one of M.'s students at the Lycée Condorcet.

239. ———. *Mémoires en vrac: au temps du Symbolisme (1880-1890).* Paris: Albin Michel, 1938. 413p.

> Chapter 10 includes personal notes on M.

240. Beck, Léon. *Poètes symbolistes et poètes d'aujourd'hui.* Paris: Delagrave, 1938. 141p.

> Includes a brief critical notice and explicatory commentary on *Apparition, Brise marine, Les Fleurs, Eventail de Mademoiselle Mallarmé,* "Le vierge, le vivace et le bel aujourd'hui...," and "Toute l'âme résumée...."

241. Chisholm, A. R. "Le Symbolisme français en Australie: Mallarmé et Brennan." *Revue de Littérature Comparée,* 18 (1938), 354-359.

> Discusses M.'s influence upon Australian poetry, particularly that of Christopher Brennan.

242. Cuénot, C. "L'origine des *Contes indiens* de Mallarmé." *Mercure de France,* 288 (1938), 117-126.

> Discusses the background of M.'s adaptation of Mary Summer's *Contes et légendes de l'Inde ancienne* (Paris, 1878). According to the author, it was Méry Laurent who suggested that M. revise these stories.

*243. Estève, Louis. *Etudes philosophiques sur l'expression littéraire.* Paris: Vrin, 1938. 275p.

244. George, Stefan. "Pages choisies: Mallarmé." *Cahiers du Sud,* 26 (1938), 265-267.

> Brief critical notes.

245. Guillaume, Michel-Maurice. *Histoire de la littérature française.* Paris: Emmanuel Vitte, 1938. 610p.

Includes a brief section on M. (pp. 552-553) in which author states: "La très haute idée qu'il avait de sa mission et le labeur acharné auquel il se livrait pour atteindre à la beauté, restent en exemple à tous les écrivains en vers."

246. Naumann, Walter. "Mallarmés 'Un Coup de Dés jamais n'abolira le Hasard.'" *Romanische Forschungen*, 52 (1938), 123-165.

Includes a brief bibliography.

247. Nobiling, Franz Julius, translator. *Mallarmé Gedichte*. Jena: W. Gronau, 1938. 59p.

248. Obaldia, René de. "L'Enfant et Stéphane Mallarmé." *La Phalange*, 11, No. 30 (1938), 92-93.

Compares M.'s conception of the universe to that of a child: "De l'enfant, Mallarmé détient la 'simplicité complexe', et les spirales qui les unissent dans un même vertige sont considérables. Tout d'abord ils ont ceci de commun... c'est qu'ils créent de toutes pièces leurs Univers."

249. Reyes, Alfonso. *Mallarmé entre nosotros*. Buenos Aires: Destiempo, 1938.

Later edition: Mexico City: Tezontle, 1955. 94p.
A collection of articles on M. and translations of his poetry, some of which appeared previously in various periodicals. Includes a bibliography of Spanish translations of M.'s works.

250. Rolland de Renéville, André. *L'Expérience poétique*. Paris: Gallimard, 1938. 173p.

Contains numerous references to M., especially concerning the relationship between M.'s thought and Oriental philosophy, including the Kabbalah. Says of M.'s poetic method: "Lorsqu'il eut assigné à son art la mission de situer le monde sensible sur un plan essentiel, et par conséquent de le ramener précisément à la limite de l'être et du non-être, il tenta d'en projeter les représentations dans les formules qui les engendraient et les niaient du même coup."

251. Schérer, Jacques. "Notes sur les *Contes indiens* de Mallarmé." *Mercure de France*, 283 (1938), 102-116.

An analysis of the *Contes indiens*. For information concerning the source of these stories, see 242.

252. Thibaudet, Albert. *Réflexions sur la littérature*. Paris: Gallimard, 1938. 265p.

> Contains "Mallarmé et Rimbaud" (pp. 157-163).

*253. Tran-Van-Tung. *L'Ecole de France*. Hanoi: Imprimerie Le-Van-Phuc, 1938.

254. Wais, Kurt. "Das *Brise Marine*-Thema von Rousseau bis Mallarmé." *Zeitschrift für Neufranzösische Sprache und Literatur*, 61 (1937-38), 211-218.

> Discusses the sea as a frequent theme in French literature from pre-Romanticism to Symbolism.

255. ———. "E. A. Poe und Mallarmés *Prose pour des Esseintes*." *Zeitschrift für Neufranzösische Sprache und Literatur*, 61 (1937-38), 23-40.

> Investigates Poe's influence upon the composition of *Prose pour des Esseintes*.

256. ———. *Mallarmé: Ein Dichter des Jahrhundertendes*. Munich: Beck'sche Verlagsbuchhandlung, 1938. 548p.

> Revised edition: *Mallarmé: Dichtung — Weisheit — Haltung*. C. H. Beck'sche Verlagsbuchhandlung, 1952. 800p.
> The first major critical study of M. incorporating biographical material. Considers in detail the evolution of M.'s poetry. Revised edition makes use of material concerning the poet which came to light after 1938.
> a) F. B., *Revue de Littérature Comparée*, 19 (1939), 198-199.
> b) M. Bémol, *Revue de Littérature Comparée*, 29 (1955), 132-136.
> c) H. Friedrich, *Romanische Forschungen* (1940), 296-303.
> d) H. Hennecke, *Kritik* (1958), 267-271.
> e) G. W. Ireland, *Modern Language Review*, 48 (1953), 476-477.
> f) E. von Jan, *Germanisch-Romanische Monatsschrift*, 5 (1955), 182-183.
> g) J. Schérer, *Modern Language Notes*, 54 (1939), 225-228.
> h) P. Van Tieghem, *Revue d'Histoire Littéraire de la France*, 38 (1938), 533-535.
> i) L. Werth, *Nouvelle Revue Française*, 56 (1942), 124-126.

1939

257. Cailliet, Emile. *Symbolisme et âmes primitives*. Paris: Boivin, 1939. 306p.

> Contains numerous references to M. in the fifth section entitled "Le mouvement symboliste."

258. Gregh, Fernand. *Portrait de la poésie moderne de Rimbaud à Valéry*. Paris: Delagrave, 1939. 264p.

> Chapter 2 is a brief essay on M.

259. Henning, George N. "The Source of Mallarmé's *L'Après-midi d'un Faune*." *Modern Language Journal*, 23 (1938-39), 506-507.

> Suggests Boucher's painting, "Pan et Syrinx," in the National Gallery (London) as the source for this poem.

*260. Hess, Gerhard. "Bermerkungen zur neueren Mallarmé-Literatur." *Neophilologische Monatsschrift* (1939), pp. 300-304.

*261. Jurénil, André. *Faux en écritures*. Paris: Editions Maurice Carton, 1939.

*262. Keferstein, Georg. "Die jüngste deutsche Mallarmé-Exegese." *Revue Germanique*, 1939, pp. 55-76.

263. Kellermann, Wilhelm. "Die jüngste deutsche Mallarmé-Exegese." *Germanisch-Romanische Monatsschrift*, 27 (1939), 55-76.

> Discusses recent German exegesis of M.'s poetry, particularly that by Franz Julius Nobiling and Kurt Wais.

264. Mondor, Henri. *L'Amitié de Verlaine et Mallarmé*. Paris: Gallimard, 1939. 274p.

> Presents the correspondence between M. and Paul Verlaine with accompanying commentary on the friendship of these two poets.

265. Temple, R. Z. "Aldous Huxley et la littérature française." *Revue de Littérature Comparée*, 19 (1939), 65-110.

> Includes a brief discussion of Huxley's references to M.

266. Thibaudet, Albert. *Réflexions sur la critique.* Paris: Gallimard, 1939. 264p.

> Contains "Epilogue à la Poésie de Stéphane Mallarmé" and "La *Lettre sur Mallarmé* de Paul Valéry."

267. Wais, Kurt. "Banville, Chateaubriand, Keats und Mallarmés *Faun.*" *Zeitschrift für Neufranzösische Sprache und Literatur,* 62 (1938-39), 178-193.

> Proposes Banville's *Diane au bois,* Chateaubriand's *Mémoires d'Outre-Tombe* (the story of the "Sylphide"), and Keats's *Endymion* as probable influences upon the composition of *L'Après-midi d'un faune.*

1940

★268. Grouas, Charles-André. "De Stéphane Mallarmé à Jean Royère." *La Phalange,* 1940.

269. Mallarmé, Stéphane. *Herodias.* Translated by Mills Clark. Prairie City, Ill.: J. A. Decker, 1940. 37p.

270. Mondor, Henri. "Verlaine et Mallarmé. Deux années de leur amitié: 1883-1884." *Revue de Paris,* 1 (1940), 450-468.

> Presents correspondence between Verlaine and M.

271. Noulet, Emilie. *L'Œuvre poétique de Stéphane Mallarmé.* Paris: E. Droz, 1940. 564p.

> A well done comprehensive study of M. First part is a general consideration of the poet, the genesis of his poetry, his poetical technique, etc. Second part is devoted to exegesis of his poems, taken in chronological order. Appendix includes a useful "Index du vocabulaire poétique de Mallarmé." (Publication of the author's thesis.)
>
> Some of the explications in this volume appear in revised form in later publications (435, 926).

272. Vossler, Karl. *Aus der romanischen Welt.* Vol. 2. Leipzig: Koehler und Amelang, 1940. 170p.

> Includes a general study of M. entitled "Mallarmé und die Seinen."

1941

273. Aish, Deborah A. K. "Le rêve de Stéphane Mallarmé d'après sa correspondance." *PMLA*, 56 (1941), 874-884.

> Concerns M.'s conception of the "Grand Œuvre." Aish says that the obsession of this dream "finit par le paralyser.... Idéaliste, Mallarmé a sacrifié tout son talent dans le vain espoir de créer le 'Grand Œuvre.' "

274. Chaigne, Louis. *Notre littérature du XIXe siècle*. Paris: J. de Gigord, 1941. 130p.

> Includes a brief section on M. (pp. 84-87) in which the author calls M. "un mystique de la poésie." Presents an explication of "Le vierge, le vivace et le bel aujourd'hui...."

275. Dresden, S. "Publications récentes sur Mallarmé." *Neophilologus*, 26 (1940-41), 185-191.

> Survey of recent M. criticism.

276. Drieu La Rochelle, Pierre. *Notes pour comprendre le siècle*. Paris: Gallimard, 1941. 189p.

> Includes brief critical remarks concerning M.'s poetry.

277. Fargue, Léon-Paul. "La classe de Mallarmé." *Nouvelle Revue Française*, 29, No. 326 (1941), 641-649.

> Personal notes on M. by Fargue, who was one of M.'s students at the Collège Rollin.

278. Faure, Gabriel. *Mallarmé à Tournon*. Grenoble: Arthaud, 1941. 91p.

> Revised edition: *Mallarmé à Tournon: lettres à Aubanel, Mistral et Cazalis*. Paris: Editions des Horizons de France, 1946. 132p.
> A presentation of M.'s correspondence with Aubanel, Mistral, and Cazalis during the poet's stay in Tournon (cf. 231).

279. Fiser, Emeric. *Le Symbole littéraire: essai sur la signification du symbole chez Wagner, Baudelaire, Mallarmé, Bergson et Marcel Proust*. Paris: Librairie José Corti, 1941. 225p.

Contains a chapter on "Le Poète du symbolisme: Stéphane Mallarmé" in which the author characterizes M. as "un des plus intenses rêveurs de la littérature moderne." States that the Mallarméan symbol is dynamic: "...il est le poème lui-même.... La création du symbole s'identifie avec la création de l'œuvre d'art symboliste. *C'est le poème qui constitue le symbole littéraire.*"

280. Fowlie, Wallace. *La Pureté dans l'art.* Montreal: Editions de L'Arbre, 1941. 153p.

> Includes four essays on M.: "Poésie," "Métaphore," "Réalité," and "Joie."

*281. Kučera, Otakar. "Stéphane Mallarmé." *Revista Psicoanalítica,* No. 7 (1941), pp. 249-294.

282. Mauron, Charles. *Mallarmé l'obscur: l'œuvre et la vie.* Paris: Denoël, 1941. xxiii, 206p.

> Later edition: *Mallarmé l'obscur.* Paris: José Corti, 1968. 152p. Presents an essay on the development of M.'s obscurity and exegesis of most of M.'s poetry based upon the author's psychocritical method (see also 486). Interprets M. by a comparative study of the texts, investigating the significance of recurring interrelated metaphors and poetical themes.

283. Mondor, Henri. "L'Intermède du Faune." *Nouvelle Revue Française,* 55-56 (1940-41), 166-178.

> Discusses the genesis of *L'Après-midi d'un faune.*

284. ————. *Vie de Mallarmé.* Paris: Gallimard, 1941. 827p.

> The definitive biography of M. Mondor uses correspondence, autograph manuscripts, family relics, and other documents which he patiently and carefully collected over a period of many years to retrace "l'aventure sans éclat, sans drame apparent, mais singulièrement ardente, d'un poète de tour d'ivoire." Introduces much previously unpublished material, especially extracts from letters. An indispensable sourcebook for M. scholars.
>
> a) A. Rolland de Renéville, *Nouvelle Revue Française,* 57 (1942), 570-576, 631-635.

285. Roger, Bernard. "Le Sâdhana de Mallarmé." *Revue Philosophique de la France et de l'Etranger,* 131 (1941), 460-462.

Concerns M.'s search for the absolute of which the author says: "A bien étudier les diverses phases de cette quête à la fois joyeuse et désespérée, nous y avons trouvé de bien curieux rapprochements avec celles qui marquent aux Indes le *sâdhana*, cette réalisation spirituelle qui s'effectue par le *yoga*, et dont le terme se trouve dans l'extase, le *samâdhi*."

286. Soulairol, Jean. "Mallarmé et la création poétique." *Divan*, 27 (1941), 71-85.

General essay.

287. Taupin, René. "Racine et Mallarmé." *French Review*, 14 (1940-41), 16-20.

Discusses Racine's influence on M. Calls *Hérodiade* "son Hommage à Racine."

1942

288. Beausire, Pierre. *Essai sur la poésie et la poétique de Mallarmé*. Lausanne: Roth, 1942. 221p.

Later edition published as *Mallarmé: poésie et poétique*. Lausanne: Mermod, 1949.
A general study of M.'s poetry and poetical techniques in which the author insists upon M.'s uniqueness in the history of letters: "Je ne pense pas que l'on trouve dans toute notre littérature poésie plus grave et plus étrange que celle de Mallarmé. Elle s'impose à nous comme un événement unique."
a) J. Rütsch, *Trivium*, 1, No. 1 (1943), 78-81.
b) P. O. Walzer, *Formes et Couleurs*, No. 3 (1942), unpaged.

289. Bounoure, Gabriel. "Destin et poésie chez Mallarmé." *Revue du Caire*, No. 43 (1942), pp. 103-111.

Concerns M.'s conceptions of "fate" and "chance."

*290. Cocteau, Jean. "Discours sur Mallarmé." *Fontaine*, 4 (1942), 83-90.

291. Croce, Benedetto. *Poesia e non poesia: note sulla letteratura europea del secolo decimonono*. Third edition. Bari: Laterza, 1942. viii, 337p.

Contains an essay on M.

292. Curtius, Ernst-Robert. "Nuit d'Idumée." *Romanische For-schungen*, 56 (1942), 180-181.

Concerns *Don du poème*.

293. Fargue, Léon-Paul. *Refuges*. Paris: Emile-Paul Frères, 1942. 306p.

Contains "La classe de Mallarmé."

294. Ghyka, Matila. "Vision analogique et composition symphonique chez Mallarmé et chez Marcel Proust." *France Libre*, 3 (1942), 386-390.

Brief comparative study: "On voit que chez Marcel Proust, comme chez Mallarmé, la recherche des correspondances, des analogies, pouvait aboutir à ce que ce dernier appelait la vision *orphique* de la vie."

295. Jean-Aubry, Georges. *Une Amitié exemplaire: Villiers de l'Isle-Adam et Stéphane Mallarmé d'après des documents inédits*. Paris: Mercure de France, 1942. 125p.

Presents the correspondence between M. and Villiers de l'Isle-Adam from October 1864 until the latter's death in August 1889.

296. Mallarmé, Stéphane. *Les Poèmes en prose*. Introduction by G. Jean-Aubry. Paris: Editions Emile-Paul, 1942. 118p.

297. Marasso, Arturo. "El pensamiento secreto de Mallarmé." *Logos*, 1 (1942), 249-260.

See 424.

298. Masur, Gerhard. "Stéphane Mallarmé: 1842-1942." *Revista de las Indias*, 15 (1942), 359-365.

A commemorative article with general commentary.

299. Matthey, Pierre Louis, *et al*. *Stéphane Mallarmé: essais et témoignages*. Neuchâtel: La Baconnière, 1942. 106p.

Contains: Jean Paul Zimmermann, "La Gloire de Mallarmé"; Pierre Jean Jouve, "La Langue de Mallarmé"; Georges Haldas, "Hommage"; Marcel Raymond, "Mallarmé"; Pierre Courthion,

"Le Poète et la vie: Stéphane Mallarmé"; Charly Guyot, "La Genèse d' 'Après-midi d'un faune.' "

300. Morrissette, Bruce A. "Early English and American Critics of French Symbolists." In *Studies in Honor of Frederick W. Shippley.* St. Louis: Washington University Studies, 1942. xi, 314p.

Includes several references to M.

301. Mortimer, Raymond. *Channel Packet.* London: Hogarth Press, 1942. 200p.

Contains a general essay on M. (pp. 132-147). Gives as an important reason for the difficulty of M.'s verse his desire that "the effort demanded of the readers would provide them with the valuable equivalent of the creative effort put forward by the poet."

302. ———. "Mallarmé." *Horizon,* 6 (1942), 247-264.

General commentary.

303. Peña Barrenechea, Enrique. "El centenario de Mallarmé." *Mercurio Peruano,* 25 (1942), 203-206.

Commemorative article concerning "el culto de Mallarmé."

*304. Raymond, Marcel. "Mallarmé." *Poésie,* 42 (May-June 1942), 65-70.

305. Rojas Paz, Pablo. "De la inspiración y la inteligencia: Mallarmé." *Nosotros,* 18 (1942), 252-268.

General commentary.

306. Romo Arregui, J. "De la Siringa de Teócrito al fauno de Mallarmé." *Cuadernos de Literatura Contemporánea,* No. 1 (1942), pp. 25-31.

An essay concerning M.'s poetry, its characteristics, and its forms. Also considers M.'s influence in Spain.

307. Royère, Jean. "Le Centenaire de Mallarmé." *Mois Suisse,* No. 41 (1942), pp. 3-13.

A commemorative article. Discusses "le musicisme de Mallarmé," which, according to the author, sees in poetry "le langage et le rythme du langage."

308. Schmidt, Albert-Marie. *La Littérature symboliste (1870-1900)*. Paris: Presses Universitaires de France, 1942. 128p.

> An excellent introductory text on Symbolism in the "Que Sais-je?" Series (No. 82). Treats M. as a "precursor" along with Rimbaud, Verlaine, and Villiers de l'Isle-Adam. Calls M. "un saint laïque dont la gloire exemplaire . . . ne cesse de s'accroître."

309. Soulairol, Jean. "Stéphane Mallarmé." *Divan*, 28 (1942), 256-258.

> Commentary on Mondor's *Vie de Mallarmé* (vol. 2).

*310. Tilliette, Xavier. "L'Aventure intérieure d'un poète unique." *Cité Nouvelle*, 25 Nov. 1942, pp. 758-776.

311. Woolley, Grange. *Stéphane Mallarmé: 1842-1898*. Madison, N. J.: Drew University, 1942. vi, 281p.

> A commemorative (centenary) publication on M. presenting a biographical sketch of the poet and English translations of many of M.'s works accompanied by commentary.

1943

*312. Benda, Julien. *Domaine français*. Geneva: Editions des Trois Collines, 1943. 445p.

313. Blanchot, Maurice. *Faux Pas*. Paris: Gallimard, 1943. 366p.

> Contains three essays concerning M.: "Le silence de Mallarmé," "La Poésie de Mallarmé est-elle obscure?" concerning Mauron's *Mallarmé l'obscur* (282), and "Mallarmé et l'art du roman," discussing "une définition de l'art du roman et une allusion chargée de gloire à ce qu'il est appelé à faire" found in M.'s writings on language and literature.

*314. Cattaui, Georges. "Mallarmé et les mystiques." *Les Lettres*, 1943, pp. 51-63.

315. Clouard, Henri, "Bilan poétique de Mallarmé." *Revue Universelle*, No. 51 (1943), pp. 180-189.

> General study.

316. Destéfano, José Rafaël. *Ocho ensayos.* Buenos Aires: El Ateneo, 1943. 143p.

> Contains "En el centenario del nacimiento de Stéphane Mallarmé (1842-1942)," a commemorative article offering general commentary concerning M. and his poetic method.

317. Dinar, André. *La Croisade symboliste.* Paris: Mercure de France, 1943. 189p.

> Contains a general study of M. (pp. 27-41). Criticizes M.'s obscurity saying that it makes his poetry totally incomprehensible: "Si la poésie est la possibilité de communiquer à autrui ses impressions, il est regrettable que Mallarmé ait poussé jusqu'à la rigueur une esthétique un peu tâtonnante...."

318. Eigeldinger, Marc. *Le Dynamisme de l'image dans la poésie française.* Neuchâtel: Editions de la Baconnière, 1943. 298p.

> Contains numerous references to M. as well as a chapter entitled "Mallarmé et le démon de l'analogie," considering M.'s esthetical principles and images of movement in his works. States that "l'imagination de Mallarmé est avant tout motrice autant par les formes qu'elle crée que par ses aspirations."

*319. Fernandat, René. "Entre Mallarmé et Platon (Louis Le Cardonnel)." *Résurrection,* 1943, pp. 31-47.

320. ———. "Mallarmé animateur de la rêverie." *Méridien,* No. 5 (1943), pp. 5-11; No. 6 (1943), pp. 3-9.

> Discusses M.'s predilection for reverie and says of the poet: "Mallarmé c'est le rêve devenu homme."

321. Lalou, René. *Les Etapes de la poésie française.* Paris: P.U.F., 1943. 127p.

> Includes numerous references to M.

322. Mallarmé, Stéphane. *L'Après-midi d'un faune.* 4 vols. Paris: Rombaldi, 1943.

> Deluxe edition of *L'Après-midi d'un faune* including 1) commentary by Henry Charpentier, 2) Debussy's score of the *Prélude à l'après-midi d'un faune,* and 3) sixteen lithographs by R. Demeurisse.

323. Mazel, Henri. *Aux beaux temps du symbolisme: 1890-1895.* Paris: Mercure de France, 1943. 197p.

> Contains "Verlaine et Mallarmé," concerning the poets' influence on the development of Symbolism.

*324. Mucci, R. "Ses purs ongles...." *Letterature*, 7, No. 2 (1943), 50-53.

325. Noulet, Emilie. "Villiers de l'Isle-Adam y Stéphane Mallarmé." *Filosofía y Lettras*, 6, No. 12 (1943), 291-300.

> Concerns Villiers de l'Isle-Adam's influence on M.

326. Roulet, Claude. *Elucidation du poème de Stéphane Mallarmé: Un Coup de dés jamais n'abolira le hasard.* Neuchâtel: Aux Ides et Calendes, 1943, 182p.

> An analysis of *Un Coup de dés* offering detailed exegesis of the poem from various aspects: structural, typographic, "photographic," musical, etc. Also contains an explication of "A la nue accablante tu...," which Roulet calls "une première édition du *Coup de Dés.*"
>
> Much of the material in this volume is republished in the author's *Traité de poétique supérieure* (633). See also 394, 464, 491, 633.
>
> a) J. Rütsch, *Trivium*, 6 (1948), 233-238.
> b) P. O. Walzer, *Formes et Couleurs*, No. 2 (1944), pp. 86-87.

327. Rousseaux, André. "Mallarmé tel qu'en lui-même: état présent des études mallarméennes." *Poésie*, 43, No. 13 (1943), 55-62.

> Survey of recent M. criticism.

328. Segond, J. "La Vocation platonicienne de Stéphane Mallarmé." *Fontaine*, 5 (1943), 382-407.

> Concerns M.'s idealism, which Segond believes is "orienté vers la vision platonicienne de la Pensée et de l'Etre."

1944

329. Francavilla, Francesco. *Il Simbolismo.* Milan: Ultra, 1944. 71p.

Contains "Verlaine e Mallarmé" (pp. 38-41) and "Un Autoritratto" (pp. 42-48), including an Italian translation of M.'s "Autobiographie."

330. Ghyka, Matila. "Of Some French Writers and Their Key Words." *Life and Letters Today*, 40 (1944), 162-167.

A classification of several French authors by their predilection for certain words. Ghyka considers M.'s frequent use of *azur*, *pur*, *or*, *vierge*, *cristal*, and *glacier*.

331. Jones, P. Mansell. "Poe, Baudelaire and Mallarmé: A Problem of Literary Judgment." *Modern Language Review*, 39 (1944), 236-246.

Considers Baudelaire's and M.'s admiration of Poe.

332. Mallarmé, Stéphane. *Poésies*. Preface by E. Noulet. Mexico City: Ediciones Quetzal, S. A., 1944. 173p.

333. Mondor, Henri. *Mallarmé plus intime*. Paris: Gallimard, 1944. 251p.

A volume which supplements Mondor's *Vie de Mallarmé* (284), furnishing a more intimate view of the poet: his life at home, family and friends.

334. Noulet, Emilie. *Etudes littéraires*. Mexico City: Talleres Gráficos de la Editorial Cultura, 1944. 159p.

Contains three essays: "L'hermétisme dans la poésie française moderne," "Influence d'Edgar Poe sur la poésie française" (both including references to M.), and "Exégèse de trois sonnets de Stéphane Mallarmé" (concerning "Quand l'ombre menaça...," "Une dentelle s'abolit...," and "A la nue accablante tu...").

335. ———. "Exégèse d'un poème de Mallarmé." *Lettres Françaises*, No. 12 (1944), pp. 30-35.

Exegesis of "A la nue accablante tu...."

336. ———. "Mallarmé y su *Hérodiade*." *Cuadernos Americanos*, 15 (1944), 198-215.

Concerns the genesis of *Hérodiade* and its importance in relation to M.'s other compositions.

337. *Le Point*, 5, Nos. 29-30 (1944), 5-98.

> Issue dedicated to M. containing: Paul Valéry, "Mallarmé";
> Henri Mondor, "Un Conte inédit de Mallarmé lycéen" ("Ce
> que disaient les trois cigognes"); Gaston Bachelard, "La Dia-
> lectique dynamique de la rêverie mallarméenne"; extracts from
> *Propos sur la poésie* (see 348); André Rouveyre, "Mallarmé,
> Matisse et le Cygne," concerning Matisse's drawings to ac-
> company "Le vierge, le vivace et le bel aujourd'hui..." (with
> reproductions); Henry Charpentier, "Etude," exegetical notes
> on several poems; André Fontainas, "La Lecture pour Stéphane
> Mallarmé"; fragments from M.'s works; H. M., "La Signature
> de Mallarmé"; Camille Soula, "Définitions," in which the
> author defends M.'s hermeticism: "Auteur difficile, oui, incom-
> préhensible, non. Ses poèmes sont de la raison en comprimés";
> "Mallarmé et la peinture de son temps" (chronological table).
> The volume includes numerous portraits, photographs, drawings,
> and reproductions of texts.

338. Vortriede, Werner. "The Conception of the Poet in the Works
of Mallarmé and Stefan George." *Summaries of Doctoral Dis-
sertations: Northwestern University*, 12 (1944), 48-50.

1945

339. Benda, Julien. *La France byzantine, ou le triomphe de la littérature pure*. Paris: Gallimard, 1945. 293p.

> Discusses M. as a notable representative of the "triomphe de
> la conception de la pure littérature," which, Benda believes,
> "répond à ce que l'homme, en principe, demande originaire-
> ment des satisfactions de la sensibilité, voire de la sensualité,
> non de l'intelligence."

340. Bo, Carlo. *Mallarmé*. Milan: Rosa e Ballo, 1945. 257p.

> Includes four essays: "Amleto," "Igitur," "Un Coup de dés,"
> and "Valvins" with a "Nota sulla bibliografia." Offers inter-
> pretations of much of M.'s poetry.

341. Borgeaud, Willy. "Aux extrêmes de la sphère d'appartenance."
Trivium, 3 (1945), 122-129.

> Exegesis of *Hérodiade*.

342. García Bacca, Juan David. "La filosofía de Husserl y el poema *Hérodiade* de Mallarmé." *Cuadernos Americanos,* 22
(1945), 77-99.

Suggests the influence of Husserl's *Méditations cartésiennes*
upon the composition of *Hérodiade.*

343. Johansen, Svend. "Le Problème d'*Un Coup de dés.*" *Orbis
Litterarum,* 3 (1945), 282-313.

A review-article concerning 326.

344. ———. *Le Symbolisme: étude sur le style des symbolistes
français.*

Includes stylistic analyses of many of M.'s poems.

345. Madaule, Jacques. "A propos de Stéphane Mallarmé." *Revue
de l'Alliance Française,* No. 9 (1945), pp. 15-16.

Brief general essay on the occasion of the publication of M.'s
Œuvres complètes. States that M. "demeure comme une stèle
qu'on ne pourra plus déplacer."

346. Mallarmé, Stéphane. *Œuvres complètes.* Edited by Henri
Mondor and G. Jean-Aubry. Bibliothèque de la Pléiade. Paris: Editions Gallimard, 1945. xvii, 1659p.

The only major publication of M.'s lifelong literary production,
although, in spite of the title, this volume does not present M.'s
"complete works." For texts not included and their location in
other publications, see Richard's *Univers imaginaire de Mallarmé* (752), pp. 623-624. Major sections are (1) Poèmes d'enfance et de jeunesse, (2) Poésies, (3) Vers de circonstance, (4)
Les Poèmes d'Edgar Poe. (5) Proses de jeunesse, (6) Poèmes
en prose, (7) Crayonné au théâtre, (8) Variations sur un sujet,
(9) Igitur, (10) Un Coup de dés, (11) Quelques médaillons et
portraits en pieds, (12) Richard Wagner, (13) Préface à Vathek,
(14) Le "Ten O'Clock" de M. Whistler, (15) Contes indiens,
(16) La Musique et les lettres, (17) Proses diverses, (18) Les
Mots anglais, (19) Les Thèmes anglais, (20) Les Dieux an-
tiques, and (21) L'Etoile des fées. Also includes a chronology,
extensive bibliography, iconography, and excellent annotation
concerning the genesis and publication of the texts, with vari-
ants. Of inestimable value for Mallarmé studies.

a) M. Gilman, *Romanic Review,* 38 (1947), 184-186.

b) A. Rolland de Renéville, *La Nef,* No. 12 (1945), 122-125.

347. Mallarmé, Stéphane. *Poésies*. Commentary by Pierre Beausire. Lausanne: Editions Mermod, 1945. 209p.

348. ———. *Propos sur la poésie*. Edited by Henri Mondor. Monaco: Editions du Rocher, 1945. 175p.

> Later edition: 1953. 235p.
> Extracts of M.'s letters (4 June 1862-August 1898) concerning thoughts on poetics, literary criticism, and the genesis of the poet's own literary production. For complete texts of most of these letters, see the three volumes of *Correspondance* (700, 855, 993).

349. ———. "Stéphane Mallarmé." *La Nef*, 2, No. 4 (1945), 92-97.

> General commentary. States that after years of mockery and derision, "la gloire de Stéphane Mallarmé est l'une des plus pures" and he can now take his place "de premier rang, avec Baudelaire et Rimbaud."

350. ———. "Un poème du lycéen Stéphane Mallarmé." *Les Lettres*, No. 2 (1945), pp. 83-87.

> Concerns *Causerie d'adieu*.

351. Teissier, Léon. *Aubanel, Mallarmé et le "Faune."* Montpellier: Editions Calendau, 1945. 16p.

> Indicates points of similarity between M.'s *L'Après-midi d'un faune* and the works of Provençal authors: Aubanel's sonnet *Patimen* and *lou Pastre*, a drama in verse, and Mistral's *Calendau* (ninth canto).

352. Vallat, H. "La Poésie de l'absence dans l'œuvre de Mallarmé." Dissertation. Montpellier, 1945.

1946

353. Blais, Jean-Ehier. "Mallarmé." *Amérique Française*, 5, No. 9 (1946), 34-37.

> General commentary on M.

354. Blanchot, Maurice. "Mallarmé et le langage." *L'Arche*, March-April 1946, pp. 134-146.

> A discussion of M.'s conception of language: "Le poète marque ... la possibilité majeure du langage: non pas exprimer un sens, mais l'incarner et finalement le créer."

*355. Chassé, Charles. "Lueurs sur Mallarmé." *Renaissance*, April 1946.

356. Fretet, Jean. *L'Aliènation poétique: Rimbaud, Mallarmé. Proust.* Paris: J. B. Janin, 1946. 332p.

> A psychoanalytical study presenting the thesis that M. was a manic-depressive schizophrenic: "L'exemple de Mallarmé montre l'association d'un fond shizoïde et d'épisodes tantôt d'excitation légère, tantôt de dépression profonde. Aux inhibitions stérilisantes du mélancolique s'ajoutent les orgueilleuses abstractions du shizoïde. Leur conjonction est à l'origine du Néant mallarméen."

357. Gide, André. "Souvenirs littéraires et problèmes actuels." *L'Arche*, Nos. 18-19 (1946), pp. 3-19.

> Contains a description of Gide's visits to the "Mardis." Gide also tells of M.'s influence upon him as an author: "... je gardais de son enseignement une sainte horreur de la facilité, de la complaisance, de tout ce qui flatte et séduit...."

358. Golffing, Francis C. "Stéphane Mallarmé: A Reconsideration." *New Mexico Quarterly Review*, 16 (1946), 63-73.

> Discusses M.'s original contributions to French poetry: "... he exhibits a rigorous classicism in all points of versification; and the steadily maintained equilibrium between this metrical orthodoxy and his revolutionary treatment of all verbal and syntactical aspects is one of the most fascinating features of Mallarmé's poetry."

359. Gutman, René-Albert. *Introduction à la lecture des poètes français.* Paris: Flammarion, 1946.

> Later edition: Librairie Nizet, 1967. 396p.
> Contains a section on M. including analyses of several poems and general critical commentary.

360. Henriot, Emile. *Poètes français de Lamartine à Valéry.* Paris: H. Lardanchet, 1946. 392p.

Contains "La Vie de Stéphane Mallarmé" (pp. 223-230) concerning Mondor's biography (284) and "Mallarmé clair et amoureux" (pp. 231-235) pertaining to a letter from M. to Cazalis about his future wife, Marie Gerhard.

361. Jaloux, Edmond. *D'Eschyle à Giraudoux.* Fribourg: Egloff, 1946. 315p.

Contains "Portrait de Mallarmé," "La Correspondance de Mallarmé," and "L'Amitié de Verlaine et de Mallarmé."

362. Mondor, Henri. "Premier entretien Mallarmé-Valéry." *Cahiers du Sud,* Nos. 276-278 (1946), pp. 49-64.

Offers details concerning M.'s friendship with Valéry and his influence on the younger poet.

363. Papadopoulo, Alexandre. "Stéphane Mallarmé." *Revue du Caire,* 9 (1946), 390-408, 520-537.

A general essay concerning primarily M.'s influence on the development of modern poetry.

364. Rousseaux, André. *Le Monde classique.* Vol. 2. Paris: Editions Albin Michel, 1946. 253p.

Contains "Mallarmé tel qu'en lui-même" (pp. 232-244).

365. Saurat, Denis. *Modern French Literature.* New York: G. P. Putnam's Sons, 1946. 192p.

Contains a somewhat unfavorable essay on M. Although Saurat recognizes the genius of the poet's literary vision, he states that "Mallarmé's great handicap is that he cannot write, either in prose or in poetry.... His poems can easily be printed in some fifty pages, and are mostly bad."

366. Secrétain, Roger. *Quand montait l'orage.* Paris: Editions du Saggitaire, 1946. 259p.

Contains "Barrès et Mallarmé," an essay concerning Barrès' unfavorable criticism of M.

367. Sells, A. Lytton. "Reflections on Stéphane Mallarmé: Some Greek and English Reminiscences." *Modern Language Review,* 41 (1946), 362-381.

Suggests possible sources from English and classical Greek literature as influences upon M., e.g., Keats, Shelley, the *Odyssey*, the *Anthologia Palatina*.

368. Simons, Hi. "Wallace Stevens and Mallarmé." *Modern Philology*, 43 (1945-46), 235-259.

Concerns M.'s influence on Stevens' poetry.

369. Souffrin, Eileen. "Un sonnet inédit de Stéphane Mallarmé." *Fontaine*, 10 (1946), 497-502.

Concerns "De l'Orient passé des Temps...," an unpublished poem which M. sent to William Bonaparte-Wyse in 1868. For a challenge to M.'s authorship of this poem, see 867.

370. Soula, Camille. *Gloses sur Mallarmé*. Preface by Jean Cassou. Paris: Editions Diderot, 1946. 304p.

A collection of previously published exegetical studies (119, 120) except for the essay on *L'Après-midi d'un faune*, which is presented for the first time.

371. Van Tieghem, Philippe. *Les Grandes Doctrines littéraires en France de la Pléiade au surréalisme*. Paris: P.U.F., 1946. 302p.

Offers a succinct discussion of M.'s poetics which, according to the author, consists of "trois éléments distincts et parfois contrariés; le mot, ou le vers, en soi comporte une valeur musicale propre; l'objet n'est désigné que par une image allusive; la matière du poème est une Idée, c'est-à-dire, une notion abstraite, intellectuelle ou émotive."

372. Zurowski, Mathieu. "Notes sur Mallarmé." *Cahiers Franco-Polonais*, Dec. 1946, pp. 64-67.

Suggests sources for several themes in M.'s poetry: Louis Bouilhet, Thalès Bernard, Charles Nodier, etc.

1947

373. Auriant. "Autour d'un sonnet de Mallarmé." *Mercure de France*, 300 (1947), 585-586.

Concerns "Au seul souci de voyager...."

374. Balakian, Anna. *Literary Origins of Surrealism: A New Mysticism in French Poetry.* New York: King's Crown Press, 1947. ix, 159p.

> Contains a section on M. as "author of *Igitur*" and a participant, with Lautréamont and Rimbaud, in the nineteenth-century spiritual crisis brought about by scientific progress. Author gives an interpretation of *Igitur*, which she claims is "the first poetic work based entirely on the materialistic mysticism which later turned out to be the basis of Surrealism and for three generations of poets replaced the concept of immortality by what they thought of as the absolute."

375. Benda, Julien. "Mallarmé und Wagner." *Lancelot,* No. 11 (1947), pp. 83-87.

> Translated extract from *Domaine français* (312).

376. Bowra, C. M. *The Heritage of Symbolism.* London: Macmillan and Co., Ltd., 1947. vii, 232.

> Introduction includes a discussion of M.'s poetical principles and their influence upon later poets. States that "in his theory and practice Mallarmé was the conclusion and crown of the Symbolist movement."

377. Brock-Sulzer, Elizabeth. "Der Dichter im Kampf mit seiner Sprache: Bemerkungen zur neueren französische Lyrik." *Trivium,* 5 (1947), 233-262.

> Contains a discussion of M. and his poetry.

378. Chassé, Charles. *Lueurs sur Mallarmé.* Paris: Editions de la Nouvelle Revue Critique, 1947. 121p.

> A collection of articles on M. by Chassé previously published in various periodicals: "Mallarmé universitaire," "Un Biographe de Mallarmé," "Lettres de Mallarmé à Mistral," "Supplément à l'article sur les lettres de Mallarmé à Mistral," "Mallarmé dans le Finistère," and "Essai d'une explication de Mallarmé."
>
> a) W. T. Bandy, *French Review,* 22 (1948), 59-60.
> b) A. Feuillerat, *Romanic Review,* 38 (1947), 365-368.

379. Chast, Denyse. "Eugénio de Castro et Stéphane Mallarmé." *Revue de Littérature Comparée,* 21 (1947), 243-253.

> Concerns M.'s influence upon the Portuguese poet.

380. Chastel, André. "Vuillard et Mallarmé." *La Nef*, 4, No. 26 (1947), 13-25.

> Concerns M.'s influence upon the artist Vuillard.

381. Clouard, Henri. *Histoire de la littérature française du symbolisme à nos jours: de 1885 à 1914*. Paris: Editions Albin Michel, 1947. 668p.

> Includes a perceptive essay on M. in which Clouard defines and analyzes the poet's personal philosophy: "Le mallarmisme situe sa matière tout à part, dans un idéalisme. Mallarmé, solitaire méditatif, en était venu à tirer son émotion des idées et ses idées se ramenaient, en manifestations diverses, à une seule que voici: le poète recrée la réalité par son rêve...."

382. Crépet, Jacques. "Un vers prêté à Mallarmé par Agrippa d'Aubigné." *Fontaine*, 11 (1947), 495-496.

> Concerns the famous line from *Le Tombeau d'Edgar Poe*: "Tel qu'en Lui-même enfin l'éternité le change...." Crépet indicates a passage with a similar expression in D'Aubigné's *Jugement dernier*.

383. Davies, Gardner. "Stéphane Mallarmé: Fifty Years of Research." *French Studies*, 1 (1947), 1-26.

> Surveys Mallarméan research from the poet's death in 1898 to 1947. Davies traces the varying critical approaches to M. from the somewhat anti-intellectual, popularizing attitude of many of his contemporaries to the careful critical analysis of Thibaudet (40), Aish (237), Wais (256), Noulet (271), Mauron (282), and others. Cites the publication of M.'s complete works in 1945 by Mondor and Jean-Aubry (346) as "the most important event in Mallarmean research in the last few years." In conclusion, calls for an even more rigorous critical method in future M. studies and decries careless and negligent research: "But whilst the few are patiently pursuing this programme of research in the best traditions of scholarship, others are busily confusing the issues.... If Mallarmé is to occupy in the history of French poetry the place to which he has a right, his obscurity must first be penetrated. Much still remains to be done."

384. Fargue, Léon-Paul. *Portraits de famille: souvenirs*. Paris: J. B. Janin, 1947. 231p.

> Includes a chapter offering personal notes on M. (pp. 107-124). Also tells of a visit to the "Mardis."

385. Fowlie, Wallace. "The Theme of Night in Four Sonnets of Mallarmé." *Modern Philology*, 44 (1946-47), 248-258.

> Traces the theme of "night" in *Le Tombeau de Baudelaire, Le Tombeau d'Edgar Poe*, "Quand l'ombre menaça...," and *Tombeau* (de Verlaine). See 550.

386. Gide, André. "La Leçon de Mallarmé." *Erasme*, 2 (1947), 145-147.

> Personal notes on M.

387. Gregh, Fernand. *L'Age d'or: souvenirs d'enfance et de jeunesse*. Paris: Bernard Grasset, 1947. 334p.

> Includes personal notes on M. (pp. 232-239).

388. Grubbs, Henry A. "Mallarmé and Bryant." *Modern Language Notes*, 62 (1947), 410-412.

> Suggests the possible influence of William Cullen Bryant's *Thanatopsis* upon M.

*389. Huxley, Aldous. *A Mirror of French Poetry*. Edited by Cecily Macworth. London: G. Rutledge, 1947. 230p.

390. Jasinski, René. *Histoire de la littérature française*. 2 vols. Paris: Boivin et Cie, 1947.

> The second volume of this literary history contains an excellent *précis* of M.'s life and work. Jasinski is quite favorable to the poet, declaring that "il mûrit lentement une œuvre d'une miraculeuse densité deux mille vers à peine, mais qui s'élèvent aux plus purs sommets de la poésie."

391. Mauron, Charles. "Gloses sur Mallarmé." *Témoignages*, No. 14 (1947), pp. 443-445.

> Concerns 370.

392. Michaud, Guy. *Message poétique du symbolisme*. Paris: Librairie Nizet, 1947. 237p.

> A comprehensive historical study of Symbolism in all of its aspects from inauspicious beginnings to its disappearance as a dominant influence in literature. Contains three major parts: (1) "L'Aventure poétique," (2) "La Révolution poétique," (3)

"L'Univers poétique." Part I devotes a chapter (5) to "Mallarmé, poète de l'absolu," but other references to M. throughout the work are numerous. The appendix, "La Doctrine symboliste," is a valuable collection of documents (extracts from newspapers, journals, and critical works of the period) pertaining to Symbolism.

393. Rivoallan, A. "Mallarmé et l'anglais." *Langues Modernes,* 41 (1947), 435-438.

> Concerns 378.

394. Roulet, Claude. *Eléments de poétique mallarméenne d'après le poème "Un Coup de dés jamais n'abolira le hasard."* Neuchâtel: Editions du Griffon, 1947. 163p.

> See 326, 464, 491, 633.
> a) T. Spoerri, *Trivium,* 6 (1948), 233-238.

395. Schérer, Jacques. *L'Expression littéraire dans l'œuvre de Mallarmé.* Paris: A. G. Nizet, 1947. 289p.

> A comprehensive study of M.'s literary style, investigating "une grammaire mallarméenne," spelling, punctuation, vocabulary, use of the parts of speech, syntax, the sentence, the verse, and the page. Also retraces the development of M.'s expression, which the author divides into six distinct phases. Final chapter is devoted to "Mallarmé et son époque."
> a) J. Boorsch, *French Review,* 21 (1948), 500-502.
> b) C. M. Bowra, *Modern Language Review,* 43 (1948), 548-549.
> c) G. Davies, *French Studies,* 2 (1948), 181-185.
> d) A. Rolland de Renéville, *La Nef,* 4, No. 36 (1947), 123-126.

396. Soulairol, Jean. "Mistral et Mallarmé." *Divan,* 31 (1947), 63-71.

> Offers details concerning M.'s friendship with Frédéric Mistral.

397. Teissier, Léon. "Le stérile Stéphane." *Marsyas,* No. 253 (1947), pp. 1324-1329.

> Challenges Fretet's psychological study of M. (see 356).

398. Thierry-Norbert. "Mallarmé et Manet." *Monde Français,* 7 (1947), 331-334.

> Discusses philosophical affinities between the two men.

399. Vortriede, Werner. "The Mirror as Symbol and Theme in the Works of Stéphane Mallarmé and Stefan George." *Modern Language Forum*, 32 (1947), 13-24.

> A comparison of the two poets' symbolic use of the mirror: "An examination of how George treated the theme reveals his indebtedness to French symbolism and especially to Mallarmé...."

400. Winters, Yvor. *In Defense of Reason*. New York: Swallow Press and W. Morrow and Co., 1947. viii, 611p.

> Contains quite unfavorable criticism of M.

1948

401. Aragon. "Mallarmé: Obscurity in Poetry." *Adam*, 16, No. 189 (1948), 5-7.

> Concerns 356, 370.

402. *Cahiers du Nord*, 21 (1948), 117-245.

> Issue dedicated to M. entitled "Stèle pour Mallarmé." Contains: Henri Mondor, "Mallarmé, Debussy et 'L'Après-midi d'un faune' "; André Bellivier, "Quelques réflexions sur Mallarmé"; Guy Lavaud, "La Vraie Leçon de Mallarmé"; André Marcou, "Mallarmé futur"; Michel Faré, "Instigations ou charmes de Mallarmé"; André Fontainas, "Les Sonnets de Mallarmé"; E. Noulet, "Exégèse d'un sonnet de Mallarmé," explication of *Le Tombeau de Verlaine*; Roget Desaise, "Mallarmé et le sens de l'universel"; Jean Royère, "L'Hermétisme de Mallarmé"; Henry Charpentier, "Legs de Mallarmé"; Antoine Orliac, "Apocalypse de Mallarmé"; Robert Vivier, "Mallarmé le Parnassien"; Charles Mauron, "Le Miroitement en dessous," a psychocritical essay concerning "Las de l'amer repos..."; Nestor Miserez, "Aveux et scrupules de Mallarmé."

403. Carrouges, Michel. *La Mystique du surhomme*. Paris: Gallimard, 1948. 436p.

> Includes several references to M.

404. Chazel, Pierre. *Figures de proue de Corneille à Valéry*. Neuchâtel: Delachaux et Niestlé, 1948. 167p.

> Contains "Sur quelques mythes de Mallarmé et de Valéry," in which author discusses the modern myths found in *L'Après-*

midi d'un faune ("le mythe du désir"), *Hérodiade* ("le mythe de l'impuissance"), and *Igitur* ("ce mythe du Prométhée moderne"). Concludes that "de tous les mythes mallarméens, le plus accompli, le plus fascinant, c'est sa vie même, haute flamme veillant sur l'œuvre en décombres."

405. Coléno, Alice. *Les Portes d'ivoire: métaphysique et poésie.* Paris: Plon, 1948. 247.

A comparative critical study of Nerval, Baudelaire, Rimbaud, and M., who were, according to the author, visionary poets expressing in their poetry the belief that "derrière ces apparences tangibles et visibles, il existe *autre chose,* un autre univers, caché à tous, sauf au poète, et dont notre univers n'est que l'ombre."

406. Duchesne-Guillemin, J. "Au sujet du 'Divin cygne.'" *Mercure de France,* 304 (1948), 62-68.

Exegesis of "Le vierge, le vivace et le bel aujourd'hui...."

407. *Empreintes,* Nov-Dec. 1948, pp. 5-95.

Special issue dedicated to M. on the occasion of the fiftieth anniversary of his death. Contains: Herman Van der Driessche, "Un peu d'histoire," concerning publication of this volume; Henry Charpentier, "Le Cinquantenaire de Mallarmé"; Benoît Dujardin, "Une Gerbe d'autographes"; E. Noulet, "Exégèses," concerning "Au seul souci de voyager..."; Robert Goffin, "L'Hermétisme freudien de Mallarmé"; J. Duchesne-Guillemin, "Encore le Divin Cygne," explication of "Le vierge, le vivace et le bel aujourd'hui..."; José Camby, "Stéphane Mallarmé en Belgique (1890)"; Fernand Verhesen, "De quelques exégèses mallarméennes," concerning recent criticism of M.'s poetry; J.-D. Garcia Bacca, "La Conception probabilistique de l'univers chez Mallarmé," exegesis of *Un Coup de dés*; Robert Vivier, "La Victoire de Mallarmé"; "Essai de bibliographie d'ouvrages à consulter sur Mallarmé"; "Echos-Documents" (concerning M.).

408. Faure, Gabriel. "Mallarmé: naissance d'*Hérodiade* et du *Faune.*" *Gazette des Lettres,* 18 Sept. 1948, pp. 1, 14.

Investigates the genesis of these poems.

409. Fontainas, André. "Rêverie à propos de Stéphane Mallarmé: l'œuvre et l'homme." *Mercure de France,* 304 (1948), 52-61.

Personal notes on M. in which Fontainas calls M. "mon maître et mon modèle."

410. Fournier, Louis. "Chroniques inconnues de Mallarmé." *Gazette des Lettres*, 18 Sept. 1948, pp. 3, 14.

> Concerns *La Dernière Mode*.

411. Fowlie, Wallace. *The Clown's Grail: A Study of Love in Its Literary Expression*. London: Dennis Dobson, 1948. 156p.

> Later edition: *Love in Literature: Studies in Symbolic Expression*. Bloomington: Indiana University Press, 1965. 155p. Introduction to this volume, entitled "The Symbolism of Mallarmé's Clown," offers an interpretation of *Le Pitre châtié*, which is, according to Fowlie, "an example of modern art where the symbol is the experience and whose literary meaning probably never existed in the poet's consciousness."

412. Goffin, Robert. *Entrer en poésie: pour mieux comprendre....* Paris: A l'Enseigne du Chat Qui Pêche, 1948. 241p.

> Contains numerous references to M.: Chap. 5, "L'Alchimie poétique"; Chap. 7, "Hermétisme et sexualité"; Chap. 19, "De Mallarmé à Ganzo par Valéry"; Chap. 20, "Rébus mallarméens," concerning exegesis of "A la nue accablante tu...."

413. Haloche, Maurice. "Cinquantenaire du décès de Stéphane Mallarmé." *Le Thyrse* (Sept. 1948), pp. 285-288.

> Commemorative article.

414. "The Hero as Artist." *Times Literary Supplement*, 47 (1948), 516.

> A commemorative article on the occasion of the fiftieth anniversary of M.'s death. States that "Mallarmé is still, with Flaubert, the hero as artist, the hero of all who dream of purity and perfection in literary form."

415. Heytens, René. "Stéphane Mallarmé herdacht." *Nieuw Vlaams Tijdschrift*, 3 (1948), 490-492.

416. Howald, Ernst. "Die absolute Dichtung im 19. Jahrhundert." *Trivium*, 6 (1948), 23-52.

> Contains numerous references concerning M. and his influence on Symbolist poetry.

417. *L'Immagine*, 2, Nos. 9-10 (1948), 502-567.

> Issue devoted primarily to M. Contains: Gianfranco Contini, "Sulla trasformazione dell'*Après-midi d'un faune*," comparing the *Monologue d'un faune* with the final version; Henri Mondor, "Mallarmé et Rodenbach"; Luigi Magnani, "Mallarmé e i miti della musica," including a discussion of similarities between M. and the composer Schönberg; Claude Edmonde Magny, "Frontière de Mallarmé," discussing M.'s obscurity; Cesare Brandi. "Psicoanalisi e poesia: Baudelaire, Mallarmé, Lautréamont"; Pierre Missac, "Sur une limite de Mallarmé," a general essay; Giuseppe Raimondi, "Mallarmé poeta di circostanza," which considers M.'s poems written after 1885 as "vers de circonstance."

418. Lannes, Roger. "Mallarmé poète de la poésie." *Synthèses*, 3, No. 1 (1948), 77-81.

> A commemorative article in which author states that M. "a été, depuis quelques années, par un mouvement unanime d'admiration et de regret, élevé presque au rang de héros et de saint." Indicates M.'s originality as a poet: "Mallarmé est le seul à avoir voulu que la poésie n'eût pas d'autre objet qu'elle-même."

419. *Les Lettres*, 3 (Special Issue, June 1948), 1-240.

> Special issue dedicated to M. on the fiftieth anniversary of his death. Contains: André Sivaire, "Présentation"; Jean Audard and Pierre Missac, "Introduction"; Paul Valéry, "Lettre à mon frère Jules Valéry"; fragments and previous versions of poems, letters by M.; Jean Starobinski, "Mallarmé et la tradition poétique française"; Henry Charpentier, " 'Mes bouquins refermés,' " concerning the books M. read and probably read; Joe Bousquet, "Mallarmé le sorcier"; Daniel-Henry Kahnweiler, "Mallarmé et la peinture," on M.'s relationship to the Impressionists; Jean Miquel, "Le phénomène futur ou le progrès d'une conscience poétique"; Claude-Edmonde Magny, "Le ramage et le plumage"; André Chastel, " 'Le théâtre est d'essence supérieure,' " on M.'s original conception of the theater; Albert-Marie Schmidt, "Mallarmé fondateur de religion," considering M.'s notion of a future national religion; Jean-Paul Roussel, "Les thèmes poétiques de Mallarmé" (*angoisse, doute, échec*); Antoine Adam, "Premières étapes d'un itinéraire," a discussion of the development of M.'s personal philosophy up to the composition of *Igitur*; E. Noulet, "La hantise d'abolir," concerning primarily *Igitur* and *Un Coup de dés*; René Nelli, " 'Igitur' ou l'argument ontologique retourné"; Charles Mauron, "Le *Coup de dés*"; Bernard Fleurot, " 'La chevelure vol d'une flamme' "; Gardner Davies, "*Salut* (essai d'exégèse raisonnée)"; Jean Audard, "Sur l'influence de Mallarmé"; Albert Béguin, "Notes sur Mal-

larmé et Claudel"; and four articles concerned with M.'s influence on foreign literatures: Cecily Mackworth, "Mallarmé en Angleterre"; Frédéric Hagen, "Mallarmé et l'Allemagne"; Guillermo de Torre, "Mallarmé en espagnol"; and Joao Gaspar Simoes, "Mallarmé et la poésie portuguaise."

a) L. Guillaume, *France-Asie*, 4, No. 31 (1948), 7-72.

b) C. A. Hackett, *French Studies*, 4 (1950), 179-187.

c) A. Patri, *Paru*, No. 46 (1948), pp. 61-62.

420. Lot, Fernand. "Mallarmé ou la poésie réfugiée dans l'obscur." *France-Asie*, 4, No. 31 (1948), pp. 10-13.

> General essay.

421. Mackworth, Cecily. "Stéphane Mallarmé and the Symbolist Attitude." *Adam*, 16, No. 189 (1948), 7-15.

> A general essay concerning M.'s poetics.

422. Mallarmé, Stéphane. *L'Après-midi d'un Faune.* Commentary by Léon-Paul Fargue. Paris: Société des Amis des Livres, 1948. 43p.

423. ———. *Poésies complètes.* Edited by Yves-Gérard Le Dantec. Paris: Editions de Cluny, 1948. 231p.

424. Marasso, Arturo. *El pensamiento secreto de Mallarmé.* Buenos Aires: Editorial Ollantay, 1948. 55p.

> Suggests possible sources for images in several of M.'s poems: Ovid, Virgil, Dante, Hugo, and others.

425. Marois, Pierre. "Les premiers vers de Mallarmé: la jeunesse du poète." *Gazette des Lettres*, 18 Sept. 1948, pp. 13-14.

> Concerns the first poem written by M. at the age of eight, six lines composed for Fanny Dubois-Davesnes, a family friend: "Ma chère Fanny / Ma bonne amie / Je te promets d'être sage / A tout âge / Et de toujours t'aimer / Stéphane Mallarmé."

426. Marino, Pierre. "Mallarmé, tel qu'en lui-même il s'est changé." *Annales du Centre Universitaire Méditerranéen*, 2 (1947-48), 235-236.

> Abstract of a lecture delivered 15 Dec. 1947.

427. Mauron, Charles. "Introduction à la psychanalyse de Mallarmé: l'aliénation poétique." *Temps Modernes*, 4 (1948), 455-478.

> See 486.

428. Miomandre, Francis de. *Mallarmé*. Mulhouse: Bader-Dufour, 1948. 207p.

> A general study of M. and his poetry in which Miomandre, attempting to dispel the legend of the poet's "literary impotency," discusses "le drame de la vie intérieure de Mallarmé" and indicates how M. made constructive use of the theme of sterility in his poems: "...il a su tirer parti d'une telle déficience, et ce dont il souffre... il en fait l'objet de sa méditation, il le célèbre et le conjure."
>
> a) E. Pognon, *Nouvelles Littéraires*, 20 Jan. 1949.

429. ———. "Notre Mallarmé." *Hommes et Mondes*, 6 (1948), 591-598.

> Extracted from 428.

430. Mondor, Henri. *L'Heureuse Rencontre de Valéry et Mallarmé*. Lausanne: La Guilde du Livre, 1948. 125p.

> Concerns the friendship between M. and his most illustrious disciple.

431. ———. *Histoire d'un faune*. Paris: Gallimard, 1948. 285p.

> A detailed study of *L'Après-midi d'un faune*, its genesis, and the two previous versions of the poem as *Monologue d'un faune* and *Improvisation d'un faune*. Also considers "l'affaire du Parnasse," Anatole France's and François Coppée's rejection of the poem for the third anthology of *Le Parnasse contemporain* in 1875.
>
> a) A. Gill, *Modern Language Review*, 45 (1950), 263-265.
> b) A. Rolland de Renéville, *La Nef*, 6, No. 51 (1949), 106-108.

*432. ———. "Mallarmé et Paul Claudel." *Revue des Deux Mondes*, 1 Dec. 1948, pp. 395-418.

433. Mora, André. "Stéphane Mallarmé et *Les Loisirs de la poste*." *Revue des Postes et Télégraphes*, 3, No. 3 (1948), 1-5.

> Concerns M.'s postal addresses in verse form.

434. Mucci, Renato. *"Il Pagliaccio punito* di Mallarmé." *Nuova Antologia,* 443 (1948), 290-295.

Exegesis of *Le Pitre châtié.*

435. Noulet, Emilie. *Dix poèmes de Stéphane Mallarmé.* Geneva: Librairie E. Droz, 1948. xv, 155p.

Detailed explications of ten poetical works by M. which were previously presented in the author's published doctoral thesis (271), but appear here in revised and corrected form.

a) C. Chassé, *Français Moderne,* 19 (1951), 307-310.

436. Orliac, Antoine. *La Cathédrale symboliste.* Vol. 2: *Mallarmé tel qu'en lui-même....* Paris: Mercure de France, 1948. 243p.

A general study of M. concentrating upon his personal philosophy and comparing M.'s thought with that found in oriental philosophy, mysticism, and the writings of modern philosophers, such as Kant, Hegel, Berkeley, etc. Discusses M.'s desire to make poetry a "religion" and concludes that "au cœur de la solitude sacrée, en ce sursaut de l'individu opposant à l'inévitable destruction l'ordre de son génie, il a dressé sa cathédrale intérieure, sanctuaire rayonnant de sa religion esthétique."

a) A. Patri, *Paru,* No. 44 (1948), pp. 57-58.

437. Patri, Aimé. "Mallarmé et la littérature." *Paru,* No. 48 (1948), pp. 7-13.

A commemorative article comparing M.'s and Jean-Paul Sartre's theories of literature.

438. Rousselot, Jean. "Mallarmé, grand prêtre et martyr du langage." *France-Asie,* 4, No. 31 (1948), 14-16.

Commemorative article. See 675.

439. Schwab, Raymond. "Elémir Bourges près de Mallarmé." *La Bouteille à la Mer,* No. 56 (1948), pp. 9-12.

Notes concerning M.'s friendship with Bourges.

440. Spoerri, Theophil. "Zu Mallarmés *Aprés-midi d'un faune.*" *Trivium,* 6 (1948), 224-232.

Exegesis, comparing the first version of the poem (1865) with its final text.

441. Tilliette, Xavier. "Quant à Mallarmé: clefs de Mallarmé."
Etudes, 259 (1948), 376-381.

Reviews various interpretations of M.'s poetry.

442. Torre, Guillermo de. "Mallarmé en español." *Asomante*, 4,
No. 3 (1948), 7-10.

Discusses parallels between Góngora and M. and considers M.'s
influence in Spain.

443. Usinger, Fritz. "Stéphane Mallarmé und die Magie der Dichtung." *Romania* (Mainz), 1 (1948), 25-35.

Includes German translations of "Surgi de la croupe et du
bond ..." and "Une dentelle s'abolit ...," with interpretative
commentary. States that "das Gedicht Mallarmés ist ein kris-
tallener Ball, den man nur als Ganzes nehmen kann."

1949

444. Adam, Antoine. "*L'Après-midi d'un faune*: essai d'explication." *L'Information Littéraire*, 1, No. 4 (1949), 137-140.

Calls M.'s poem "le chef-d'œuvre de la poésie parnassienne."

445. Aigrisse, Gilberte. "Mallarmé tel qu'en lui-même." *Action
et Pensée*, 25, No. 1 (1949), 14-16.

Concerns 436.

446. Bénichou, Paul. "Mallarmé et le public." *Cahiers du Sud*, 30
(1949), 272-290.

Discusses M.'s attitude toward the public which, according to
Bénichou, "est partie intégrante de sa pensée, ou mieux de sa
manière d'être, plutôt que conséquence de son art poétique.
L'un et l'autre ont leur source dans une conscience troublée,
qui vit un drame de séparation et d'exil, et qui s'efforce de le
surmonter."

447. Blanchot, Maurice. *La Part du feu*. Paris: Gallimard, 1949.
374p.

Contains "Le Mythe de Mallarmé," an essay in which Blanchot
attacks what he considers mythopoeic treatments of M., particularly by Valéry, and attempts to "demythologize" the con-

ception of M. of whom he says, "Nul poète n'a plus fortement senti que tout poème, si mince qu'en fût le prétexte, était nécessairement engagé dans la création du langage poétique et peut-être de tout langage."

448. Chassé, Charles. "L'Erotisme de Mallarmé." *Cahiers de la Lucarne*, No. 4 (1949), pp. 2-15.

Considers erotic imagery in M.'s poetry based on the author's premise that M. used words according to their etymology (see 565).

449. ———. "Essai d'une interprétation objective du *Tombeau d'Edgar Poe* ou Mallarmé traduit par Mallarmé lui-même." *Revue de Littérature Comparée*, 23 (1949), 97-109.

450. ———. "La source occultiste de la Prose pour des Esseintes de Mallarmé." *Quo Vadis*, 2, Nos. 16-17 (1949), 10-21.

Suggests that "c'est de la bouche de ses amis occultistes que Mallarmé a bien probablement reçu les thèmes dont il a fait état dans la *Prose pour Des Esseintes*."

451. Clarke, Margaret. "The Symbolism of Brennan and of Mallarmé: A Comparison." *Southerly*, 10 (1949), 219-226.

Underlines common points found in the two poets' works.

452. Cohn, Robert Greer. *Mallarmé's "Un Coup de dés": An Exegesis*. New Haven: Yale French Studies, 1949. 139p.

Offers quite detailed syntactical and linguistic analysis of *Un Coup de dés*. (Publication of the author's dissertation presented at Yale University.)
a) E. Kern, *Comparative Literature*, 6 (1954), 275-279.
b) S. A. Rhodes, *Romantic Review*, 41 (195), 223-229.

453. Croce, Benedetto. "Il 'segreto' di Mallarmé." *Quaderni della "Critica*," No. 14 (1949), pp. 90-97.

Concerns Noulet's exegesis of M. See 271.

454. Decorte, Bert. "Gedichten van Stéphane Mallarmé." *Nieuw Vlaams Tijdschrift*, 3 (1949), 1047-1051.

455. Fowlie, Wallace. *Mallarmé as Hamlet: A Study of "Igitur."*
Yonkers, N. Y.: Alicat Bookshop Press, 1949. 22p.

A brief analysis and interpretation of *Igitur.*

456. ———. "Three Masks of Mallarmé." *Zéro,* No. 1 (1949),
pp. 4-15.

Offers exegesis of *Le Pitre châtié,* "Le vierge, le vivace...,"
and "M'introduire dans ton histoire...."

457. Lefèvre-Roujon, Mme. C., editor. *Correspondance inédite de
Stéphane Mallarmé et Henry Roujon.* Geneva: Pierre Cailler,
1949. 71p.

Includes editorial commentary.

458. Lemonnier, Léon. "Baudelaire et Mallarmé traducteurs d'Edgar
Poe." *Langues Modernes,* 43 (1949), 47-57.

A comparative study of Baudelaire's and M.'s translations of
Poe's works. Indicates unusual and erroneous translations of
words and phrases.

459. Luzi, Mario. "Mallarmé e la poesia moderna." *Rassegna
d'Italia,* 4 (1949), 899-909.

Investigates M.'s profound influence upon the development of
modern poetry.

460. Mallarmé, Stéphane. *Divagations.* Edited by E. M. Souffrin.
Paris: Bibliothèque Charpentier, Fasquelle Editeurs, 1949.
375p.

461. Messières, René de. "Stéphane Mallarmé." *French Review,*
22 (1948-49), 362-370.

A commemorative article on the fiftieth anniversary of M.'s
death. Reviews the radical change of perspective concerning
M. from the first few years after the poet's death, during which
time Thibaudet's thesis on M. was rejected at the Sorbonne
"comme une plaisanterie de mauvais goût," to the present when
M. is readily accepted as an "initiateur de la nouvelle poésie."

462. Patriconi, Hellmuth. "Das Meer und der Tod in drei Gedichten von Mallarmé, Rimbaud, Claudel." *Romantisches
Jahrbuch*, 2 (1949), 282-295.

  Concerns *Brise Marine*.

463. Rolland de Renéville, André. "Sur Stéphane Mallarmé." *Revue
du Caire*, 12, No. 117 (1949), 179-184.

  General essay.

464. Roulet, Claude. *Version du poème de Mallarmé "Un Coup
de dés jamais n'abolira le hasard."* Neuchâtel: Editions du
Griffon, 1949. 82p.

  See 326, 394, 491, 633.

465. Roy, Claude. *Descriptions critiques*. Vol. 1. Paris: Gallimard,
1949. 319p.

  Contains "Mallarmé revisité" (pp. 21-28).

466. Ruchon, François, editor. *L'Amitié de Stéphane Mallarmé et
de Georges Rodenbach*. Preface by Henri Mondor. Geneva:
Pierre Cailler, Editeur, 1949. 169p.

  Presents the correspondence between M. and Georges Rodenbach (1887-1898), as well as other documents concerning their
  friendship.

1950

467. Aigrisse, Gilberte. "Vers une psychanalyse de Mallarmé."
Action et Pensée, 26, No. 4 (1950), 114-118.

  Concerns 486.

468. Bellivier, André. "Mallarmé et l'unité de l'esprit." *Vie, Art,
Cité*, No. 4 (1950), pp. 16-18.

  General commentary.

469. Carrouges, Michel. "Poursuite de l'ombre." *Table Ronde*,
Nos. 32-33 (1950), pp. 101-108.

Discusses Poe's influence on M. Compares *The Raven* and *Igitur.*

470. Chassé, Charles. "La clé de Mallarmé est chez Littré." *Quo Vadis,* 3, Nos. 20-22 (1950), 3-16.

See 565.

471. ———. "Explication objective du poème de Mallarmé sur *L'Eventail de Méry Laurent.*" *Daphné,* 1 Dec. 1950.

472. Croce, Benedetto. " 'L'Après-midi' di un fauno de Mallarmé e in Pietro Bembo." *Quaderni della "Critica,"* No. 16 (1950), pp. 56-60.

Compares the Faun in M.'s poem to the one found in several of Pietro Bembo's elegies, indicating the basic differences between the two as literary symbols.

473. Dauzat, Albert. "La langue et le style de Mallarmé." *Le Français Moderne,* 18 (1950), 244.

Concerns Gengoux's thesis on M. (478).

474. Davies, Gardner. *Les "Tombeaux" de Mallarmé: essai d'exégèse raisonnée.* Paris: Librairie José Corti, 1950. 233p.

Exegesis of six "commemorative poems" by M.: *Toast funèbre; Le Tombeau d'Edgar Poe;* "Sur les bois oubliés"; *Hommage* (à Wagner); *Le Tombeau de Charles Baudelaire; Tombeau* (de Verlaine). Concluding chapter is an essay on the elements of M.'s obscurity.

Publication of the author's thesis presented in Paris in 1949 under the title: "Les Poèmes commémoratifs de Mallarmé: essai d'exégèse raisonnée."

a) V. Daniel, *Erasmus,* 4 (1951), cols. 284-288.

b) J. D. Hubert, *Romanic Review,* 43 (1952), 300-302.

c) G. W. Ireland, *Modern Language Review,* 46 (1951), 276-281.

475. Douglas, Kenneth. "A Note on Mallarmé and the Theatre." *Yale French Studies,* No. 5 (1950), pp. 108-110.

Considers M.'s unfavorable opinion of the theater of his day and his desire for a new conception of the dramatic art.

476. Fernández de la Mora, Gonzalo. "La rebelde impotencia de Mallarmé." *Arbor,* 115 (1950), 489-497.

> Discusses M.'s "rebellion" against his feeling of poetic impotence and his significance as an archetype of the modern poet.

477. Fowlie, Wallace. "Mallarmé's Island Voyage." *Modern Philology,* 47 (1949-50), 178-190.

> Exegesis of *Prose pour des Esseintes.*

478. Gengoux, Jacques. *Le Symbolisme de Mallarmé.* Paris: Nizet, 1950. 269p.

> Offers exegesis of most of M.'s poetry and a useful index to recurring themes and symbols in these poems. Of M.'s symbolism Gengoux says, "Différent du romantisme par la soumission à tous les faits de la Vie, différent du réalisme par sa préoccupation constante de l'Idée, le symbolisme de Mallarmé synthétise (en le précisant) le Vague Idéal du premier et la fidélité (intériorisée) au Réel, du second."

479. Gros, Bernard. "Notes sur trois phrases de Mallarmé." *Revue des Sciences Humaines,* Nos. 57-60 (1950), pp. 277-278.

> Commentary on three sentences in M.'s reply to Jules Huret's *Enquête sur l'évolution littéraire.*

480. Grubbs, Henry A. "Mallarmé's 'Ptyx' Sonnet: An Analytical and Critical Study." *PMLA.* 65 (1950), 75-89.

> Concerns "Ses purs ongles...."

481. Jean, Marcel, and Arpad Mezei. *Genèse de la pensée moderne dans la littérature française: essai.* Paris: Corrêa, 1950. 231p.

> Includes "Mallarmé et le néant," concerning M.'s conception of "nothingness" and its place within the poetic framework of his poetry: "Mallarmé découvre que le négatif, n'est que l'inversion de la positivité, qui se continue alors et s'approfondit indéfiniment tandis que la vie perd son caractère transitoire et fuyant"; "Méditation orientale et classicisme occidental," discussing points of similarity between M.'s thought and that of Oriental philosophy.

482. Keim, Albert. *Le Demi-siècle: souvenirs de la vie littéraire et politique (1876-1946).* Paris: Albin Michel, 1950. 299p.

Contains a brief section on M. (pp. 62-65) offering personal commentary and observations.

483. Lehmann, Andrew George. *The Symbolist Aesthetic in France: 1885-1895.* Oxford: Basil Blackwell, 1950.

> Later edition: 1968. 328p.
> Contains numerous references to M. among which the most noteworthy are sections discussing M. and Schopenhauer. Lehmann notes that "Mallarmé's Idea is Schopenhauer's in one respect: it is an object of pure contemplation or intuition." He comments also on M.'s solipsistic philosophy, musical aspects in M.'s poetry, his views on *vers libre,* and his reaction to the "Wagnerian synthesis."

484. Luzi, Mario. *"Igitur,* un'ipotesi." *Paragone,* 1, No. 6 (1950), 3-10.

> Concerns the genesis and significance of *Igitur.*

485. Maurevert, Georges. "Nostradamus et Mallarmé." *Marsyas,* No. 281 (1950), pp. 1630-1633.

> Suggests Nostradamus' *Centuries* as possible sources for certain themes and images in M.'s poetry.

486. Mauron, Charles. *Introduction à la psychanalyse de Mallarmé.* Neuchâtel: Editions de la Baconnière, 1950. 249p.

> Later edition: 1968. 256p.
> A psychocritical study which investigates the "metaphores obsédantes" throughout M.'s work, from "Ce que disaient les trois cigognes" to his later writings. Mauron bases his analysis on M.'s early traumatic experience of losing his mother and sister and traces its subsequent literary expression in M.'s personal symbolism. Second edition also includes supplemental essays on M. and Taoism and the poet's unfinished project: "the Book."

487. Petrucciani, Mario. "Stéphane Mallarmé: precursore dell' 'ermetismo' italiano." *Rivista di Critica,* 1, No. 1 (1950), 19-25.

> Concerns M.'s influence upon Italian poetry.

488. Poulet, Georges. "Espace et temps mallarméens." *Deucalion,* 3 (1950), 203-252.

> Concerns M.'s conception of time and space. See also 539.

489. Pradal-Rodríguez, Gabriel. "La técnica poética y el caso Góngora-Mallarmé." *Comparative Literature*, 2 (1950), 269-280.

> A comparison of M.'s and Góngora's poetic method: "...la transcendencia de la poesía de Mallarmé nos explica mejor la transcendencia de la poesía de Góngora."

490. Queneau, Raymond. *Bâtons, chiffres et lettres*. Paris: Gallimard, 1950.

> Revised edition: 1965. 370p.
> In his essay on "Littérature potentielle," Queneau uses "Le vierge, le vivace et le bel aujourd'hui..." and "Ses purs ongles très haut..." to illustrate the "haï-kaïsation" of poetry, i.e., keeping only the rhyming sections of each line, thereby obtaining a new poem (in the form of a *bout-rimé*). Queneau also constructs an "isomorphic" sonnet based upon "Le vierge, le vivace...": "Le liège, le litane et le sel aujourd'hui...."

491. Roulet, Claude. *Nouveaux éléments de poétique mallarméenne au delà du poème: "Un coup de dés jamais n'abolira le hasard."* Neuchâtel: Editions du Griffon, 1950. 127p.

> A continuation of author's exegetical studies on *Un Coup de dés*. See 326, 394, 464, 633.

492. Sewell, Elizabeth. "Stéphane Mallarmé and Infinity." *Life and Letters*, 64 (1950), 105-114.

> Investigates M.'s revolutionary use of language. Believes that "this French experimenter... discovered a secret, perhaps the secret, of poetry which to all infinity had not been known before."

493. Souffrin, Eileen. "Une œuvre de jeunesse inédite de Mallarmé." *French Studies*, 4 (1950), 38-44.

> See 369.

494. Valéry, Paul. *Ecrits divers sur Stéphane Mallarmé*. Paris: Editions de la N.R.F., 1950. 159p.

> A collection of Valéry's numerous articles, lectures, prefaces, letters, etc., concerning M.

1951

495. Adam, Antoine. "Pour l'interprétation de Mallarmé." In *Mélanges d'histoire littéraire offerts à Daniel Mornet, professeur honoraire à la Sorbonne, par ses anciens collègues et ses disciples français.* Paris: Librairie Nizet, 1951. xxiv, 231p.

> An article criticizing "metaphysical exegesis" of M.: "Souvent, l'obscurité des poèmes mallarméens naît des constructions métaphysiques dont nous les surchargeons." Offers more literal interpretations of several poems.

496. Austin, L. J. " 'Le principal pilier': Mallarmé, Victor Hugo et Richard Wagner." *Revue d'Histoire Littéraire de la France,* 51 (1951), 154-180.

> Discusses M.'s attitude toward Wagner and his aesthetic theories. Includes an analysis of *Richard Wagner: rêverie d'un poète français* and exegesis of *Hommage* (à Wagner).

497. Bernard, Suzanne. "Le *Coup de dés* de Mallarmé replacé dans la perspective historique." *Revue d'Histoire Littéraire de la France,* 51 (1951), 181-195.

> Investigates the genesis of *Un Coup de dés.*

498. Billy, André. *L'Epoque 1900: 1885-1905.* Paris: Tallandier, 1951. 484p.

> The chapter on Symbolism contains a discussion of M. in the section entitled "Trois précurseurs."

499. Bonnet, Henri. *Roman et poèsie: essai sur l'esthétique des genres.* Paris: Librairie Nizet, 1951. 244p.

> Contains several references to M.

500. Bonora, Ettore. "Il Mallarmé: la poesia pura e la critica crociana." *Belfagor,* 6 (1951), 314-323.

> Discusses Benedetto Croce's criticism of M.

501. Bordeaux, Henry. *Histoire d'une vie.* Vol. 1: *Paris, aller et retour.* Paris: Plon, 1951. 310p.

Contains personal notes on M. in the chapter entitled "Amitiés et amours."

*502. Chassé, Charles. "Le Thème du soleil chez Mallarmé." *Quo Vadis*, Oct.-Dec. 1951, pp. 51-56.

503. ———. "Les thèmes de l'éventail et de l'éclairage au gaz dans l'œuvre de Mallarmé." *Revue des Sciences Humaines*, Nos. 61-64 (1951), pp. 333-344.

*504. Chaumeix, André. *Littérature française*. Vol. 2. Paris: Larousse, 1951.

505. Chisholm, A. R. "Substance and Symbol in Mallarmé." *French Studies*, 5 (1951), 36-39.

Warns against reading too much into M.'s poetry. Chisholm says that "it is surely necessary to discover what the images mean *in their primary form*; that is to say, as images, as poetic realities, as things visible to the eyes of the reader." Chisholm explicates "A la nue accablante tu ..." from this critical standpoint.

506. Cohn, Robert Greer. *L'Œuvre de Mallarmé: Un Coup de dés*. Paris: Les Lettres, 1951, 495p.

A revision of the author's previous study of *Un Coup de dés* (see 452) translated by René Arnaud.

507. Cornell, Kenneth. *The Symbolist Movement*. New Haven: Yale University Press, 1951. viii, 217p.

Contains numerous references to M., especially concerning the significant rôle the poet played during the development of Symbolism as a dominant influence in literature.

508. Delfel, Guy. *L'Esthétique de Stéphane Mallarmé*. Preface by Etienne Souriau. Paris: Flammarion Editeur, 1951. 209p.

Attempts to establish M.'s "aesthetic system." Delfel determines three major principles which guided M.'s literary creation: "1) l'Art transfigure le temps en vérité; 2) l'Art est une recherche de la vérité; 3) l'Art fait passer du hasard au nécessaire." Also considered are M.'s "religion," ideas on the arts and language, and his philosophy of "the Book." Concludes that M. actually has no systematized aesthetic thought: "Plus qu'une 'esthétique', la pensée mallarméenne aboutit à une vue complète du monde strictement unifiée."

a) I. W. Alexander, *Modern Language Review*, 48 (1953), 477-478.

509. Duchet, René. "Le drame de la création mallarméenne." *Synthèses*, 5, No. 58 (1951), 76-85.

Investigates the genesis of M.'s poetry.

510. Fowlie, Wallace. "Mallarmé as Ritualist." *Sewanee Review*, 59 (1951), 228-253.

A study of M.'s complete devotion to his poetry: "His cult of poetry and his belief in the poet emphasized the sacredness of his vocation. His life, his style, his themes all make him into an extraordinary figure, composite of poet, professor, magician. Ritualist is perhaps the word which includes all the aspects of his character."

511. Gavelle, Robert. "Goethe et Mallarmé, ou les secrets du Faune." *Cahiers du Sud*, 34 (1951), 150-154.

Presents possible sources for *L'Après-midi d'un faune* from Goethe's *Faust* (Part II).

512. Luzi, Mario. "Hérodiade." *Letterature Moderne*, 2 (1951), 544-549.

513. ———. "Tra *Igitur* e il *Coup de dés*." *Trivium*, 9 (1951), 154-170.

Analysis of the sonnets which M. wrote between *Igitur* and *Un Coup de dés* ("Plusieurs sonnets").

514. Mallarmé, Stéphane. *Afternoon of a Faun: A Pastoral Poem.* Introduction and translation by Eugene Delroi. Chicago: Taurus Press, 1951. 33p.

515. Mondor, Henri. *L'Affaire du Parnasse: Stéphane Mallarmé et Anatole France.* Paris: Editions Fragrance, 1951. 134p.

A study of M.'s relationship with Anatole France. Considers in some detail France's rejection of *L'Après-midi d'un faune* as unsuitable for the third volume of *Le Parnasse contemporain*.

*516. Mondor, Henri, editor. *Cent inédits de et autour de Mallarmé*. Brussels: L'Ecran du Monde, 1951.

517. ———. "Mallarmé et Anatole France." *Revue de Paris*, 58 (Jan. 1951), pp. 10-25.

>See 515.

518. ———. "Stéphane Mallarmé et Claude Debussy." *Journal Musical Français*, 25 Sept. 1951, pp. 1-2.

>Concerns primarily Debussy's "Prélude pour l'après-midi d'un faune" and its reception by music critics.

1952

519. Sewell, Elizabeth. *The Structure of Poetry*. London: Routledge & Kegan Paul, 1951.

>Later edition: 1962. 196p.
>Contains "Mallarmé and the World of the Sonnets" (pp. 137-157), a detailed phonological analysis of *Hommage* (à Wagner), "Le vierge, le vivace ...," and "Ses purs ongles."

520. Bigongiari, Pietro. *Il Senso della lirica italiana e altri studi*. Florence: Sansoni, 1952. 290p.

>Contains "Mallarmé non si allontana" (pp. 185-188).

521. Blanchot, Maurice. "Mallarmé et l'expérience littéraire." *Critique*, 8 (1952), 579-591.

>A review-article concerning 539.

522. Chassé, Charles. "Du nouveau sur Mallarmé (à propos de *La Chevelure*)." *Figaro Littéraire*, 26 April 1952.

523. ———. "Existe-t-il une clé de Mallarmé?" *Revue d'Histoire Littéraire de la France*, 52 (1952), 352-366.

>Chassé presents further evidence for his thesis that M. used Litté's dictionary in the composition of his poems and that this work can serve as a "key" to M.'s hermetic poetry.

524. Chassé, Charles. "Quelle est la source de *L'Après-midi d'un faune?*" *Marsyas*, No. 294 (1952), pp. 1795-1798.

Indicates Banville's *Diane au bois* as the source for the poem.

525. Chisholm, A. R. "Mallarmé: 'Ses purs ongles....' " *French Studies*, 6 (1952), 230-234.

526. Ernoult, Claude. "Mallarmé et l'occultisme." *Revue Métapsychique*, No. 17 (1952), pp. 32-50.

Text of a lecture presented at the Institut de Métapsychique in Paris. Considers parallels between M.'s philosophy and occultist thought.

527. Follain, Jean. "Découverte de Mallarmé." *Table Ronde*, No. 51 (1952), pp. 140-141.

Review-article concerning 452 and 508.

528. Fowlie, Wallace. "Mallarmé." *Poetry*, 80 (1952), 37-41.

General commentary.

529. Fraenkel, Ernest. "*Le Coup de dés* de Mallarmé: ce 'bel album d'imagerie abstraite.' " In *Mélanges d'esthétique et de science de l'art offerts à Etienne Souriau*. Paris: Nizet, 1952. 279p.

See 719.

530. Gutia, Joan. "Ungaretti e Mallarmé." *Rivista di Letterature Moderne*, 3 (1952), 245-259.

Presents details concerning M.'s influence on Ungaretti.

531. Hatzfeld, Helmut A. *Literature Through Art: A New Approach to French Literature*. New York: Oxford University Press, 1952. xiii, 247p.

A volume attempting "to elucidate French literature with the help of pictorial art." In a section comparing the techniques of the Symbolist poets to those of their artist counterparts, characterizes M.'s "Victorieusement fui le suicide beau" as a "verbally beautiful still life" in which "the striking feature is that the wishfully distorted word order and the purposefully obscure metaphors hinder the perspective that logical syntax would convey in a clear manner."

532. Lanson, Gustave. *Histoire de la littérature française*. Edited by Paul Tuffrau. Paris: Librairie Hachette, 1952. xviii, 1441p.

> Seriously revises Lanson's treatment of M. in the earlier edition (53). Cites M.'s greatest contribution as having affirmed, "plus vigoureusement que Baudelaire, la nécessité d'éliminer toutes les scories et de rechercher l'essence propre de la Poésie, qui doit désormais, plutôt que de décrire les choses, suggérer leur notion épurée ou l'impression que nous en recevons...."

533. Lebois, André. *Les Tendances du symbolisme à travers l'œuvre d'Elémir Bourges*. Paris: L'Amitié par le Livre, 1952. 414p.

> Contains numerous references to M. Pp. 392-395 compare M. and Bourges.

534. Luzi, Mario. *Studio su Mallarmé*. Florence: G. C. Sansoni, Editore, 1952. 133p.

> A general study of M. and his poetry with particular consideration of *Hérodiade, Igitur*, and *Un Coup de dés*.

535. Mallarmé, Stéphane. *Lettres et autographes*. Edited by B. Dujardin. Preface by Henri Mondor. Brussels: L'Ecran du Monde, 1952. 135p.

536. Miller, Richard R. "Mallarmé's 'Quand l'ombre menaça.' " *Explicator*, 10 (1952), explication 48.

537. Munro, Thomas. "*The Afternoon of a Faun* and the Interrelation of the Arts." *Journal of Aesthetics and Art Criticism*, 10 (1951-52), 95-111.

> Concerns the ballet, *The Afternoon of a Faun*, as "an excellent example of cooperation and synthesis among different arts."

538. Patri, Aimé. "Mallarmé et la musique du silence." *Revue Musicale*, No. 210 (1952), pp. 101-111.

> Concerns M.'s opinions on music, both favorable and unfavorable, and his unusual conception of the "music of silence."

539.   Poulet, Georges. *Etudes sur le temps humain.* Vol. 2: *La Distance intérieure.* Paris: Plon, 1952. ii, 357p.

> Contains a brilliant treatment of M. showing a profound understanding and appreciation of the poet's personal philosophy and its manifestations within his poetry. Using *Les Fenêtres* and a few other works as a critical point of departure, expounds upon the "Mallarméan method" founded upon "cette fiction en vertu de laquelle on veut croire que ce qui est n'existe pas, en sorte que ce qui n'est pas, existe." Discusses the concept of simultaneity, or instantaneity, found throughout M.'s writings: "La durée mallarméenne tend à se ramener à la création d'un moment éternel." In conclusion, indicates M.'s attempt to establish a perfect "reciprocity" between the poem and its reader from which both derive their only existence and authenticity: "... poème et lecteur se fondent en une même pensée, qui est tout simplement la pensée réflexive."

540.   Rogivue, Ernest. "Exégètes et glossateurs de Mallarmé." *Revue de Suisse,* No. 8 (1952), pp. 124-126.

> Brief survey of recent M. criticism.

541.   Rolland, Romain. *Le Cloître de la rue d'Ulm.* Paris: Albin Michel, 1952. xvi, 395p.

> Includes several unfavorable critical remarks concerning M.

1953

542.   Assunto, Rosario. "Postilla mallarmeana." *Letteratura,* 1, No. 2 (1953), 70-71.

> Concerns Hegel's influence on M.

543.   Austin, L. J. "Mallarmé et le rêve du 'Livre.'" *Mercure de France,* 317 (1953), 81-108.

> Discusses M.'s conception of "the Book." Suggests that Hegel was a primary influence on the development of M.'s aesthetic philosophy.

544.   Ayda, Adile. *L'Influence de Victor Hugo sur Stéphane Mallarmé.* Istanbul: "Dialogues," 1953. 25p.

> Indicates specific parallels between Hugo's and M.'s poetry. Citing common symbols and themes, author concludes that

"l'influence de Victor Hugo sur Mallarmé est donc indéniable et fondée sur une affinité réelle de tempérament et de nature."

545. Blanchot, Maurice. "L'Expérience d'*Igitur*." *Nouvelle Nouvelle Revue Française*, Nos. 4-6 (1953), pp. 1075-1085.

An analysis of this work.

546. Chassé, Charles. "Les Thèmes de la stérilité et de la virginité chez Mallarmé." *Revue des Sciences Humaines*, Nos. 69-72 (1953), pp. 171-182.

547. Chisholm, A. R. "A Working Exegesis of Mallarmé's *Coup de dés*." *AUMLA*, No. 1 (1953), pp. 2-14.

548. Clancier, Georges-Emmanuel. *De Rimbaud au surréalisme: panorama critique*. Paris: Pierre Seghers, 1953. 501p.

Contains an essay on M. in the section entitled "Les Phares," including commentary on several poems.

549. Davies, Gardner. *Vers une explication rationnelle du "Coup de Dés": essai d'exégèse mallarméenne*. Preface by Henri Mondor. Paris: Librairie José Corti, 1953. 208p.

An attempt at a "rational analysis" of M.'s masterwork. First part discusses the genesis of the poem. The author bases his study upon the premise that M. was influenced by the philosophy of Hegel, whom M. had discovered in 1866: "Sans savoir dans quelle mesure Mallarmé avait approfondi le système de Hegel, nous pouvons affirmer que la méthode de la conciliation des contraires et le développement général de la métaphysique hégélienne laissèrent une empreinte durable sur son esprit." Second part is a detailed explication of the poem, taken phrase by phrase.

In his prefatory remarks, Mondor states: "Le livre indispensable et entraînant de M. Gardner Davies montrera la pénétration, l'ingéniosité, la cohérence d'un esprit australien penché sur des pages particulièrement difficiles de la littérature française." Preface also concerns the chronology of composition and general commentary of the work in question.

550. Fowlie, Wallace. *Mallarmé*. Chicago: University of Chicago Press, 1953. 299p.

An excellent comprehensive study of M. including a biographical introduction, a thematic analysis of M.'s poetry (the blue sky, hair, the void, the closed book, night, the three masks of clown, swan, and hero); intelligent critical exegesis of *Igitur, Hérodiade, L'Après-midi d'un faune, Toast funèbre, Prose pour des Esseintes, Un Coup de dés,* and other works; a consideration of M. as "ritualist" (cf. 510) and a discussion of M.'s place within the Symbolist movement and his influence on Valéry, Claudel, and other poets. Provides careful translation of all texts considered.

a)   J. Frank, *New Republic*, 128 (13 July 1953), 19-20.

b)   J. H. Meyer, *Poetry*, 83 (1953), 279-282.

c)   G. D. Painter, *New Statesman and Nation*, 45 (1953), 675-676.

551.   Jamati, Georges. "Stéphane Mallarmé et le drame de la conscience." *Critique*, 9 (1953), 99-107.

Review-article concerning 508.

552.   Junker, Albert. "Mallarmé im Urteil heutiger Forschung." *Neueren Sprachen*, 2 (1953), 49-63.

A critical review of recent M. criticism.

553.   Marvardi, Umberto. "Poetica e poesia di Stéphane Mallarmé." *Dialoghi*, 1, Nos. 4-5 (1953), 58-79.

General essay.

554.   Michaud, Guy. "A propos de la genèse de l'œuvre littéraire, deux exemples : Gide et Mallarmé." *Cahiers de l'Association Internationale des Etudes Françaises*, 3-5 (1953), 239-251.

A comparison of Gide's and M.'s processes of literary creation.

555.   ———. *Mallarmé: l'homme et l'œuvre*. Paris : Hatier-Boivin, 1953.

Revised edition : Hatier, 1958. 192p.

An excellent introductory text by the author of *Message poétique du symbolisme* (392). Provides valuable critical insight into much of M.'s writing, although Michaud's major aim in this volume is to propose "une *introduction à la lecture et à la connaissance de Mallarmé* : étude ouverte sur le futur, surtout attentive à fixer des jalons qui permettent de situer les diverses investigations déjà tentées, tout en suggérant des itinéraires pour des recherches ultérieures."

Also contains a detailed chronology of the composition of M.'s poems, indicating first publications, subsequent versions, etc.

a) M. Bémol, *Revue de Littérature Comparée,* 28 (1954), 499-502.

b) *Bulletin Critique du Livre Français,* 99 (1954), 189.

556. Miller, Richard R. "Mallarmé's 'Le vierge, le vivace.'" *Explicator,* 12 (1953), explication 6.

*557. Mondor, Henri. "Proust et Mallarmé." *Le Disque Vert,* Jan. 1953.

558. Mucci, Renato. "Il mondo poetico di Mallarmé." *Dialoghi,* 1, No. 3 (1953), 47-58.

General essay on M.'s poetic principles.

559. Sartre, Jean-Paul. "Mallarmé (1842-1898)." In *Les Ecrivains célèbres.* Vol. 3. Paris: Editions d'Art Lucien Mazenod, 1953.

Later edition: 1966.
See 1006.

560. Smith, Madeleine. "Mallarmé and the Chimères." *Yale French Studies,* 11 (1953), 59-72.

Investigates M.'s sentiments "with regard to the theme of man's weakness for woman."

561. Tamara. "Mallarmé et la danse." *Revue du Caire,* 16 (1954), 260-271.

Indicates that M.'s conception of the dance as a pure art form prefigures the development of contemporary ballet.

562. Vanwelkenhuyzen, Gustave. *Mallarmé et la Belgique.* Brussels: Palais des Académies, 1963. 15p.

Publication of a lecture given 12 June 1953 concerning M.'s friendship with such Belgian poets as Rodenbach, Mockel, Verhaeren, and Maeterlinck, and his visit in 1890 to Belgium where he presented his lectures on Villiers de l'Isle-Adam in several major cities.

1954

563. Austin, L. J. "Mallarmé et son critique allemand." *Revue d'Histoire Littéraire de la France*, 54 (1954), 184-194.

Concerns Kurt Wais's criticism of M.

564. ———. "Mallarmé, Huysmans et la *Prose pour des Esseintes*." *Revue d'Histoire Littéraire de la France*, 54 (1954), 145-182.

A critical review of previous interpretations of this poem followed by author's own exegesis.

565. Chassé, Charles. *Les Clés de Mallarmé*. Paris: Aubier, 1954. 240p.

Presents the thesis that M.'s hermetic poetry can be explained "philologically" using as a basis for analysis Littré's *Dictionnaire de la langue française*, which, Chassé believes, M. "compulsait assidûment... tirant profit et des rubriques étymologiques et de divers sens des mots au travers des siècles comme aussi des citations d'auteurs. Même s'il advenait à Littré de faire fausse route dans ses suppositions, Mallarmé le suivait aveuglément."

a) *Bulletin Critique du Livre Français*, 102 (1954), 432-433.

b) E. Noulet, *Nouvelle Nouvelle Revue Française*, 2, No. 21 (1954), 493-499.

c) *Times Literary Supplement*, 8 Oct. 1954, p. 642.

566. ———. "Mallarmé connaisseur d'oiseaux." *Lettres Nouvelles*, 2 (1954), 924-927.

Identifies the bird in *Petit Air II* as a woodpecker.

*567. Dommarco, Alessandro. *Il Fauno*. Rome: 1954.

See 597.

568. Jaloux, Edmond. *Visages français*. Preface by Henri Mondor. Paris: Editions Albin Michel, 1954. 254p.

Contains several references to M. in "Regards sur le Symbolisme."

569. Lamont, Rosette. "The Hamlet Myth in French Symbolism." Dissertation. Yale University, 1954.

Discusses M.'s contributions to the "Hamlet myth."

570. Larrauri, Agustín D. *Mallarmé, poeta símbolo*. Buenos Aires: Francisco A. Colombo, 1954. 90p.

> General study.

571. McLuhan, Marshall. "Joyce, Mallarmé, and the Press." *Sewanee Review*, 62 (1954), 38-55.

> Includes a discussion of M.'s attitude toward journalism and the press: "...it was Mallarmé who formulated the lessons of the press as a guide for the new impersonal poetry of suggestion and implication...."

572. Madaule, Jacques. "Mallarmé, clásico." *Sur*, No. 229 (1954), pp. 16-19.

> General commentary.

573. Mallarmé, Stéphane. *Pages choisies*. Edited by Guy Delfel. Paris: Hachette, 1954.

574. Mondor, Henri. *Mallarmé lycéen*. Paris: Gallimard, 1954. 361.

> Supplements Mondor's *Vie de Mallarmé* (284). A closer consideration of M.'s years at the Lycée de Sens. Presents "Entre quatre murs," a previously unpublished collection of early poems written in 1859 and 1860; describes three notebooks which M. called "Glanes," a personal anthology of favorite authors and poems; and includes M.'s first prose poem, "Ce que disaient les trois cigognes," published also in Mondor's *Mallarmé plus intime* (323).
> a) E. Noulet, *Marginales*, 47 (April, 1956), 43-45.
> b) Y. Gandon, *Arts*, 2-8 Feb. 1955, p. 8.

575. ———. "Précocité de Mallarmé." *Revue de la Pensée Française*, 13, No. 6 (1954), 5-8.

> Concerns M.'s early translations of Poe's poetry while a student at the Lycée de Sens.

576. ———. "Sur la *Symphonie littéraire* de Mallarmé." In *Mélanges d'histoire littéraire et de bibliographie offerts à Jean Bonnerot, conservateur en chef honoraire de la Bibliothèque de la Sorbonne, par ses amis et collègues*. Paris: Librairie Nizet, 1954. 551p.

577.   Mondor, Henri. "Un sonnet inconnu de Mallarmé." *Nouvelle Nouvelle Revue Française*, Nos. 13-15 (1954), pp. 188-192.

    Concerns *Alternative*, a sonnet which Mondor believes is a first or second version of "Quelle soie aux baumes de temps. . . ."

578.   Poggioli, Renato. "Pagine da un commento a Mallarmé." *Letteratura*, 2, Nos. 11-12 (1954), 16-28.

    Exegesis of *Prose pour des Esseintes*.

579.   Ragusa, Olga. "Mallarmé in Italy: A Study of Literary Influence and Critical Response." *Dissertation Abstracts*, 14 (1954), 1420.

    See 657.

*580.   Rousselot, Jean. *La Poésie*. Paris: Nouvelle Editions Debresse, 1954.

581.   Sanna, Luigi. "Stefano Mallarmé — 'Il mistero nelle lettere.' " *Galleria*, 4 (May-June 1954), pp. 52-54.

582.   Taupin, René. "The Myth of Hamlet in France in Mallarmé's Generation." *Modern Language Quarterly*, 14 (1954), 432-447.

    Includes a discussion of M.'s understanding of the "Hamlet myth" and his contributions to it.

583.   Teissier, Léon. "De Mistral à Mallarmé." *Marsyas*, No. 310 (1954), pp. 1971-1972.

    Concerns 565.

584.   Thompson, Mariana. "Mallarmé et ses amis britanniques." Dissertation. Paris, 1954.

585.   Valeri, Diego. *Il simbolismo francese da Nerval a de Régnier*. Padua: Livian Editrice, 1954. 151p.

    Contains a brief essay on M. and Italian translations of *L'Azur*, *Brise Marine*, *Hérodiade* (Scène), *L'Après-midi d'un faune*, *Le Tombeau d'Edgar Poe*, and "Le vierge, le vivace et le bel aujourd'hui. . . ."

586. Zimmermann, Eléonore M. "Mallarmé et Poe: précisions et aperçus." *Comparative Literature,* 6 (1954), 304-315.

> Presents detailed notes concerning points of similarity between Poe and M.: "En vertu d'une osmose inconsciente mais sélective, Mallarmé ... a pris chez Poe ce qui convenait le mieux à ses conceptions littéraires et à son tempérament propre."

1955

587. Austin, L. J. "Du nouveau sur la *Prose pour des Esseintes* de Mallarmé." *Mercure de France,* 323 (1955), 84-104.

588. Ayda, Adile. *Le Drame intérieur de Mallarmé, ou l'origine des symboles mallarméens.* Istanbul: Editions "La Turquie Moderne," 1955. xxx, 288p.

> A study of the genesis of M.'s poetical themes, based upon the psychocritical method. Making special use of M.'s earliest compositions, Ayda explores the effects of M.'s traumatic losses of his sister Maria and his friend Harriet Smyth upon the development of his hermetic symbolism, convinced that "il fallait connaître intégralement la pensée de Mallarmé de la période claire et que les symboles contenus dans les textes hermétiques devaient avoir leurs germes dans ceux qui appartiennent à l'époque d'avant l'hermétisme." The fifth chapter is a glossary of Mallarméean symbols classified into three main groups: "1) Symboles se rattachant à la notion du Ciel, 2) Symboles se rattachant à l'image de Maria, 3) Symboles se rattachant à l'image de Harriet."

589. Blanchot, Maurice. *L'Espace littéraire.* Paris: Gallimard, 1955. 382p.

> Contains "L'Expérience de Mallarmé," an essay which considers M.'s "expérience littéraire" as beginning "au moment où il passe de la considération de l'œuvre faite, celle qui est toujours tel poème particulier, tel tableau, au souci par lequel l'œuvre devient la recherche de son origine et veut s'identifier avec son origine...."

590. Castex, Pierre-Georges, editor. *Autour du symbolisme: Villiers, Mallarmé, Verlaine, Rimbaud.* Paris: José Corti, 1955. 321p.

> Contains: Alan W. Raitt, "Autour d'une lettre de Mallarmé," concerning a letter to Villiers de l'Isle-Adam; Charles Chassé,

"Le thème de Hamlet chez Mallarmé" (see 593); Léon Cellier, "'Sur les bois oubliés·...' ou Mallarmé l'humain" (see 591, 592).

591.   Cellier, Léon. " 'Sur les bois oubliés ...' ou Mallarmé l'humain." *Revue des Sciences Humaines,* Nos. 77-80 (1955), pp. 170-176.

592.   ———. " 'Sur les bois oubliés ...' ou Mallarmé l'humain: exemple d'exégèse." In *Autour du symbolisme: Villiers de l'Isle-Adam, Mallarmé, Verlaine, Rimbaud.* Edited by Pierre Castex. Paris: José Corti, 1955. 321p.

593.   Chassé, Charles. "Le thème de Hamlet chez Mallarmé." *Revue des Sciences Humaines,* Nos. 77-80 (1955), pp. 157-169.

> Investigates the themes of Hamlet in M.'s works other than *Igitur* and *Un Coup de dés.*

594.   Chisholm, A. R. "Mallarmé's *Sainte*: An Epitome of Symbolism." *AUMLA,* No. 3 (1955), pp. 1-4.

595.   ———. "Three difficult sonnets by Mallarmé." *French Studies,* 9 (1955), 212-217.

> Explication of "Tout Orgueil fume-t-il du soir...," "Surgi de la croupe et du bond...," and "Une dentelle s'abolit...."

596.   Davies, Gardner. "The Demon of Analogy." *French Studies,* 9 (1955), 197-211, 326-347.

> An examination of M.'s use of analogy in his poetry.

597.   Dommarco, Alessandro. *Il Fauno.* Rome: Edizione Fuori Commercio, 1955. xiv, 81p.

> Translation of *L'Après-midi d'un faune* including commentary.

598.   Gill, A. "From 'Quand l'ombre menaça' to 'Au seul souci de voyager': Mallarmé's Debt to Chateaubriand." *Modern Language Review,* 50 (1955), 414-432.

> Discusses Chateaubriand's influence on M., examining the above sonnets from this standpoint. Calls "Au seul souci..." "Mallarmé's *Tombeau de Chateaubriand.*"

599. Küchler, Walter. "Weltgefühl and Formtrieb — Mallarmé und Valéry." In *Actes du Cinquième Congrès International des Langues et Littératures Modernes.* Florence: Valmartina Editeur, 1955. xv, 546p.

Compares M.'s and Valéry's personal philosophies.

600. Lebois, André. "Station Littré! ... Mallarmé continue." *Quo Vadis,* 8, Nos. 77-79 (1955), 36-41.

Concerns 565.

601. "The Making of a Poet." *Times Literary Supplement,* 54 (1955), 742.

Review-article concerning 514.

602. Man, Paul de. "Le néant poétique: commentaire d'un sonnet hermétique de Mallarmé." *Monde Nouveau,* 10, No. 88 (1955), 63-75.

Concerns "Une dentelle s'abolit...."

603. Mucci, Renato. "Il concetto del libro in Mallarmé." *Ausonia,* 10, No. 1 (1955), 8-16.

See 795.

604. Parreaux, André. "Le Tombeau de Beckford par Stéphane Mallarmé." *Revue d'Histoire Littéraire de la France,* 55 (1955), 329-338.

Concerns M.'s "Préface" to Beckford's *Vathek.*

605. Ramsey, Warren. "A View of Mallarmé's Poetics." *Romanic Review,* 46 (1955), 178-191.

A general study of M.'s poetical principles. States that "the poetics of Mallarmé presents a few variables among many constants. We will continue to think of him, and rightly, as the poet of the crystal-like Idea, the obsessive Absence."

606. Roujon, Jacques. "Whistler et Mallarmé: 1888-1898." *Mercure de France,* 325 (1955), 631-660.

A discussion of M.'s friendship with Whistler, including fragments from their correspondence.

607. Siciliano, Italo. *Il romanticismo francese da Prévost ai nostri giorni.* Venice: La Goliardica, 1955. 494p.

> Contains a chapter on M.

608. Souffrin, Eileen. "La source des Thèmes anglais de Mallarmé." *Revue de Littérature Comparée,* 29 (1955), 107-108.

> Presents as the source for M.'s text a collection of English proverbs entitled *A Handbook of English Proverbs...* (1855), edited by Henry Bohn.

609. Souriau, Michel. *Le Mystère de Mallarmé.* Lille: Revue des Sciences Humaines, 1955. 24p.

> Text of a lecture presented at the Université Populaire de Lille on 30 Jan. 1955.

1956

610. Austin, Lloyd James. "Les 'Années d'apprentissage' de Mallarmé." *Revue d'Histoire Littéraire de la France,* 56 (1956), 65-84.

> Considers M.'s *juvenilia* and his personal anthology which he entitled "Glanes."

*611. Ayda, Adile. "Les Sources d'*Hérodiade*." *Dialogues,* 4 (1956), 97-113.

612. Bernard, Suzanne. "La Clef de Mallarmé est-elle dans Littré?" *Revue d'Histoire Littéraire de la France,* 56 (1956), 85-93.

> Challenges Chassé's thesis that Littré's dictionary is the "key" to M.'s poetry (see 565).

613. Blanchot, Maurice. "Joubert et Mallarmé." *Nouvelle Nouvelle Revue Française,* Nos. 37-39 (1956), pp. 110-121.

> See 685.

614. Brereton, Geoffrey. *An Introduction to the French Poets.* London: Methuen and Co., Ltd., 1956.

> Later edition: 1960. xv, 302p.
> Chapter 17 is a general essay on M.

615. Champigny, Robert. "Mallarmé's Relation to Platonism and Romanticism." *Modern Language Review*, 51 (1956), 348-358.

> Author sees M.'s personal interpretation of Platonic philosophy as "a conclusion, a sober one, to the evolution of Romanticism."

616. Chassé, Charles. "Ce que Mallarmé pensait de la danse." *Lettres Nouvelles*, 4, No. 40 (1956), 118-130.

> Concerns M.'s conception of the dance as an art form. States that M. "est beaucoup plus un visuel qu'un auditif."

617. ———. "Une source inattendue de Mallarmé: *Les Mésaventures de Jean-Paul Choppart*." *Revue des Sciences Humaines*, Nos. 81-84 (1956), pp. 333-336.

> Proposes Desnoyers' *Les Mésaventures de Jean-Paul Choppart* as a source for *La Marchande d'herbes aromatiques*.

618. Chiari, Joseph. *Symbolisme from Poe to Mallarmé: The Growth of a Myth*. Foreword by T. S. Eliot. London: Rockliff, 1956. x, 198p.

> An investigation of the problem concerning the influence of Edgar Allan Poe on M. Reviews previous critical appraisals of Poe's influence and then seeks internal evidence of it in M.'s own writings. Final chapters are devoted to expositions of "Edgar Allan Poe's poetry and aesthetics" and "Mallarmé's poetry and aesthetics" in which comparisons are made of the two poets. Conclusion states that although the influence of Poe, both direct and indirect, was considerable, in the final analysis M. went his own way and surpassed Poe in this literary genre: "Mallarmé was bent on a journey which obviously he would have made and in fact did make without Poe. The knowledge that another traveller had taken a similar road encouraged him and helped him by the trail he left behind. But Mallarmé soon overtook all forerunners and reached bourns which no human being had ever visited before."

619. Cook, Bradford, translator. *Mallarmé: Selected Prose Poems, Essays, and Letters*. Baltimore: Johns Hopkins Press, 1956. xxii, 168p.

> Annotated translations of much of M.'s prose, including prose poems and extracts from letters.

620. Fongaro, Antoine. "*L'Après-midi d'un faune* et le *Second Faust.*" *Revue des Sciences Humaines,* Nos. 81-84 (1956), pp. 327-332.

> Suggests Goethe's *Faust* (Part II) as a source for *L'Après-midi d'un faune.*

621. Friedrich, Hugo. *Die Struktur der moderne Lyrik: von Baudelaire bis zur Gegenwart.* Hamburg: Rohwohlt, 1956. 216p.

> Contains a general essay on M. including explications of several poems.

622. Fromilhague, R. "Nouvelle exégèse mallarméenne: 'L'Ouverture ancienne d'Hérodiade.' " *Littératures,* 4 (1956), 21-33.

623. Goffin, Robert. *Mallarmé vivant.* Paris: Librairie Nizet, 1956. 293p.

> Discusses M.'s relationship with Méry Laurent and the rôle she played in the creation of his poetry. Goffin believes that Méry Laurent was not M.'s mistress, as many have previously supposed.
>
> a) A. Ayguesparse, *Marginales,* 47 (April 1956), 52-53.
> b) C. Chassé, *Revue d'Histoire Littéraire de la France,* 58 (1958), 410-413.
> c) K. Cornell, *Romanic Review,* 47 (1956), 227-228.
> d) E. Noulet, *Lettres Nouvelles,* 4 (1956), 421-424.

624. ———. "Propos sur Mallarmé." *Bulletin de l'Académie Royale de Langue et de Littérature Françaises,* 34 (1956), 229-241.

> Exegetical notes.

625. Graaf, Daniel A. de. "Mallarmé tributaire de Flaubert." *Neophilologus,* 40 (1956), 314-315.

> Presents themes in *Madame Bovary* which possibly inspired certain of those found in *Brise Marine.*

626. Hayman, David. *Joyce et Mallarmé.* 2 vols. Paris: Lettres Modernes, 1956.

> A detailed examination of M.'s influence upon James Joyce. First volume, *Stylistique de la suggestion,* shows how M.'s use of "suggestion" in poetry affected the development of Joyce's

literary theories, particularly in the composition of *Ulysses* and *Finnegans Wake*. Second volume, *Les Eléments mallarméens dans l'œuvre de Joyce*, discusses Mallarméan elements in Joyce's works, with special consideration of *Finnegans Wake*, which Hayman compares with *Un Coup de dés*, indicating analogical passages, similar images, phrases, structures, etc. (Publication of the author's thesis, *Les Eléments mallarméens dans l'œuvre de Joyce*, presented in Paris in 1955.)

   a) W. Fowlie, *Symposium*, 11 (1957), 328-332.

   b) J. Jacquot, *Etudes Anglaises*, 12 (1959), 39-41.

627. Kemp, Robert. *La Vie du théâtre*. Paris: Editions Albin Michel, 1956. 333p.

   Contains a section concerning *Hérodiade* (pp. 18-25).

628. Mallarmé, Stéphane. *Un Coup de dés jamais n'abolira le hasard*. Translated into English by Daisy Aldan. New York: Tiber Press, 1956. Unpaged.

   The first published English translation of *Un Coup de dés*. Follows typographic disposition of the original, which is included.

629. Nardis, Luigi de. "Il sonetto della Sibilla." *Letterature Moderne*, 6 (1956), 607-610.

   Exegesis of "A la nue accablante tu. . . ."

630. Orr, John. "*L'Après-midi d'un faune*; Mallarmé's Debt to Chateaubriand." *Modern Language Review*, 51 (1956), 77-80.

   Suggests a passage from Chateaubriand's *Mémoires d'Outre-Tombe* as a source for *L'Après-midi d'un faune*.

631. Ragusa, Olga. "La *Voce*, Mallarmé e 'Tendenze' di Onofri." *Esperienza Poetica*, Nos. 9-11 (1956), pp. 54-60.

   Discusses similarities between M.'s and the Italian poet Onofri's poetic theories.

632. Rodrigue, G. M. "Ombres et lumières sur Mallarmé." *Le Thyrse*, 58 (1956), 256-262.

   Survey of recent M. studies.

633. Roulet, Claude. *Traité de poétique supérieure: Un Coup de dés jamais n'abolira le hasard.* Neuchâtel: Editions H. Messeiller, 1956. 434p.

> A comprehensive analysis of *Un Coup de dés* offering detailed exegesis of the poem from various aspects: "mimetic profiles" of vocabulary and syntax, orchestration, architecture, etc. Uses numerous graphs and sketches to illustrate the intricate, but unified structure of the work.
>
> See also 326, 394, 464, 491.
>
> a) L. J. Austin, *Revue d'Histoire Littéraire de la France*, 59 (1959), 244-246.
>
> b) H. Hatzfeld, *Deutsche Literaturzeitung*, 78 (1957), 510-513.

634. Siciliano, Italo. "Mallarmé, o il narcisismo della parola." *Letterature Moderne*, 6 (1956), 7-21, 156-175.

> An essay on M. and his poetic method extracted from *Il romanticismo francese da Prévost ai noi giorni* (607).

635. Viatte, Auguste. "La première version imprimée du *Don du poème.*" *Revue d'Histoire Littéraire de la France*, 56 (1956), 94-96.

> Author tells of discovering an unsigned version of *Don du poème* in a Louisiana periodical, *L'Avant-Coureur*, dated 2 Feb. 1867. The poem was not published in France until 1883.

636. Weinberger, M. E. "The Linguistic Implications in the Theory and Poetry of Mallarmé." *Dissertation Abstracts*, 16 (1956), 1447-1448.

1957

637. Angioletti, Giovanni Batista. *L'anatra alla normanna.* Milan: Fratelli Fabbri, Editori, 1957. 236p.

> A collection of essays on French literature containing "Mallarmé nella foresta," which discusses M.'s appreciation of the forest and countryside around Valvins where he could shed his anxiety and tension, freeing his mind for poetic creativity: "A Valvins si sentiva più protetto, più libero di pensare e scrivere come gli piaceva."

638. Beauverd, J. "L'herbier de des Esseintes." *Littératures,* 5 (1957), 13-19.

Exegetical notes on *Prose pour des Esseintes.*

639. Charpier, J. "Un échec exemplaire." *Lettres Nouvelles,* 5, No. 52 (1957), 340-342.

Concerns 658.

640. Chassé, Charles. "Le vocabulaire nautique de Mallarmé." *Revue des Sciences Humaines,* Nos. 85-88 (1957), pp. 451-459.

An examination of M.'s use of nautical terms: "Il semble que le vocabulaire nautique n'ait pris que petit à petit de l'importance dans l'œuvre de Mallarmé et surtout à partir du moment où, devenu propriétaire d'une embarcation à Valvins..., il eût pris vraiment goût à la navigation en rivière."

641. Dussort, Henri. "L'artiste dépassé par l'art (note sur Mallarmé et Heidegger)." *Revue Philosophique de la France et de l'Etranger,* 147 (1957), 41-46.

Notes on M.'s philosophy of literature.

642. Fraenkel, Ernest. "Mallarmé, peintre abstrait qui s'ignore." *Revue d'Esthétique,* 10 (1957), 87-92.

Notes on a lecture given 16 Feb. 1957 during a meeting of the Société Française d'Esthétique. Concerns the unusual typography of *Un Coup de dés.*

643. Girolamo, Nicola di. "La Lezione della 'Rue de Rome.'" *Capitoli,* 1 (1957), 234-248.

Concerns 658.

644. Glissant, Edouard. "L'attente du poème." *Lettres Nouvelles,* 5, No. 52 (1957), 342-344.

Concerns 658.

645. Goffin, Robert. "A propos de Mallarmé." *Nos Lettres,* 21, No. 4 (1957), 13-15.

Concerns *Prose pour des Esseintes.*

646. Graaf, Daniel A. de. "Le Tournant dans la vie de Mallarmé."
      Synthèses, 12, Nos. 137-139 (1957), 91-95.

      Discusses the influence of the painter Regnault on M.

647. Hellens, Franz. "Stéphane Mallarmé et l'éditeur Deman."
      Synthèses, 11, Nos. 130-132 (1957), 47-51.

      Discusses M.'s relationship with his publisher, E. Deman.

648. Lüders, Eva Maria. "Sechzig Jahre Mallarmé-Forschung."
      Romantisches Jahrbuch, 8 (1957), 146-176.

      A critical survey of M. criticism.

649. Mallarmé, Stéphane. *Œuvres choisies*. Edited by Luigi de
      Nardis. Rome: Signorelli, 1957. 180p.

650. ———. *Selected Poems*. Translated by C. F. MacIntyre.
      Berkeley and Los Angeles: University of California Press,
      1957. xi, 169.

      Verse translations of forty-one poetical works with interpreta-
      tive annotation. Includes the original French versions on op-
      posite pages.

651. "Mallarmé: The Man and the Dream." *Times Literary Sup-
      plement*, 56 (1957), 506.

      Review-article concerning 658.

652. Mannoni, O. "Poésie et psychanalyse." *Psychanalyse*, 3 (1957),
      139-163.

      Contains several references to M.

653. Muner, M. *Note mallarmeane*. Cremona: Pizzorni, 1957. 16p.

      Contains "Carattere di centralità di 'Prose pour des Esseintes'
      nell'opera di Mallarmé" and "Gli 'Eventails' di casa Mallarmé."

654. Nardis, Luigi de. *Impressionismo di Mallarmé*. Rome: Edi-
      zioni Salvatore Sciascia, 1957. 153p.

      Discusses M.'s relationship with the Impressionist painters (Ma-
      net, Monet, Morisot, and others) and similarities between the
      techniques M. used in his poetry and those used by the artists.

655. Nardis, Luigi de. *Mallarmé in Italia.* Milan: Società Editrice Dante Alighieri, 1957. 101p.

> Presents revised versions of previously published essays on M.:
> "Del tradurre Mallarmé," "Momenti mallarmeani in Ungaretti,"
> "Alcuni modi di tradurre Mallarmé," and "Un sonnetto di
> Mallarmé" (an explication of "A la nue accablante tu...").
> Also includes a bibliography of M. studies in Italy for the
> period 1885-1955.

656. Poggioli, Renato. "Pagine da un commento a Mallarmé." *Letteratura,* 5, Nos. 27-28 (1957), 20-39.

> Exegesis of *Un Coup de dés.*

657. Ragusa, Olga. *Mallarmé in Italy: Literary Influence and Critical Response.* New York: S. F. Vanni, 1957. 228p.

> A meticulous study of M.'s influence in Italy from the time
> Vittorio Pica first introduced the poet there in 1886 through
> the first half of the twentieth century. Considers in detail both
> critical reaction to M. and his effect upon Italian poetry. In-
> cludes as an appendix an annotated list of Italian translation
> of M.'s works and an extensive bibliography containing a sec-
> tion devoted to Italian criticism of M.
>
> a) R. G. Cohn, *Modern Language Notes,* 74 (1959), 375-377.
> b) J. A. Scott, *Romanic Review,* 50 (1959), 150-152.

658. Schérer, Jacques. *Le "Livre" de Mallarmé: premières recherches sur des documents inédits.* Preface by Henri Mondor. Paris: Gallimard, 1957. xxiv, 382p.

> Presents the text of an unfinished manuscript consisting of notes
> and drafts for M.'s grandiose literary project which he often
> referred to as "the Book." Introductory chapter discusses M.'s
> conception of the work, its format, content and intention, and
> details concerning the publication of the manuscript.
>
> a) L. J. Austin, *Revue d'Histoire Littéraire de la France,* 59
> (1959), 409-412.
> b) R. G. Cohn, *Modern Language Notes,* 75 (1960), 689-692.
> c) A. Gill, *Revue de Littérature Comparée,* 33 (1959), 130-133.
> d) E. Noulet, *Lettres Nouvelles,* 5 (1957), 334-340; 6 (1958),
> 110-115.
> e) ————. *Revue de l'Université de Bruxelles,* 11 (1958-59),
> 57-68.
> f) J. Robichez, *L'Information Littéraire,* 9 (1957), 218-219.
> g) G. Saba, *Ausonia,* 13, No. 4 (1958), 32-37.

h) *Times Literary Supplement,* 23 Aug. 1957, p. 506.

i) J.-P. Weber, *Parisienne,* 6 (1958), 271-275.

659. Vigée, Claude. "Les Artistes de la faim." *Table Ronde,* No. 112 (1957), pp. 43-64.

See 730.

660. Weinberg, Kurt. "Heine, Baudelaire, Mallarmé: Atavism and Urbanity." *Western Review,* 21 (1956-57), 119-135.

A comparison of Heine, Baudelaire, and M. from the standpoint of their common "quest for origins of the universe, organized life, society, language, and the arts."

1958

661. Brickwood, J. D. "The Influence of Mallarmé and Rimbaud on James Joyce." Dissertation. Cambridge, 1957-1958.

662. Cellier, Léon. "Le pâle Vasco." *Revue d'Histoire Littéraire de la France,* 58 (1958), 510-522.

Exegesis of "Au seul souci de voyager...."

663. Chisholm, Alan Rowland. *Mallarmé's "Après-midi d'un faune": An Exegetical and Critical Study.* Melbourne: Melbourne University Press, 1958. 35p.

A meticulous explication of *L'Après-midi d'un faune* considering particularly its unusual "musicality" expressed in three main themes: 1) sensuality, 2) dream, and 3) memory.

a) R. G. Cohn, *Modern Language Notes,* 75 (1960), 632-634.

b) C. A. Hackett, *French Studies,* 15 (1961), 78-80.

664. François, C. R. "Analogies et sources bibliques du *Tombeau d'Edgar Poe* de Mallarmé." *Revue d'Histoire Littéraire de la France,* 58 (1958), 65-68.

Presents commentary on *Le Tombeau d'Edgar Poe* with reference to analogical themes and images found in the New Testament describing Christ. Suggests these Biblical texts as a probable source of the poem.

665. Gill, A. "Mallarmé et l'antiquité: *L'Après-midi d'un faune.*" *Cahiers de l'Association Internationale des Etudes Françaises,* 10 (1958), 158-173.

666. Gombet, G., and J. Pommier. "Du Tombeau de Charles Baudelaire." *Mercure de France,* 333 (1958), 751-753.

> Concerns exegesis of the second quatrain of this poem. See also 674.

667. Haug, Gerhart. "Stéphane Mallarmé: 1842-1898." *Welt und Wort,* 13 (1958), 67-70.

> General commentary.

668. Hyppolite, Jean. "Le *Coup de dés* de Stéphane Mallarmé et le message." *Etudes Philosophiques,* 13 (1958), 463-468.

> Discusses the "message" of M.'s *Coup de dés,* of which the author says "Chez Mallarmé le message est sans fin; il est 'l'ultérieur démon immémorial' qui n'aboutit qu'à lui-même et peut-être à sa survie gratuite."

669. Juliet, Charles. "Reverzy ou le vestige du non-être." *Lettres Nouvelles,* 6, No. 62 (1958), 85-96.

> Investigates Mallarméan elements in the novels of Jean Reverzy.

670. Lawler, James R. "Mallarmé's *L'Après-midi d'un faune.*" *Meanjin,* 17 (1958), 429-431.

671. ———. "A Reading of Mallarmé's 'Le vierge, le vivace et le bel aujourd'hui.'" *AUMLA,* 9 (1958), 78-83.

672. Lebois, André. *Admirable XIXe siècle.* Paris: L'Amitié par le Livre, S.A.B.R.I., 1958. 317p.

> Contains essays concerning Camille Mauclair's *Le Soleil des morts,* the hero of which, Calixte Armel, is a literary portrait of M.; M.'s politics; and criticism of Chassé's theories presented in *Les Clefs de Mallarmé* (565).

673. Noël, Jean. "George Moore and Mallarmé." *Revue de Littérature Comparée,* 32 (1958), 363-376.

Concerns M.'s friendship with George Moore. Author believes that M.'s influence upon the English author was slight.

674. Pommier, Jean. "*Le Tombeau de Charles Baudelaire* de Mallarmé." *Mercure de France,* 32 (1958), 656-675.

675. Rousselot, Jean. *Présences contemporaines: rencontres sur les chemins de la Poésie.* Paris: N. E. D. Editeur, 1958. 328p.

> Contains "Stéphane Mallarmé: grand prêtre et martyr du langage," an essay on M.'s unique use of language in poetry and his contribution to literature: "... Mallarmé nous a montré le premier que la fiction ... peut prétendre à marcher en avant du rêve dans l'insurrection de l'esprit contre le réel et nous a fait entrevoir l'étendue des pouvoirs réformateurs que la littérature-entendez l'Art — peut exercer sur la vie...." Also includes a "Notice bio-bibliographique sur Stéphane Mallarmé."

676. Ryan, Mariana. "John Payne et Mallarmé: une longue amitié." *Revue de Littérature Comparée,* 32 (1958), 377-389.

> Presents details concerning M.'s friendship with the English translator of Villon.

677. Scarfe, Francis. "La *Prose pour des Esseintes* de Mallarmé." *Le Bayou,* 22 (1958), 65-72.

678. Souffrin, Eileen. "Coup d'œil sur la bibliothèque anglaise de Mallarmé." *Revue de Littérature Comparée,* 32 (1958), 390-396.

> Concerns the English books that were in M.'s library at Valvins at the time of his death. Author is surprised to find only about one hundred English texts in this collection.

679. Wais, Kurt. *An den Grenzen der Nationalliteraturen: vergleichende Aufsätze.* Berlin: W. De Gruyter, 1958. 416p.

> Contains "E. A. Poe und Mallarmés *Prose pour Des Esseintes,*" "Mallarmés *Des Esseintes*-Gedicht im Verständnis der vierziger und fünfziger Jahre," and "Übersetzung und Nachdichtung. Zur Bewertung neuer Ubertragungen von Mallarmés Lyrik."

680. ———. "Zwei Gedichte Mallarmés und ihre Vorgänger." In *Französische Marksteine von Racine bis Saint-John Perse.* Berlin: Walter De Gruyter, 1958. 363p.

> Concerns *Brise Marine* and *L'Après-midi d'un faune.* See 254.

1959

681. "Accustomed to Dream." *Times Literary Supplement,* 58 (1959), 617-618.

> Review-article concerning 689 and 700.

682. Austin, L. J. "Le Cantique de Saint-Jean." *AUMLA,* No. 10 (1959), pp. 46-59.

683. Barthelme, M. M. "Formation et mise en œuvre de la pensée de Mallarmé sur le théâtre." Dissertation. Paris, 1959.

684. Bernard, Suzanne. *Mallarmé et la musique.* Paris: Librairie Nizet, 1959. 184p.

> Investigates M.'s conception of music and its influence upon the poetical techniques used in his later works, which the author sees as " 'musicalisation' poétique." Defends the thesis that M.'s aesthetic principles were not an adaptation of Wagner (cf. 187).
>
> a) A. Fongaro, *Studi Francesi,* 5 (1961), 504-508.
> b) E. Noulet, *Cahiers du Sud,* 50 (1960), 297-301.

685. Blanchot, Maurice. *Le Livre à venir.* Paris: Gallimard, 1959. 374p.

> Contains several references to M. as well as a comparative essay on Joubert and M., underlining points of similarity between their "expériences poétiques."

686. Block, Haskell M. "Dramatic Values in Mallarmé's *Herodiade.*" In *Stil- und Formprobleme in der Literatur.* Heidelberg: Carl Winter, 1959. 524p.

> Cf. 782.

687. Cellier, Léon. "Gautier et Mallarmé devant le miroir de Venise." *Cahiers de l'Association Internationale des Etudes Françaises,* 11 (1959), 121-133.

> Compares Gautier's and M.'s thematic use of mirrors in their writings.

688. Cellier, Léon. "Las de l'amer repos." *L'Information Littéraire,* 11 (1959), 41-44.

689. ———. *Mallarmé et la morte qui parle.* Paris: P.U.F., 1959. 225p.

> A study devoted primarily to the images of death and related themes in M.'s poetry. Like Mauron (486) and Ayda (588), Cellier sees M.'s traumatic losses of his mother, his sister, and his friend Harriet Smyth as having a profound effect upon the development of his personal symbolism.
>
> a) L. J. Austin, *Romanic Review,* 51 (1960), 127-129.
> b) ———. *French Studies,* 14 (1960), 373-374.
> c) R. Champigny, *Modern Language Notes,* 75 (1960), 377.
> d) A. R. Chisholm, *Revue d'Histoire Littéraire de la France,* 62 (1962), 121-123.
> e) A. Fongaro, *Studi Francesi,* 6 (1962), 510-513.
> f) P. M. Jones, *Modern Language Review,* 55 (1960), 454-456.
> g) E. Noulet, *Bulletin de l'Académie de Langue et de Littérature Française,* Aug. 1960.
> h) J. Onimus, *Revue des Sciences Humaines,* No. 103 (1961), pp. 444-446.

690. Chassé, Charles. "Mallarmé et l'étymologie." *Cahiers de l'Association Internationale des Etudes Françaises,* 11 (1959), 367-370.

> Chassé uses Littré's dictionary to explain some of M.'s more difficult symbols.

691. Chisholm, A. R. "Mallarmé: 'Quelle soie aux baumes de temps' (1885)." *AUMLA,* 12 (1959), 17-19.

692. Cornell, J. G. "Apologia pro exegetice." *AUMLA,* No. 10 (1959), pp. 21-27.

> Defends the exegesis of M.'s poetry provided it is "reverent and sincere."

693. Davies, Gardner. "An Exegesis of Mallarmé's 'M'introduire dans ton histoire. . . . " *AUMLA,* 10 (1959), 32-45.

694. ———. *Mallarmé et le drame solaire: essai d'exégèse raisonnée.* Paris: Librairie José Corti, 1959. 301p.

Presents exegesis of eight poems which reflect M.'s fascination with "le drame solaire": "Le soleil, à son apparition à l'est, en pleine trajectoire, et plus encore au moment de son coucher, est sans doute l'image de la Nature à laquelle il est le plus sensible." Conclusion discusses the significant rôle of this theme in M.'s aesthetics.

a) L. J. Austin, *French Studies*, 14 (1960), 374-375.

b) L. J. Austin, *Romanic Review*, 51 (1960), 123-127.

c) R. Champigny, *Modern Language Notes*, 75 (1960), 731-732.

d) A. R. Chisholm, *AUMLA*, 12 (1959), 84-85.

e) P. M. Jones, *Modern Language Review*, 55 (1960), 454-456.

f) E. Noulet, *Bulletin de l'Académie de Langue et de Littérature Françaises*, Aug. 1960.

695. Davies, Gardner. "Mallarmé: *Les Noces d'Hérodiade*." *Nouvelle Revue Française*, 13 (1959), 178-192.

See 701.

696. Duchet, René. "La Rencontre inattendue: Mallarmé et Voltaire." *Synthèses*, 14, Nos. 160-162 (1959), 218-223.

Discusses M.'s admiration for Voltaire and indicates points of similarity between the two basically different authors.

697. Gill, Austin. "Le Symbole du miroir dans l'œuvre de Mallarmé." *Cahiers de l'Association Internationale des Etudes Françaises*, 11 (1959), 159-181.

A thematic study.

698. Girolamo, N. di. "*Ouverture ancienne d'Hérodiade*": *studio critico storico*. Siena: Maia, 1959. 135p.

a) A. Fongaro, *Studi Francesi*, 5 (1961), 116-118.

b) G. Montagna, *Ausonia*, 15, No. 4 (1960), 86.

699. Lethève, Jacques. *Impressionnistes et symbolistes devant la presse*. Paris: Armand Colin, 1959. 302p.

An interesting presentation of critical reaction to the Impressionist painters and the Symbolist poets appearing in newspapers and reviews of the period. Contains several references to M.

700.   Mallarmé, Stéphane. *Correspondance: 1862-1871.* Edited by Henri Mondor and Jean-Pierre Richard. Paris: Gallimard, 1959. 381p.

> Annotated edition of M.'s correspondence from 17 Jan. 1862 to 20 May 1871.

701.   ————. *Les Noces d'Hérodiade.* Edited by Gardner Davies. Paris: Gallimard, 1959. 237p.

> Presents the unfinished texts and notes that M. intended for a long dramatic poem, *Les Noces d'Hérodiade.*
> a) L. J. Austin, *French Studies,* 14 (1960), 375-376.
> b) A. Fongaro, *Studi Francesi,* 4 (1960), 381.

702.   Nardis, Luigi de. "Voile sur la rivière." *Letteratura,* 7, Nos. 37-38 (1959), 24-28.

> Concerns M.'s "yole" and its symbolic significance (see 724).

703.   Nelson, R. J. "Mallarmé's Mirror of Art: An Explication of 'Ses purs ongles....'" *Modern Language Quarterly,* 20 (1959), 49-56.

704.   Noulet, Emilie. *Suite mallarméenne.* 2 vols. Brussels: Editions des Artistes, 1959.

> Contains "La Hantise d'abolir," an essay which appeared in *Les Lettres* (1948), and book reviews previously published in various periodicals.

705.   St. Aubyn, F. C. "Hérodiade: Eine Frau mit Schatten." *Revue de Littérature Comparée,* 33 (1959), 40-49.

> A comparison of M. and Hofmannsthal, who experienced similar mental crises. St. Aubyn differentiates the use of "shadow" as a symbol in *Hérodiade* and in *Die Frau ohne Schatten.*

706.   Senior, John. *The Way Down and Out: The Occult in Symbolist Literature.* Ithaca: Cornell University Press, 1959. xxvi, 217p.

> In a section on M. (pp. 133-144), states that this poet "belongs in a study of the occult in symbolisms chiefly because of his use of language...." Indicates striking parallels between M.'s thought and occultist philosophy, but does not establish any direct esoteric influences.

707. Souffrin, Eileen. "La Rencontre de Wilde et de Mallarmé." *Revue de Littérature Comparée*, 33 (1959), 529-535.

> Concerns Oscar Wilde's meeting with Mallarmé in Feb. 1891.

708. Wais, Kurt. "Die Errettung aus dem Schiffbruch: Melville, Mallarmé und einige deutsche Voraussetzungen." In *Comparative Literature: Proceedings of the Second Congress of the International Comparative Literature Association.* Edited by Werner P. Friedrich. 2 vols. Chapel Hill: University of North Carolina Press, 1959.

> Article's principal concern is a comparison of similar themes in *Moby Dick* and *Un Coup de dés*.

1960

709. Abril, Xavier. *Dos estudios.* Bahía Blanca: Cuadernos del Sur, 1960. 39p.

> Contains "Vallejo y Mallarmé (La estética de Trilce y Una jugada de dados jamás abolirá el azar)."

710. Austin, Lloyd James. "Mallarmé on Music and Letters." *Bulletin of the John Rylands Library*, 42 (1959-60), 19-39.

> Discusses M.'s opinions on music and literature. Concludes that "it may well be that Mallarmé's meditations on Music and Letters as the reciprocal 'means of mystery' and, still more, his dream of the supreme Book, are to be taken as an allegory of the ultimate ideal inspiring every artist, whether he knows it or not."

711. Boulay, Daniel. *L'Obscurité esthétique de Mallarmé et la "Prose pour des Esseintes."* Vitry-sur-Seine: Imprimerie R. Léger, 1960. 70p.

> An essay based upon the thesis that M.'s obscurity "n'est pas l'obscurité d'une ininintelligibilité absolue, mais celle d'une esthétique pénétrable au prix de quelque patience." Second section is "un exemple de cette patience," a detailed explication of one of M.'s most hermetic poems, *Prose pour des Esseintes*.
>
> a) E. Noulet, *Revue de l'Université de Bruxelles*, 13 (1960-61), 372-376.

712. Burnshaw, Stanley, editor. *The Poem Itself*. New York: Holt, Rinehart, and Winston, 1960. xiv, 338p.

> Presents commentary and explications of six poems by M.: *Don du poème* (S. Burnshaw), *Sainte* (Henri Peyre), *Toast funèbre* (H. P.), "Le vierge, le vivace..." (H. P.), *Autre Eventail de Mademoiselle Mallarmé* (H. P.), *Le Tombeau d'Edgar Poe* (H. P.).

713. Butor, Michel. *Essais sur les modernes*. Paris: Gallimard, 1960. 377p.

> Contains "Mallarmé selon Boulez," on Boulez's "musical portrait" of M.

714. Chadwick, Charles. "Mallarmé et la tentation du lyrisme." *Revue d'Histoire Littéraire de la France*, 60 (1960), 188-198.

> Discusses the evolution of M.'s thought and the importance of taking this into account when interpreting his poems.

715. Chisholm, A. R. "Mallarmé's Edens." *AUMLA*, No. 13 (1960), pp. 3-22; No. 14 (1960), pp. 3-22.

> A discussion of M.'s search for four "Edens," which Chisholm calls the "four worlds of the spirit that Mallarmé endeavoured to substitute for the banality of terrestrial existence: namely, an ideal love, beyond the hazards and the storm of passion; an exquisite subtlety of expression, enriched by correspondences; a poetic absolute, and a world of genius luminous enough to outshine the materiality of the cosmos."

716. ———. "Victorieusement fui le suicide beau...." *French Studies*, 14 (1960), 153-156.

717. Cohn, Robert Greer. *The Writer's Way in France*. Philadelphia: University of Pennsylvania Press, 1960. 447p.

> Contains numerous references to M.

718. Fowlie, Wallace. *Dionysus in Paris: A Guide to Contemporary French Theater*. New York: Meridian Books, 1960. 314p.

> Contains "Mallarmé and the Aesthetics of Theater," an examination of M.'s thought concerning the dramatic art. Concludes that "drama for Mallarmé arises out of a conflict between two protagonists: the hero (or Igitur) who is capable of producing

a work, and chance (or Le Hasard), which seems to represent a synthesis of all the forces in the world bent upon opposing the hero in the creation of his work."

719. Fraenkel, Ernest. *Les Dessins trans-conscients de Stéphane Mallarmé: à propos de la typographie de "Un Coup de dés."* Preface by Etienne Souriau. Paris: Librairie Nizet, 1960. 44p.

A psychological study of the visual designs presented by the typographical configurations of *Un Coup de dés.*

720. Graaf, Daniel A. de. "La genèse d'un poème en prose de Mallarmé." *Synthèses,* 15, Nos. 169-170 (1960), 402-407.

Concerns *La Gloire.*

721. Guiette, Robert. "Max Elskamp et Mallarmé." *Mercure de France,* 339 (1960), 253-260.

Concerns M.'s friendship with Elskamp and his influence upon the Belgian poet.

722. Hermans, Georges. "C'est Mallarmé qui *découvrit* Maeterlinck." *Le Livre et l'Estampe,* No. 22 (1960), pp. 138-141.

Indicates that M. recommended Maeterlinck to Octave Mirbeau, who made the young poet an immediate success by his quite favorable criticism.

723. Mucci, R. "Panama et Mallarmé." *Letteratura,* 8, Nos. 43-45 (1960), 253-255.

Concerns M.'s article on the Panama Canal scandal which first appeared in the *National Observer* (25 Feb. 1893) and was later revised and published as *Or.*

724. Nardis, Luigi de. *Il sorriso di Reims e altri saggi di cultura francese.* Rocca San Casciano: Cappelli Editore, 1960. 315p.

Contains "Il 'Libro' di Mallarmé," a discussion of J. Schérer's *Le "Livre" de Mallarmé* (658), and " 'Voile sur la rivière,' " an essay concerning M.'s "yole," painted by Berthe Morisot and others and the central image in Valéry's sonnet *Valvins* as a symbol of the Mallarméan aesthetic.

725. Noulet, E. "Du nouveau sur Mallarmé?" *Bulletin de l'Académie Royale de Langue et de Littérature Françaises*, 38 (1960), 37-59.

> Survey of recent M. studies.

726. ————. *Du nouveau sur Mallarmé?* Brussels: Palais des Académies, 1960. 28p.

> See 725.

727. Rat, Maurice. "Stéphane Mallarmé." *Vie et Langage*, No. 94 (1960), pp. 315-320.

> General essay praising M.'s literary achievement: "Son incomparable mérite, c'est, dans les poèmes les plus *liés* qu'on ait écrits en France, et qui n'ont d'égal dans la littérature latine et grecque que les odes d'Horace et de Callimaque, d'avoir *lié* ses rimes aux vertus du contexte, musical, sensoriel, idéal et symbolique, de l'œuvre."

728. Roedig, Charles F. "Musical Instruments in Mallarmé's *Poésies*." *Kentucky Foreign Language Quarterly*, 7 (1960), 219-225.

> Discusses the rôle of various musical instruments in M.'s poetry: flutes, trumpets, cymbals, harps, etc.

729. Usinger, Fritz. *Welt ohne Klassik: Essays.* Darmstadt: E. Roether, 1960. 159p.

> Contains "Die Dichtung Stéphane Mallarmés" (pp. 22-36).

730. Vigée, Claude. *Les Artistes de la faim: essais.* Paris: Calmann-Lévy, 1960. 275p.

> Contains an essay comparing M., Kafka, and T. S. Eliot.

731. Weber, Jean-Paul. *Genèse de l'œuvre poétique.* Paris: Librairie Gallimard, 1960. 563p.

> Contains a psychocritical thematic study of M. According to Weber's thesis, the numerous images of birds, wings, feathers, flight, etc. found in M.'s poetry (enumerated in detail in the text) are the result of the poet's feelings of guilt for having participated as a young boy in the killing of small birds in their nests.

732. Weber, Jean-Paul. "Le thème de l'oiseau mort dans l'œuvre de Stéphane Mallarmé." *Revue de Métaphysique et de Morale,* 65 (1960), 475-510.

    See 731.

1961

*733. Angeli, Dina d'. "Du fait à l'idéal avec Mallarmé." *Culture Française* (Bari), 8 (1961), 301-306.

734. Austin, Lloyd James. "*L'Après-midi d'un faune* de Mallarmé: lexique comparé des trois états du poème." In *Langue et littérature: Actes du VIIIe Congrès de la Fédération Internationale des Langues et Littératures Modernes.* Paris: Les Belles Lettres, 1961. 448p.

    A brief vocabulary study of the three versions of the poem (1865, 1875 and 1876).

735. Chisholm, A. R. "Mallarmé: 'Quand l'ombre menaça...' " *French Studies,* 15 (1961), 146-149.

736. *L'Esprit Créateur,* 1 (1961), 109-155.

    Contains: A. R. Chisholm, "Mallarmé and the Art of Creation," in which author says that M. "goes as close to the art of creation as any mortal can hope to go"; Bernard Weinberg, "A Suggested Reading of *Le Tombeau d'Edgar Poe*"; Robert Greer Cohn, "A Propos du *Coup de Dés*"; Lloyd James Austin, "The Mystery of a Name," which discusses M.'s poetic practice of refusing to name an object in order to *suggest* it more perfectly and studies "curious exceptions to this rule of suggestion without designation"; Grange Woolley, "Comments on Mallarmé's Cubism and Preciosity," concerning "Mallarmé's transitional role between symbolism and cubism"; Robert Champigny, "The *Swan* and the Question of Pure Poetry," analysis of "Le vierge, le vivace et le bel aujourd'hui..." of which Champigny says: "The poem is a worthy example of how far concurrence of contexts and polyvalence of words can be pushed. As such, it is an extreme, rather than standard, example of pure poetry."

737. Fongaro, Antoine. "Notes sur Mallarmé." *Studi Francesi,* 5 (1961), 490-491.

Concerns typographical errors in editions of M.'s texts and exegesis of *Tombeau* (de Verlaine).

738. Gill, Austin. "Esquisse d'une explication de la *Vie d'Igitur*." *Saggi e Ricerche di Letteratura Francese*, 2 (1961), 163-199.

739. Girard, Raymond. "Mallarmé et l'autre versant." *Lettre Ouverte*, No. 3 (1961), pp. 12-21.

> Concerns M.'s unusual theories on language which the author calls "une très pure métaphysique du langage."

740. Haley, Martin. "Brennan and Mallarmé: A Footnote." *Quadrant*, 5, No. 18 (1961), 16-17.

> A note concerning M.'s relationship with Christopher Brennan.

741. Jourdain, Louis. "Complément à la *Prose pour des Esseintes*." *Tel Quel*, No. 4 (1961), pp. 38-56; No. 5 (1961), pp. 79-91; No. 6 (1961), pp. 71-80.

742. Mallarmé, Stéphane. *Antología: verso y prosa*. Edited by Xavier Abril. Montevideo: Ediciones Front, 1961. 119p.

743. ———. *Divagations*. Preface by Georges Perros. Paris: Club Français du Livre, 1961. xix, 307p.

744. ———. *Opere scelte*. Edited by Luigi de Nardis. Parma: Guanda, 1961. xxiv, 213p.

745. ———. *Pour un tombeau d'Anatole*. Edited by Jean-Pierre Richard. Paris: Editions du Seuil, 1961. 320p.

> Presents the unfinished manuscript which M. began after the death of his eight-year old son Anatole. Richard says of these unusual pages: "A travers ce poème tout abstrait, il eût certainement tenté de se persuader lui-même que son enfant n'était pas mort vraiment, et qu'avec courage, de la patience, et un suffisant 'génie', il pouvait lui être donné de le faire revivre en lui." (Publication of author's *thèse complémentaire*.)
>
> a) H. Amer, *Nouvelle Revue Française*, 20 (1962), 322-324.
>
> b) L. J. Austin, *Romanic Review*, 54 (1963), 144-147.
>
> c) R. G. Cohn, *Revue d'Histoire Littéraire de la France*, 63 (1963), 691-693.
>
> d) E. Mora, *Revue des Deux Mondes* (Sept.-Oct. 1962), 455-460.

746. Missac, Pierre. "Tel que jamais en lui le temps ne l'a changé." *Critique*, 17 (1961), 675-690.

> A review-article concerning 684, 694, 700, 701, 711, 726.

747. Mondor, Henri. *Autres précisions sur Mallarmé et inédits.* Paris: Gallimard, 1961. 277p.

> Previously unpublished prose poems by M., manuscripts, variant versions of poems, and details concerning M.'s poetic career.

748. ———. *Sur un poème de Mallarmé.* Paris: Editions Estienne, 1961. 33p.

> A study of *Brise marine* retracing its composition and comparing the five versions of the poem.

749. Mondor, Henri. "Un des derniers sonnets de Stéphane Mallarmé." *La Voix de Poètes*, No. 7 (1961), pp. 33-36.

> Notes concerning "A la nue accablante tu...."

750. Noulet, E. "Exégèse d'un sonnet de Mallarmé, *Tombeau.*" In *Studi in onore di Vittorio Lugli e Diego Valeri.* 2 vols. Venice: N. Pozza, 1961.

> Exegesis of the *Tombeau* for Verlaine.

751. Poulet, Georges. *Les Métamorphoses du cercle.* Paris: Plon, 1961. xxi, 525p.

> Chapter 15 is a detailed discussion of M.'s *Prose pour des Esseintes* considering in particular its circular structure.

752. Richard, Jean-Pierre. *L'Univers imaginaire de Mallarmé.* Paris: Editions du Seuil, 1961. 654p.

> A comprehensive thematic study of M.'s entire literary production. Richard's analysis is based upon the premise that the "key" to M.'s hermetic writing, especially his poetry, is not an external one, but is to be found within the texts themselves: "Que chaque poème se réduise à un cryptogramme, telle est au fond la présupposition commune à tous les efforts de déchiffrage terme à terme. Il nous semble pourtant que si l'hermétisme doit s'éclairer fructueusement par endessous, une recherche des architectures a plus de chance d'y réussir qu'une traduction juxtalinéaire." Accordingly, M.'s symbols, by and in themselves, mean little; it is rather M.'s work taken as a

concerted whole, his "univers imaginaire," which endows them with enduring significance.

a) I. W. Alexander, *Modern Language Review*, 61 (1966), 330-332.

b) H. Amer, *Nouvelle Revue Française*, 20 (1962), 322-324.

c) L. J. Austin, *Revue d'Histoire Littéraire de la France*, 63 (1963), 493-497.

d) H. M. Block, *Romanic Review*, 56 (1965), 70-73.

e) L. Cellier, *Studi Francesi*, 9 (1965), 510-513.

f) M. de Dieguez, *Critique*, 19 (1963), 517-535.

g) M. Foucault, *Annales*, 19 (1964), 996-1004.

h) E. Mora, *Revue des Deux Mondes*, Sept-Oct. 1962, pp. 455-460.

i) J. Pfeiffer, *Synthèses*, 17, No. 202 (1963), 230-238.

j) X. Tilliette, *Etudes*, 316 (1963), 376-383.

753. Spitzer, Leo. *Interpretationen zur Geschichte der französischen Lyrik*. Edited by Helga Jauss-Meyer and Peter Schunck. Heidelberg: Selbstverlag des Romanischen Seminars der Universität Heidelberg, 1961. 188p.

Contains an explication of *Autre Eventail de Mademoiselle Mallarmé*.

754. Steland, Dieter. "Die Kritische Prosa Mallarmés: Studien, Kommentare und Übersetzungen zu *Office* und *Bucolique*." Dissertation. Freiburg, 1961.

a) M. Arrivé, *Revue d'Histoire Littéraire de la France*, 68 (1968), 133.

b) H. M. Block, *French Review*, 42 (1968-69), 766-767.

c) P. Bürger, *Romantisches Jahrbuch*, 17 (1966), 222-224.

d) H. Charney, *Romanic Review*, 58 (1967), 234-235.

e) H. G. Tuchel, *Romanische Forschungen*, 79 (1967), 411-418.

1962

755. Alexander, Jean. "Poe's *For Annie* and Mallarmé's *Nuit d'Idumée*." *Modern Language Notes*, 77 (1962), 534-536.

Discusses M.'s interpretation of *For Annie* "as a Symbolist poem, almost as an allegory of Mallarmé's own long, intermittent spiritual crisis."

756. Bird, Edward. A. "Stéphane Mallarmé: la poésie et la musique." *Bulletin of the Humanities Association of Canada,* 12 (1962), 92-97.

> Discusses the influence of music on M. Author believes that "la conception mallarméenne de la musique est à la fois idéaliste et religieuse; idéaliste en ce sens qu'elle permet à l'artiste, au moyen du silence et de la suggestion, de s'approcher de plus près de l'idée, essence des choses; religieuse au sens d'un drame mystique...."

757. ————. *L'Univers poétique de Stéphane Mallarmé.* Paris: Librairie A. G. Nizet, 1962. 225p.

> An investigation of the principles of the Symbolist movement as well as a detailed study of M. as its principal exponent. First part centers attention on the essential elements of M.'s aesthetic and literary development within the context of the Symbolist movement; second part describes M.'s "aventure poétique, caractérisée par le renouvellement constant des procédés d'expression"; final part considers the "situation" of M. within his own lifetime and subsequently, touching upon his originality, ideas on other art forms, and influence on later writers. (Publication of the author's thesis presented in Paris in 1955 under the title "La Pensée littéraire de Stéphane Mallarmé.")

758. Camon, Ferdinando. "Letture di Mallarmé." *Ausonia,* 17, No. 2 (1962), 33-38.

> Italian translations of three poems with brief commentary: *Apparition, Angoisse,* and *Tristesse d'été.*

*759. ————. "Le Poesie d'amore di Mallarmé." *Langues Modernes,* 12 (1962), 568-578.

760. ————. "Questioni mallarméane." In *Romania: scritti offerti à Francesco Piccolo nel su LXX cumpleanno.* Naples: Armanni, 1962. 536p.

> Considers M.'s "reflections" on poetry.

761. Chadwick, Charles. *Mallarmé: sa pensée dans sa poésie.* Paris: Librairie José Corti, 1962. 157p.

> Exegesis of M.'s poetry taking into special consideration each poem's date of composition and place within the development of the poet's thought.

a) L. Cellier, *Revue d'Histoire Littéraire de la France*, 66 (1966), 531-532.

b) J. Follain, *Mercure de France*, 346 (1962), 472-474.

c) H. Laitenberger, *Zeitschrift für Französische Sprache und Literatur*, 73 (1963), 238-242.

762. Chadwick, Charles. "Méry Laurent dans la poésie de Mallarmé." *Revue des Sciences Humaines*, Nos. 105-108 (1962), pp. 251-261.

> Discusses M.'s relationship with Méry Laurent and her appearance as a poetic theme in several of M.'s poems.

763. Chisholm, Alan Rowland. "Brennan and Mallarmé: A Study of Mallarmé's Influence on Christopher Brennan." *Southerly*, 21, No. 4 (1961), 2-11; 22, No. 1 (1962), 23-35.

> An investigation of Brennan's literary debt to M. States that Brennan's "poetry would have been very different from what it is if he had not been influenced by the poetic theory and practice of Stéphane Mallarmé."

764. ———. *Mallarmé's "Grand œuvre."* Manchester: Manchester University Press, 1962. viii, 139p.

> An analysis of M.'s major poems from the standpoint that these works make up what M. called his "Grand Œuvre" and not some unrealized project as Jacques Schérer has argued (see 658). Chisholm believes that these poems show "evidence of the poet's long and patient effort to transmute baser substances into pure beauty, to fuse the phenomenal world and the Absolute."
>
> a) A. Gill, *Modern Language Review*, 58 (1963), 122-123.
>
> b) J. Roger, *Arbor*, 53 (1962), 511-512.

765. Chisholm, Alan Rowland. "A Study of Mallarmé's *Toast funèbre*." *AUMLA*, No. 17 (1962), pp. 53-61.

766. ———. "Two Heretical Notes." *AUMLA*, No. 18 (1962), pp. 229-232.

> Part I is "Mallarmé's Inkpot," suggesting "inkstand" as the meaning of *ptyx* in "Ses purs ongles...."

767. ———. "Le vierge, le vivace...." *French Studies*, 16 (1962), 359-363.

768. Cohen, J. "L' 'obscurité' de Mallarmé." *Revue d'Esthétique,* 15 (1962), 64-72.

769. Douchin, Jacques. "La *Prose pour des Esseintes* ou l'examen de conscience de Mallarmé." *Orbis Litterarum,* 17 (1962), 82-99.

770. Follain, Jean. "Connaissance de Mallarmé." *Mercure de France,* 346 (1962), 472-477.

Review-article concerning 752 and 761.

771. Genette, Gérard. "Bonheur de Mallarmé?" *Tel Quel,* No. 10 (1962), pp. 61-65.

Review-article concerning 752.

772. Grubbs, Henry A., and J. W. Kneller. *Introduction à la poésie française.* Boston: Ginn and Company, 1962. 276p.

Furnishes explicatory comments on "Toute l'âme résumée...," *Apparition, L'Azur,* "Las de l'amer repos...," *Le Pitre châtié, Autre Eventail de Mademoiselle Mallarmé,* "Le vierge, le vivace et le bel aujourd'hui...," and *L'Après-midi d'un faune.*

773. Lethève, Jacques. "Mallarmé sur les chemins de Des Esseintes." *Bulletin de la Société Joris-Karl Huysmans,* 35, No. 43 (1962), 370-375.

Concerns M.'s interest in interior decorating.

774. Mannoni, O. "Mallarmé relu." *Temps Modernes,* 18 (1962), 864-883.

Review-article concerning 752.

*775. Miguet, Thierry. "Mallarmé, poète du néant musicien. *Bulletin des Professeurs du Lycée d'Etat de Garçons de Mulhouse,* No. 1 (1962), pp. 19-23.

776. Mondor, Henri, and Lloyd James Austin, editors. *Les "Gossips" de Mallarmé.* Paris: Gallimard, 1962. 123p.

Presents M.'s artistic and literary *chroniques* written for the London *Athenaeum* during the winter of 1875-1876.

777. Nardis, Luigi de. *L'ironia di Mallarmé*. Rome: Salvatore
      Sciascia Editore, 1962. 309p.

> A collection of studies on M. Contains "Crisi e ironia: la situa-
> zione del poeta," an investigation of M.'s use of irony in his
> poetry and other writings, taking as a critical point of depar-
> ture, M.'s article "Sur le chapeau haut de forme." Also includes
> "La tradizione e il nulla," "Oggettività e intellettualismo: l'es-
> perienza impressionista," "Tra Naturalismo e Simbolismo: la
> situazione del critico," and in the appendices: "Mallarmé bizan-
> tino," "Momenti mallarmeani in Ungaretti," "Bibliogaphia degli
> studi mallarmeani in Italia (1885-1961)," and exegesis of "A la
> nue accablante tu."
>
> a) C. Chassé, *Revue d'Histoire Littéraire de la France*, 65
> (1965), 138-140. Incorrectly gives author's name as "Luigi de
> Nittis."
>
> b) M. Colesanti, *Letteratura*, 60 (Nov.-Dec. 1962), 96-99.
>
> c) E. Fiorioli, *Culture Française*, 10 (1963), 143-145.

778. Piazzolla, Marino. "Purreza di Mallarmé." *Sestante Letterario*,
      1, Nos. 3-4 (1962), 29-31.

> General essay concerning M.'s *"poésie pure."*

779. Ragusa, Olga. "Ancora sui rapporti tra Mallarmé e Vittorio
      Pica." *Studi Francesi*, 6 (1962), 94-95.

> Concerns the two authors' literary relationship.

1963

780. Austin, L. J. "Les moyens du mystère chez Mallarmé et
      chez Valéry." *Cahiers de l'Association Internationale des Etu-
      des Françaises*, 15 (1963), 103-117.

> Contains an interpretation of "Quelle soie aux baumes de
> temps...."

781. Bandy, W. T. "Mallarmé's Sonnet to Poe: The First Text?"
      Revue de Littérature Comparée, 37 (1963), 100-101.

> Presents a poem, with the title *Au Tombeau d'Edgar Poe*,
> which the author discovered in the Alderman Library of the
> University of Virginia. Suggests that this text without the revi-
> sions of the later versions may be "a faithful replica of the
> original sonnet, as Mallarmé first set it down on paper."

782. Block, Haskell M. *Mallarmé and the Symbolist Drama.* Detroit: Wayne State University Press, 1963. vii, 164p.

A detailed investigation of M.'s dramatic theories and their influence upon the Symbolist theater of Maeterlinck and others.
a) S. D. Braun, *Romanic Review*, 56 (1965), 309-311.
b) C. Chadwick, *Revue d'Histoire Littéraire de la France*, 65 (1965), 332-333.
c) A. Fongaro, *Studu Francesi*, 8 (1964), 581-582.
d) M. J. Friedman, *French Review*, 38 (1964-65), 269-271.
e) H. Goldar, *Comparative Literature*, 17 (1965), 182-184.
f) R. L. Peters, *Journal of Aesthetics and Art Criticism*, 23 (1964-65), 507-508.
g) R. O. J. Van Nuffel, *Annales de la Fondation Maurice Maeterlinck*, 10 (1964), 72-73.

783. "The Cult of Mallarmé." *Times Literary Supplement*, 62 (1963), 665-667.

Review-article concerning 745, 752, 770, and 776.

784. Davies, Gardner. "Note on Banville and Mallarmé." *AUMLA*, No. 19 (1963), pp. 107-111.

A comparative study of Banville's *La Femme aux roses* and M.'s *Mysticis umbraculis*, indicating Banville's influence on M.

785. ———. "Paradox and Dénouement in Mallarmé's Poetry." *French Studies*, 17 (1963), 351-357.

Discusses dramatic elements found in *L'Après-midi d'un faune*, *Hérodiade*, and *Un Coup de dés*.

786. Douchin, Jacques. "Mallarmé technicien du vers: notes sur les deux versions du Sonnet en -YX." In *Etudes romanes dédiées à Andreas Blinkenberg*. Copenhagen: Librairie Munksgaard, 1963. 271p.

Concerns "Ses purs ongles...."

787. Dubief, Henri. "Mallarmé et Pontus de Tyard: à propos d'une lettre inédite." *Revue d'Histoire Littéraire de la France*, 63 (1963), 119-121.

A note on M.'s interest in Pontus de Tyard.

788.   Gan, Peter. "Stéphane Mallarmé: 'Der Facher.'" *Merkur*, 17 (1963), 57-58.

Concerns *Autre Eventail de Mademoiselle Mallarmé.*

789.   Gill, A. "Les vrais bosquets de la *Prose pour des Esseintes*." *Cahiers de l'Association Internationale des Etudes Françaises*, 15 (1963), 87-102.

Exegesis.

790.   Goffin, Robert. "Théodore de Banville et Mallarmé." *Journal des Poètes*, 33, No. 6 (1963), 2.

Concerns influence of Banville's *Diane au bois* on the composition of *L'Après-midi d'un faune.*

791.   Guichard, Léon. *La Musique et les lettres en France au temps du wagnérisme.* Paris: Presses Universitaires de France, 1963. 354p.

Contains a section entitled "Mallarmé, admirateur distant, inquiet et réservé," discussing M.'s relationship to the Wagnerian aesthetic as it was known and interpreted in France during the last half of the nineteenth century. Comments on M.'s "Rêverie d'un poète français" and *Hommage* (à Richard Wagner). Concludes that "esthétiquement, Mallarmé n'accepte pas le complexe wagnérien des arts, l'influence de la musique de Wagner sur son esthétique propre est nulle."

792.   Maione, Italo. "La poesia di Mallarmé." *Il Baretti*, 4, Nos. 22-23 (1963), 3-17.

General critical remarks.

793.   Mallarmé, Stéphane. *Opere: poemi in prosa e opere critica.* Edited by F. Piselli. Introduction by M. Luzi. Milan: Lerici, 1963. lii, 553p.

794.   Mauron, Charles. *Des Métaphores obsédantes au mythe personnel: introduction à la psychocritique.* Paris: Librairie José Corti, 1963. 380p.

Contains three chapters on M. Using author's psychocritical method, analyzes the *réseaux* of "obsessing metaphors" in M.'s poetry and considers their place within his "mythe personnel," which, according to Mauron, has its principal source in M.'s traumatic loss of his sister.

795. Mucci, Renato. "Il Libro strumento spirituale in Mallarmé." *Academie e Biblioteche d'Italia,* 31 (1963), 508-517.

Concerns M.'s conception of "the Book."

796. Nicolas, Henry. *Mallarmé et le symbolisme.* Nouveaux Classiques Larousse. Paris: Librairie Larousse, 1963. 126p.

An introductory text including biographical and interpretative sections, as well as poems and extracts from prose works, which help to establish M.'s place within the context of the Symbolist movement.

797. Pfeiffer, Jean. "Trajectoire de Mallarmé." *Synthèses,* 17, No. 202 (1963), 230-238.

Review-article concerning 752.

798. Poggioli, Renato. "Decadence in Miniature." *Massachusetts Review,* 4 (1962-63), 531-562.

Contains a discussion of "Las de l'amer repos...."

799. Richard, J.-P. "L'Univers imaginaire de Mallarmé." *L'Information littéraire,* 15, No. 1 (1963), 1-9.

Author discusses the object, critical method, and major conclusions of his study of the same title (see 752).

800. Tânger Corrêa, Manuel. "Mallarmé e Fernando Pessoa: perante o 'Corvo' de Edgar Allan Poe." *Occidente,* 65, No. 303 (1963), 4-20.

Considers Poe's influence on the French and Portuguese poets and compares their translations of *The Raven.*

801. Tilliette, Xavier. "L'aventure de Mallarmé." *Etudes,* 316 (1963), 376-383.

Review-article concerning 752.

802. Vortriede, Werner. "Novalis und Mallarmé." *Antaios,* 5 (1963), 64-78.

A comparative study pointing out similar symbolism found in Novalis' *An Tieck* and M.'s *Prose pour des Esseintes.*

803. Walzer, Pierre-Olivier. *Essai sur Mallarmé.* Paris: Editions Pierre Seghers, 1963. 256p.

> Using a biographical framework, offers a perceptive analysis of M.'s most significant literary production, amply supported by quotations from correspondence and critical writings, comparisons with variant versions, and stylistic considerations. Also presents interesting photographs, facsimiles, etc., concerning M.
>
> a) L. J. Austin, *Revue d'Histoire Littéraire de la France,* 65 (1965), 718-719.

1964

804. Aigrisse, Gilberte. "Mallarmé, maître et ombre." *Le Thyrse,* 66, No. 2 (1964), 62-65.

> Concerns 689.

805. Bailey, Helen Phelps. *Hamlet in France from Voltaire to Laforgue.* Geneva: Librairie Droz, 1964. xv, 181p.

> Contains a discussion of M.'s "vision" of Hamlet. (Publication of the author's dissertation, Columbia University, 1950.)

806. Baudoux, Luce. "L'inconscient concerté: syntaxe et lexique dans l'œuvre de Mallarmé." *Revue d'Esthétique,* 17 (1964), 105-119.

> A stylistic study.

807. Bays, Gwendolyn. *The Orphic Vision: Seer Poets from Novalis to Rimbaud.* Lincoln: University of Nebraska Press, 1964. ix, 303p.

> In several references, links M. with the "Orphic tradition" in literature, which regards the poet as a seer.

808. Bigeard, Guy. "Explication française. Mallarmé: *Brise marine.*" *L'Ecole,* 29 Feb. 1964.

809. Brown, Calvin S. "De Quincey and the Participles in Mallarmé's *Coup de dés.*" *Comparative Literature,* 16 (1964), 65-69.

> Suggests two essays by Thomas De Quincey in *The English Mail-Coach* as possible sources for the unusual combination of present participles in *Un Coup de dés.*

*810. Cartier, Marius. "La prose de Verlaine et de Mallarmé." In *Contribution à l'étude de la prose des symbolistes français: quelques problèmes de langue et de stylistique.* Bern: Städt Gymnasium, 1964. 66p.

811. Chevalier, J.-C. "Quelques remarques sur le vocabulaire du *Toast funèbre* de St. Mallarmé." *Cahiers de l'Association Internationale des Etudes Françaises,* 16 (1964), 9-19, 285.

> Exegetical notes.

812. Chisholm, A. R. "Le Démon de l'analogie." *Essays in French Literature,* No. 1 (1964), pp. 1-6.

> An analysis of this prose poem.

813. Davies, Gardner. "Mallarmé's *Le Cantique de Saint Jean.*" *Essays in French Literature,* No. 1 (1964), pp. 7-29.

814. ———. "The 'Prelude' of *Les Noces d'Hérodiade.*" *Australian Journal of French Studies,* 1 (1964), 71-95.

> See 701.

815. Evans, Calvin. "Mallarméan Antecedents of the Avant-garde Theater." *Modern Drama,* 6 (1963-64), 12-19.

> Discusses M.'s unfavorable opinions of the theater of his day and his recognition of "the need for a new theatrical order," anticipating the development of the avant-garde theater.

816. Eymard, J. "*La Prose pour des Esseintes,* hymne ou narration?" *Littératures,* 11 (1964), 7-23.

817. Fongaro, Antoine. "Mallarmé et les verbes." *Studi Francesi,* 8 (1964), 101-102.

Challenges Richard's statement that there are "few verbs" in M.'s poetry. By a sample count, author establishes that "il y a autant de verbes dans la poésie de Mallarmé ... que chez n'importe quel autre poète!"

818. Goffin, Robert. *Fil d'Ariane pour la poésie.* Paris: A. G. Nizet, 1964. 280p.

Contains five chapters concerning M.: "Mallarmé — la sœur et l'Idumée," on *Don du poème*; "Problèmes mallarméens," "Anastase" and "Pulchérie," exegesis of *Prose pour des Esseintes*; and "Mallarmé et Banville."

819. Jourdain, Louis. "Le concept psychique de Mallarmé." *Cahiers du Sud,* 58 (1964), 9-28.

Discusses M.'s personal philosophy.

820. Lamont, Rosette. "The Hamlet Myth." *Yale French Studies,* No. 33 (1964), pp. 80-91.

Discusses M.'s contributions to the "Hamlet myth": "For Mallarmé, Hamlet is the hero par excellence, a prototype of the modern intellectual, and the most perfect incarnation on the stage — both the living stage and the superior one of the mind and the imagination." See 569.

821. Laurent, M. "Explication française. Mallarmé: *Apparition.*" *L'Ecole,* 11 April 1964.

822. Lawler, James R. "Mallarmé and the 'Monstre d'or.'" *Romanic Review,* 55 (1964), 98-110.

A thematic study tracing the motif of the "monstre d'or" (cf. *Toast funèbre*) in M.'s poetry.

823. Lins, Alvaro. "O exemplo-Mallarmé." In *Orelógio e o quadrente: obras, autores e problemas de literatura estangeira. Ensaios e estudios (1940-1960).* Rio de Janeiro: Editora Civilizacão Brasileira, S. A., 1964. 414p.

824. McLaren, James C. "Criticism and Creativity: Poetic Themes in Mallarmé and Valéry." *Esprit Créateur,* 4 (1964), 222-227.

Underlines differences between M. and Valéry: "... they differ sharply in their goals and methods as poet-critics."

825. Mallarmé, Stéphane. *Recueil de "Nursery Rhymes."* Edited by Carl Paul Barbier. Paris: Gallimard, 1964. 157p.

> Presents a collection of English nursery rhymes with corresponding French themes written by M. intended for use in the teaching of English.

826. Mallarmé, Stéphane, and James McNeill Whistler. *Correspondance.* Edited by Carl Paul Barbier. Paris: A. G. Nizet, 1964. 307p.

> Presents the correspondence between M. and his friend Whistler from 18 March 1888 to 31 May 1898, with editorial commentary.

827. Mauron, Charles. *Mallarmé par lui-même.* Paris: Editions du Seuil, 1964. 190p.

> A good introductory text. As is usual with the "par lui-même" series, draws heavily upon correspondence and autobiographical documents. Second section contains selections from M.'s poetry and prose works. The collection of photographs, drawings, and facsimiles concerning M. and his family is particularly noteworthy.
> a) *Bulletin Critique du Livre Français,* 24 (1969), 125.
> b) J. Demougin, *Mercure de France,* 353 (1965), 331-333.

828. Missac, Pierre. "Note sur l'usage de la préposition 'à' chez Mallarmé." *Cahiers du Sud,* 58 (1964), 34-50.

829. Morawska, Ludmila. *L'Adjectif qualificatif dans la langue des symbolistes français (Rimbaud, Mallarmé, Valéry).* Poznan: Uniwersytet Im. Adama Mickiewicza w Poznania, 1964. 170p.

> A comprehensive stylistic study of the use of qualificative adjectives by Rimbaud, Mallarmé and Valéry. Among the many aspects considered are agreement, degree of intensity, degree of comparison, function, position, alliteration, and repetition.

830. ———. "La couleur chez Mallarmé." *Filologia,* 5 (1964), 145-165.

> Includes stylistic analysis of M.'s use of qualificative adjectives of color in his poetry. States that among the poets of his age, "c'est Mallarmé qui a été particulièrement sensible à la couleur."

831. Mossop, D. J. "Mallarmé's *Prose pour Des Esseintes.*" *French Studies,* 18 (1964), 123-135.

832. Noulet, Emilie. "Remémoration d'amis belges." *Australian Journal of French Studies,* 1 (1964), 96-103.

833. ———. *Suites: Mallarmé, Rimbaud, Valéry.* Paris: A. G. Nizet, 1964. 267p.

   A collection of articles and book reviews published in various periodicals.

834. Orlando, Francesco. "Mallarmé e la fede perduta." *Rivista di Letterature Moderne e Comparate,* 17 (June 1964), 85-97.

   Exegesis of *Sainte.*

835. Paxton, N. "Stéphane Mallarmé and Stefan George." *Modern Languages,* 45 (1964), 102-104.

   Discusses M.'s influence on George, whom author calls "a German Mallarmé."

836. Pevel, Henri. "Résonances mallarméennes du nouveau roman." *Méditations,* No. 7 (1964), pp. 95-113.

   Considers Mallarméan elements in the works of Alain Robbe-Grillet, Claude Mauriac, Jean Ricardou, Marguerite Duras, and others. Indicates how these writers have adopted M.'s principle of "ambiguity" which Pevel defines as "un glissement constant et invisible de la description d'un objet à un autre, de façon à ce que, comme par frottement, ils s'usent l'un l'autre et finissent par s'annuler."

837. Richard, Jean-Pierre. "Mallarmé et le rien, d'après un fragment inédit." *Revue d'Histoire Littéraire de la France,* 64 (1964), 633-644.

   Presents the unfinished text of a projected poem by M.: "Je veux épouser la notion...."

838. Roudaut, Jean. "Mallarmé et Butor, *a gossip.*" *Cahiers du Sud,* 58 (1964), 29-33.

   Treats M.'s influence on Michel Butor.

839. Tortel, Jean. "Note brève sur le regard de Mallarmé." *Cahiers du Sud*, 58 (1964), 3-8.

> Concerns M.'s use of language: "Le langage de Mallarmé n'est qu'un regard, mais son regard n'est que langage."

1965

840. Bolle, L. "Mallarmé, Igitur et Hamlet." *Critique*, 21 (1965), 853-863.

> A review-article concerning 689, 752, and 803.

841. Bürger, Peter. "Der *orgueil* bei Mallarmé." *Romantisches Jahrbuch*, 16 (1965), 163-168.

> Investigates M.'s use of the word *orgueil*.

842. Cattaui, Georges. *Orphisme et prophétie chez les poètes français: 1850-1950*. Paris: Plon, 1965. 329p.

> Contains "Mallarmé et les mystiques," an essay in which Cattaui shows the relationship of M.'s thought to that found in the mystic tradition, particularly Oriental mysticism: "...plus encore qu'à nos mystiques chrétiens d'Occident — qui trouvent dans un recueillement passif de tous les sens la source de leur expérience — nous fait-il songer aux *Soufis*, aux *Yoghis*, aux *Taoïstes* par la concentration volontaire, active de la conscience."

843. Chiaromonte, Nicola. "Mallarmé e la situazione moderna." *Tempo Presente*, No. 1 (1965), pp. 5-12.

> Discusses the contemporary significance of M.'s aesthetics.

*844. Christin, A. M. "Thèmes baudelairiens et mallarméens dans l'œuvre de Manet." *Sévriennes d'aujourd'hui* (March 1965), pp. 14-19.

845. Coeuroy, André. *Wagner et l'esprit romantique: Wagner et la France, le wagnérisme littéraire*. Paris: Gallimard, 1965. 380.

> Chapter entitled "Les symbolistes" includes a discussion of M.'s attitude toward Wagner. States that "le contact avec Wagner reste limité au vocabulaire.... Mallarmé n'a pas été un wagnérien."

846.   Cohn, Robert Greer. *Toward the Poems of Mallarmé.* Berkeley: University of California Press, 1965. x, 284p.

> Exegesis of thirty-four of M.'s poetical works in which the author uses meticulous linguistic analysis to support his interpretations.
> a) C. S. Brown, *Modern Philology*, 64 (1966-67), 371-373.
> b) A. Fongaro, *Studi Francesi*, 10 (1966), 587-588.
> c) A. H. Greet, *French Review*, 39 (1956-66), 945-947.
> d) R. T. Neely, *Esprit Créateur*, 7 (1967), 155-156.
> e) W. N. Ince, *Symposium*, 21 (1967), 271-273.
> f) C. G. Whiting, *Modern Language Journal*, 50 (1966), 574.
> g) *Times Literary Supplement*, 64 (1965), 1208.

847.   Davies, G. "A quel psaume de nul antique antiphonaire...." *AUMLA*, No. 24 (1965), pp. 183-219.

> Discusses the third and final section of the "Prélude" to *Les Noces d'Hérodiade* which begins with this line.

848.   Fongaro, Antoine. "Mallarmé et Victor Hugo." *Revue des Sciences Humaines*, Nos. 117-120 (1965), pp. 515-527.

> Treats Hugo's influence on M. Reviews previous suggestions of sources and parallels.

849.   ———. "Pour l'exégèse de *Sainte*." *Studi Francesi*, 9 (1965), 485-490.

850.   Gill, Austin. "Mallarmé on Baudelaire." In *Currents of Thought in French Literature: Essays in Memory of G. T. Clapton.* Oxford: Basil Blackwell, 1965. xi, 370p.

> An essay which does not directly treat the problem of Baudelaire's influence on M.'s poetry, but rather the impact on his thought, particularly during the period 1862-1867. Gill uses textual analysis of M.'s writings to show that although M.'s admiration for Baudelaire's poetry "is asserted by obvious imitation ... his ideas as Mallarmé understands them are opposed," and concludes that "traced back to their origins, then, Mallarmé's thoughts on Baudelaire are those of a young poet on a lost leader."

851.   Graaf, Daniel A. de. "De doolhof van Mallarmé of gedichten als Sterrenbeelden." *De Vlaamse Gids*, 49 (1965), 789-793.

852. Hartley, Anthony, translator. *Mallarmé*. Baltimore: Penguin Books, 1965. xxxi, 240p.

> Prose translations of much of M.'s poetry and prose. Includes the original French versions with translations below. The volume is introduced by a perceptive essay in which Hartley says that "for Mallarmé his poems were the only earnest of an absolute without which he himself would be swallowed up in the gulf into whose depths he had once gazed with terror."

853. Kesting, Marianne. *Vermessung des Labyrinths: Studien zur modernen Ästhetik*. Frankfort on the Main: S. Fischer Verlag, 1965. 182p.

> Includes "Entwurf des absoluten Buches: über Stéphane Mallarmé," an essay concerning M.'s conception of "the Book."

854. Lawrence, Joseph. "Mallarmé et son amie anglaise." *Revue d'Histoire Littéraire de la France*, 65 (1965), 457-478.

> Concerns Ettie Yapp.

855. Mallarmé, Stéphane. *Correspondance: 1871-1885*. Edited by Henri Mondor and Lloyd James Austin. Paris: Gallimard, 1965. 337p.

> Annotated edition of M.'s correspondence from 12 Aug. 1871 to 20 Dec. 1885. Contains supplemental letters for the period covered in the previous volume (700).

856. ———. *Dice Thrown Will Never Abolish Chance*. Translated by Brian Coffey. Chester Springs, Pa.: Dufour Editions, Inc., 1965. Unpaged.

> A translation of *Un Coup de dés* which follows the typographic format of the original. Also includes a translation of M.'s "Preface" and a brief introduction.

857. Merle, Pierre. "Les 'vers uniques,' les 'vers joyaux' de Mallarmé." *L'Auvergne Littéraire*, No. 186 (1965), pp. 57-64.

> Isolates and lists sixty verses taken from M.'s poetry which the author considers "vers uniques" and "vers joyaux," with philosophical significance independent of the context of the entire poems.

858. Nardis, Luigi de. "L'Influence de Lamartine sur les poèmes de jeuness de Mallarmé." In *Actes du Congrès: Secondes Journées Européennes d'Etudes Lamartiniennes.* Mâcon: Comité Permanent d'Etudes Lamartiniennes, 1965. 141p.

> An article (pp. 35-43) which investigates the influence of Lamartine's poetry on M.'s early verse found in *Entre quatre murs* (see 574). According to the author, "Lamartine, le doux Lamartine, avec son lyrisme éloquent et musical, avec le flou de ses images, avec son idéalisme vague et captivant, correspondait parfaitement aux vagues épanchements de l'âme mallarméenne, aut tâtonnements de sa naissante vocation poétique."

859. Raitt, A. W. *Life and Letters in France: The Nineteenth Century.* London: Nelson, 1965. xxx, 177p.

> Chapter 17 discusses M.'s "Les Fenêtres," which the author says, "in its amalgam of Baudelairean borrowings, specifically Mallarméan features... and representative indications of contemporary preoccupations, is a rich and powerful evocation of some of the currents of emotion which eddied through literature in the second half of the century."

860. ———. *Villiers de l'Isle-Adam et le mouvement symboliste.* Paris: Librairie José Corti, 1965. 419p.

> Includes a chapter on M. Discusses Villiers de l'Isle-Adam's influence on M. and the friendship between the two men.

861. Remacle, Madeleine. "La poésie obscure dans les classes supérieures: trois essais d'interprétation." *Cahiers d'Analyse Textuelle,* 7 (1965), 25-44.

> Includes an explication of *Autre Eventail de Mademoiselle Mallarmé.*

862. Steland, Dieter. *Dialektische Gedanken in Stéphane Mallarmés "Divagations."* Munich: Wilhelm Fink Verlag, 1965. 86p.

> A study of the dialectical process of M.'s thought in his *Divagations.* Considers in detail M.'s ideas on poetry, the dance, the theater of the future, and the relationship of art to nature as expressed in his "poèmes critiques."

863. Wellek, René. *A History of Modern Criticism: 1750-1950.* Vol. 4: *The Later Nineteenth Century.* New Haven: Yale University Press, 1965. vi, 671p.

Includes an excellent section on M. summarizing his major aesthetic principles. Insists upon M.'s originality: "He is... the first writer who is radically discontent with the ordinary language of communication and attempts to construe an entire separate poetic language."

1966

864. Adams, Robert Martin. *Nil: Episodes in the Literary Conquest of Void during the Nineteenth Century.* New York: Oxford University Press, 1966. 249p.

Contains a chapter concerning M.'s "sense of void."

865. Agosti, Stefano. "Mallarmé e il linguaggio dell'ontologia." *Sigma,* No. 10 (1966), pp. 17-37.

A stylistic study investigating M.'s personal philosophy and its poetic expression.

866. Austin, L. J. "Mallarmé and the *Prose pour des Esseintes.*" *Forum for Modern Language Studies,* 2 (1966), 197-213.

867. Barbier, Carl Paul. "Mallarmé: A Correction and a New Prose Poem." *French Studies,* 20 (1966), 341-342.

Shows that the composition E. Souffrin presented as "une œuvre de jeunesse inédite" (see 369) is actually a translation of an English sonnet. Also presents an unpublished early prose poem, *Sextillion.*

868. Borum, Poul. *Poetisk modernisme: en kritisk introduktion.* Copenhagen: S. Vandelkaer, 1966. 278p.

869. Bürger, Peter. "Zum 'poème critique' bei Mallarmé." *Romantisches Jahrbuch,* 17 (1966), 150-154.

Concerns M.'s *Divagations* and other critical articles.

870. Burke, Kenneth. *Language as Symbolic Action: Essays on Life and Literature and Method.* Berkeley and Los Angeles: University of California Press, 1966. xiv, 514p.

Includes an essay which investigates "images of catharsis" in M.'s poetry, using Wallace Fowlie's exegesis as a critical basis.

871. Chisholm, A. R. *"Don du poème."* Essays in French Liter-
      ature, No. 3 (1966), pp. 33-37.

872. ———. "Mallarmé's 'Vasco Sonnet.' " French Studies, 20
      (1966), 139-143.

      Exegesis of "Au seul souci de voyager...."

873. Cohn, Robert Greer. *Mallarmé's Masterwork: New Findings.*
      The Hague: Mouton, 1966. 114p.

      A volume supplementing and updating Cohn's previous work
      on *Un Coup de dés.* Reviews other criticism concerning this
      poem and considers M.'s adolescent poems, *Le Tombeau d'Ana-
      tole* (see 745), and the fragments called "le Livre" (cf. 658) in
      connection with the genesis of *Un Coup de dés.* Also includes
      photographic reproductions of the proof sheets of the Lahure
      edition, which the poet was correcting just before his death,
      and the author's comments there.

      a) A. Fongaro, *Studi Francesi,* 12 (1968), 385.

      b) J. L. Forestier, *Esprit Créateur,* 8 (1968), 170-171.

      c) H. A. Grubbs, *French Review,* 41 (1967-68), 746.

874. Cordié, Carlo. "Mallarmé." *Cultura e Scuola,* No. 20 (1966),
      pp. 57-65.

      Discusses recent M. criticism.

875. Damase, Jacques. *La Révolution typographique depuis Mal-
      larmé.* Geneva: Editions Motte, 1966. 220p.

      Contains references to *Un Coup de dés.*

876. Ferré, André. "Obscurité de syntaxe et syntaxe d'obscurité
      chez Mallarmé." *Vie et Langage,* No. 169 (1966), pp. 182-
      189.

      A stylistic study concerning the syntactical elements of M.'s
      obscurity: Latin word order, ellipsis, etc.

877. Fischler, Alexander. "The Ghost-making Process in Mallar-
      mé's 'Le vierge, le vivace,' *Toast funèbre,* and 'Quand l'ombre
      menaça.' " *Symposium,* 20 (1966), 306-320.

      Exegesis of the above poems. Defines "ghost-making" as a
      "remarkably consistent abstraction of subject and setting by al-
      lusion."

878. Fowlie, Wallace. "Mallarmé and the Painters of His Age." *Southern Review*, 2 (1966), 542-558.

> Discusses M.'s relationship with Manet, Monet, Degas, Morisot, Renoir, and Whistler. Also considers the points of similarity between M.'s aesthetic principles and those of the Impressionist painters.

879. Gill, Austin. " 'L'être aux ailes de gaze' dans la doctrine esthétique de Mallarmé." In *Studi in onore di Italo Siciliano*. 2 vols. Florence: L. S. Olschki, 1966.

> Concerns chiefly Banville's influence on M.'s poetry and on his conception of the theater.

880. Haugen, Arne Kjell. *Mallarmés poetikk*. Oslo: Johan Grundt Tanum Forlag, 1966. 160p.

881. Jones, Rhys S. "The Selection and Usage of Symbols by Mallarmé and Valéry." *Trivium*, 1 (1966), 44-45.

> Investigates M.'s influence on Valéry from a thematic and stylistic standpoint.

882. Lockspeiser, Edward. "Mallarmé and Music." *Musical Times*, 107 (1966), 212-213.

> Program notes on Boulez's *Pli selon pli*, in which the composer claims to have carried on in music M.'s aesthetic principles.

883. Mallarmé, Stéphane. *Poesie*. Edited and translated by Luciana Frezza. Milan: G. G. Feltrinelli, 1966. xxi, 329p.

884. ———. *Poesie d'amore*. Edited and translated by Ferdinando Camon. Padua: Rebellato, 1966. 60p.

885. ———. *Poésies*. Preface by Jean-Paul Sartre. Paris: Gallimard, 1966. 190p.

886. *Les Mardis: Stéphane Mallarmé and the Artists of His Circle.* Foreword by Marilyn Stokstad and Bret Waller. Miscellaneous Publications by the Kansas Museum of Art, No. 61, 1966. 67p.

A pamphlet complementing an art exhibition at the Kansas Museum of Art, concerning the famous "Mardis" and M.'s artist friends who frequently attended: Manet, Monet, Renoir, Morisot, Gauguin, Rodin, Munch, Whistler, Degas, Redon, and Puvis de Chavannes. Contains four articles devoted to M. and the Symbolist Movement: 1) James L. Connelly, "The World of Mallarmé's Circle — The Historical Ambience: 1870-1914"; 2) Robert T. Neely, "Endymion in France: A Brief Survey of French Symbolist Poetry"; 3) Jeanne A. Stump, "Varieties of Symbolism"; and 4) Klaus Berger, "Mallarmé and the Visual Arts."

887. Orlando, Francesco, and Antoine Fongaro. "Ancora sull'esegesi critica di *Sainte*." *Studi Francesi*, 10 (1966), 87-90.

> Authors discuss their basic differences concerning the interpretation of *Sainte*.

888. Park, Ynhui. "Dilemme mallarméen." *Revue d'Esthétique*, 19 (1966), 149-160.

> A philosophical discussion of M.'s insoluble dilemma between the "desire to create" and the "desire of self-justification."

889. ———. *L' "Idée" chez Mallarmé, ou la cohérence rêvée.* Paris: Centre Documentation Universitaire, 1966. 164p.

> An investigation of M.'s lifelong pursuit of the absolute, which he called "l'Idée": "...Mallarmé n'a cessé sa recherche de l'Absolu à tel point qu'il tente jusqu'à la fin de sa vie de l'exprimer dans *le Livre*. Il est donc certain que l'Idée constitue le pivot de l'univers mallarméen et de son aventure."

890. Paxton, Norman. "Stéphane Mallarmé: Five Prose Poems." *Kolokon*, No. 1 (1966), pp. 26-31.

> Five prose poems (*Le Phénomène futur, Plainte d'automne, La Pipe, Le Nénuphar blanc,* and a brief poetic piece inspired by Baudelaire taken from the "Divagations"), translated and introduced by Norman Paxton.

891. Pia, Pascal. "Un sonnet contesté de Mallarmé." *Quinzaine Littéraire*, 1 April 1966, p. 15.

> Concerns the sonnet "Parce que de la viande était à point rôtie...." Pia believes that this poem was not written by M. and presents evidence for this thesis.

892. Pollmann, Leo. "Paul Claudel und Mallarmé." *Zeitschrift für Französische Sprache und Literatur*, 76 (1966), 1-8.

> Concerns M.'s influence on Paul Claudel. Studies Claudel's *Jour d'automne* from this standpoint.

893. Saillet, Maurice. "Villiers, pair de Mallarmé." *Quinzaine Littéraire*, 15 April 1966, p. 12.

> Concerns M.'s appraisal of Villiers de l'Isle-Adam in his lecture "Villiers de l'Isle-Adam."

894. Schaffner, R. "Die Salome, Dichtungen von Flaubert, Wilde und Mallarmé, Vergleichende Gestalt- und Stilanalyse." Dissertation. Würzburg, 1966.

895. Schulze, J. "Ein Preisgedicht in der Weise des Gepriesenen: Mallarmés *Tombeau de Charles Baudelaire*." *Archiv für das Studium der Neueren Sprachen und Literaturen*, 203 (1966), 97-117.

896. Sollers, Philippe. "Littérature et totalité." *Tel Quel*, No. 26 (1966), pp. 81-95.

> Concerns M.'s philosophy of literature: "L'expérience de Mallarmé... peut être définie brièvement comme une action créatrice et critique portant sur la symbolique du livre (de la fin du livre et de son absence) et de l'écriture...."

897. Stempel, Wolf-Dieter. "Syntax in dunkler Lyrik." In *Immanente Ästhetik, ästhetische Reflexion: Lyrik als Paradigma der Moderne.* Edited by W. Iser. Munich: Fink, 1966. 543p.

> Concerns "A la nue accablante tu..." (pp. 33-46).

898. Strauss, Walter A. "The Reconciliation of Opposites in Orphic Poetry: Rilke and Mallarmé." *Centennial Review*, 10 (1966), 214-236.

> A comparison of M.'s and Rilke's personal philosophies: "The encounter with death and nothingness in Mallarmé leads to the discovery of beauty; in Rilke this encounter leads to the discovery of the unity of true being...."

899. Veri, Margot. "Contribution à l'explication d'un poème de Mallarmé." *Moderna Språk*, 60 (1966), 55-58.

> Concerns *Autre Éventail de Mademoiselle Mallarmé.*

900. Weinberg, Bernard. *The Limits of Symbolism: Studies of Five Modern French Poets.* Chicago: University of Chicago Press, 1966. ix, 430p.

> Offers quite extensive studies on *L'Après-midi d'un faune,* "Le vierge, le vivace et le bel aujourd'hui," *Toast funèbre, Le Tombeau d'Edgar Poe,* and *Un Coup de dés.*

901. Williams, Thomas A. "Mallarmé's *Plusieurs Sonnets,* IV (Ses purs ongles très haut...)." *The Explicator,* 25 (1966), explication 28.

> A brief explication of "Ses purs ongles..." in which the author demonstrates that three main symbols (the room, the mirror, and the constellation) offer the key to this sonnet.

902. Zaubitzer, Hannelore. "Clownmetaphern bei Baudelaire, Mallarmé und Michaux." *Neueren Sprachen,* 15 (1966), 445-456.

> A thematic study comparing Baudelaire's, M.'s, and Michaux's use of the clown as a metaphor in their poetry.

903. Zillmer, Herman Lawrence. "A Study of the Use of the Symbol in the Dramatic Aesthetic of Mallarmé, Maeterlinck, Valéry and Claudel." *Dissertation Abstracts,* 26 (1966), 5600.

1967

904. Agosti, Stefano. "Interpretazioni d'un sonetto di Mallarmé: 'Quand l'ombre menaça de la fatale loi.'" *Strumenti Critici,* 1 (1967), 295-312.

905. Anderson, Richard. "Hindu Myths in Mallarmé: *Un Coup de Dés.*" *Comparative Literature,* 19 (1967), 28-35.

> Suggests several Indian myths found in the *Bhagavata Purana* as sources for themes found in *Un Coup de dés.*

906. Austin, L. J. "Mallarmé disciple de Baudelaire: 'Le Parnasse contemporain.' " *Revue d'Histoire Littéraire de la France*, 67 (1967), 437-449.

> Investigates Baudelaire's influence upon the composition of eleven of M.'s poems which appeared in the first *Parnasse contemporain*.

907. Balakian, Anna. *The Symbolist Movement*. New York: Random House, 1967. ix, 208p.

> In a chapter on "Mallarmé and the Symbolist *Cénacle*," investigates M.'s relationship with the poets often called the Symbolist "school." States that M. was "not, historically speaking, a Symbolist," and far from being the acclaimed Master of a group of fawning, adulating "disciples," as he has frequently been described, M. remained entirely independent of any real obligations of leadership and often exhibited views quite contrary to the "official" Symbolist doctrine of the day.

908. Brown, Clavin S. "The Musical Analogies in Mallarmé's *Un Coup de Dés.*" *Comparative Literature Studies*, 4 (1967), 67-79.

> An examination of M.'s musical analogies in *Un Coup de dés* "in order to see just what they involve, what their limitations and strengths are, how far they are valid logically, and whether logical validity is a necessary part of aesthetic utility."

909. Castoldi, Alberto. "La nozione di 'impersonalità' in Mallarmé." *ACME*, 20 (1967), 349-371.

> Concerns M.'s conception of "impersonality" as a fundamental element of his literary philosophy.

910. Charvet, Patrick Edward. *A Literary History of France*. Edited by P. E. Charvet. Vol. 5: *The Nineteenth and Twentieth Centuries: 1870-1940*. New York: Barnes and Noble, Inc., 1967. xvi, 315p.

> In a section on Symbolism, treats M., along with Verlaine and Rimbaud, as a "pre-Symbolist." Divides M.'s poems into two groups: "the early poems leading up to 'L'Après-Midi d'un Faune' and the remainder." The first group, according to the author, "do not for the most part raise any problems of interpretation." With *L'Après-midi d'un faune*, however, M. "gradually shifts from direct statement to esoterism, from discursiveness ... to intense compression, from definition of things to suggestions. ..."

911. Davies, G. "The 'Scène intermédiaire' in *Les Noces d'Héro-diade*." *Australian Journal of French Studies*, 4 (1967), 270-286.

> See 701.

912. Fowlie, Wallace. *Climates of Violence: The French Literary Tradition from Baudelaire to the Present*. New York: Macmillan Company, 1967. xi, 274p.

> In a perceptive essay, "Mallarmé's Purity," offers an excellent interpretation of M.'s aesthetic principles. Compares the poet to an alchemist or magician: "... Mallarmé enunciated this belief in many ways and on many occasions — that poetry is something akin to magic. It is a talisman which may open up the way to a metaphysical life in man." Also discusses the relationship of Symbolism to Impressionism in the plastic arts.

913. Françon, Marcel. "Mallarmé et la poésie du XVIᵉ siècle." *Zagadnienia Rodzajów Literackich*, 10, No. 18 (1967), 98-107.

> Concerns the poems of sixteenth-century poets found in M.'s personal anthology of favorite poems (see 574). Author notes the conspicuous absence of Ronsard. Also considers M.'s early use of poems of fixed form: sonnets, triolets, rondeaux, etc.

914. Frey, Hans-Jost. "Mallarmé und die Neue Musik." *Schweizer Monatshefte*, 46 (1966-67), 575-598.

> Concerns the influence of M.'s aesthetics upon contemporary music.

915. Garnier, Pierre. "Poésie expérimentale: Un Coup de dés jamais n'abolira le hasard." *Poésie Vivante*, No. 24 (1967), p. 76.

> States that with *Un Coup de dés* M. "ouvre une nouvelle époque à l'occident où peu à peu la lecture de la phrase sera remplacée par la vision, et où le groupe sacré sujet — verbe — complément sera rompu."

916. Gaughan, Gerard Charles. "Wallace Stevens and Mallarmé: A Comparative Study in Poetic Theory." *Dissertation Abstracts*, 27 (1966-67), 3453A.

917. Gay-Crosier, Raymond. "Le sonnet en -yx de Mallarmé." *Culture,* 28 (1967), 285-292.

Concerns "Ses purs ongles...."

918. Gill, Austin. "*Le Tombeau de Charles Baudelaire* de Mallarmé." *Comparative Literature Studies,* 4 (1967), 45-65.

919. Glauser, Alfred. *Le Poème-symbole de Scève à Valéry.* Paris: A. G. Nizet, 1967. 221p.

Sixth chapter compares Hugo's *Le Satyre* and M.'s *L'Après-midi d'un faune.* Says of the Satyr and the Faun. "Tous les deux sont victimes de leur créateur et ont été forcés à des aveux contraires: chez Hugo, c'est celui du poète total, qui ignore les hésitations et les remords, chez Mallarmé celui du poète stérile, qui vit de ces hésitations et de ces remords."

920. Gsteiger, Manfred. *Poesie und Kritik: Betrachtungen über Literatur.* Bern: Francke Verlag, 1967. 190p.

Includes a brief discussion of M.'s *Autre Eventail de Mademoiselle Mallarmé.*

921. Guglielmi, Joseph. "Comme une lecture d'*Un Coup de dés.*" *Manteia,* 1 (1967), 4-12.

Exegesis.

922. Jaeckle, Erwin. *Zirkelschlag des Lyrik.* Zurich: Fretz & Wasmuth Verlag, 1967. 302p.

Contains a brief general essay on M. entitled "Offenbarung aus den Sprachwurzeln: Stefan Mallarmé."

923. Mallarmé, Stéphane. *Poesie.* Edited and translated by Antonio Corsaro. Rome: A. Curcio, 1967. 623p.

924. Martino, Pierre. *Parnasse et symbolisme.* Paris: Librairie Armand Colin, 1967. 192p.

Contains numerous references to M. including a general study of M. and his poetic principles.

925. Nerlich, Michael. "La Finestra: note a Mallarmé, Kafka e Gide." *Sigma,* No. 14 (1967), pp. 61-75.

Compares the use of the window as a symbol in the works of
Mallarmé, Kafka, and Gide.

926. Noulet, Emilie. *Vingt poèmes de Mallarmé*. Geneva: E. Droz,
1967. xvi, 284p.

> Detailed explications of twenty poetical works by M. which
> were presented in the author's published doctoral thesis (271)
> and in her *Dix poèmes de Stéphane Mallarmé* (435), but ap-
> pear here in revised and corrected form.
> a) *Bulletin Critique du Livre Français*, 22 (1967), 947.
> b) W. Hirdt, *Studi Francesi*, 13 (1969), 579-581.
> c) M. J. Lefebve, *Synthèses*, 22, Nos. 256-257 (1967), 98-100.
> d) A. Soreil, *La Vie Wallone*, 43 (1969), 57-59.

927. Rasmusson, Torkel. " 'Pages and — here! Lemme show you':
Mallarmé och boken." *BLM*, 36 (1967), 651-658.

928. Read, Herbert. *Poetry and Experience*. New York: Horizon
Press, 1967. 160p.

> Contains "The Resurrection of the Word," in which the author
> states: "A problem exists for the modern poet... which Mal-
> larmé was the first to formulate and attempts to overcome — the
> evident fact that the language of our western civilization had
> become too corrupt for poetic use." Also discusses original
> contributions of M.'s poetic theory.

929. Rose, Marilyn Gaddis. "The Daughters of Herodias in *Hérodiade, Salomé*, and *A Full Moon in March*." *Comparative
Drama*, 1 (1967), 172-181.

> Compares the heroines of M.'s *Hérodiade*, Oscar Wilde's *Salomé*,
> and W. B. Yeats's *A Full Moon in March*.

930. Shartar, I. Martin. "The Theatre of the Mind: An Analysis
of Works by Mallarmé, Yeats, Eliot, and Beckett." *Dissertation
Abstracts*, 27 (1966-67), 2161A.

931. Surer, Paul. "Explication de texte: *L'Azur*." *L'Information
Littéraire*, 19 (1967), 92-96.

932. Todrani, Jean. "Libre cours." *Manteia*, 1 (1967), 31-37.

> Concerns M.'s influence upon contemporary poetics.

933. Vernois, Paul, editor. *Le Réel dans la littérature et dans la langue.* Paris: Librairie C. Klincksieck, 1967. v, 324p.

> Contains abstracts of the following papers: A. Gill, "Du fait à l'idéal: une transposition mallarméenne"; Lloyd James Austin, "Mallarmé et le réel." See 966.

934. Wais, Kurt. "Bulwer-Lytton und der *Igitur* von Mallarmé." *Zeitschrift für Französische Sprache und Literatur*, 77 (1967), 296-331.

> Suggests a novel by Bulwer-Lytton, *Zanoni*, as a possible influence upon the composition of *Igitur*.

935. ————. "*Igitur*: Gegengenungen Mallarmés mit seinen Vorgängern: I." *Comparative Literature Studies*, 4 (1967), 35-43.

> A discussion of themes similar to those in *Igitur* found in the works of earlier French authors, including Balzac, Gautier, Hugo, Musset, and others.

936. Walzer, Pierre-Olivier. "Prolégomènes à toute exégèse future de la *Prose*." In *Festgabe Hans von Greyerz zum sechzigsten Geburtstag: 5 April 1967.* Edited by Ernest Walder. Bern: Herbert Lang, 1967. xx, 849p.

> Concerns exegesis of *Prose pour des Esseintes*.

937. Williams, Thomas Andrew. "Mallarmé and the Language of Mysticism; A Concordance to the Poems of Mallarmé." *Dissertation Abstracts*, 27 (1966-1967), 217A.

> See 1048.

1968

938. Assunto, Rosario. *L'automobile di Mallarme e altri ragiomenti intorno alla vocazione odierna delle arti.* Rome: Edizioni dell'Ateneo, 1968. 177p.

> The essay "L'automobile di Mallarmé" concerns M.'s brief article "Sur le Beau et l'Utile."

939. Barbier, Carl Paul, editor. *Documents Stéphane Mallarmé.* Vol. 1. Paris: Librairie Nizet, 1968. 129p.

Presents unpublished manuscripts, variant versions of poems, letters, and other *Mallarméana.*

940. Betz, Dorothy Katherine Marshall. "Baudelairian Imagery and Rhetoric in the Works of Several Later Nineteenth-Century Poets." *Dissertation Abstracts,* 28 (1968), 4163A.

Discusses Baudelaire's influence on M.

941. Biès, J. "Poésie incantatoire, poésie jaculatoire: Mallarmé et Péguy." *Littératures,* 15 (1968), 69-84.

A comparative study: "Si Mallarmé a voulu redécouvrir plutôt une *langue* paradisiaque, et Péguy, plutôt un *temps* paradisiaque, tous deux ont connu le même désir de rejoindre... ce cœur du monde où établir leur demeure, de dépasser les contingences et les limitations humaines pour recouvrer une espèce de condition divine."

942. Breillat, Pierre. "*Le Guignon* de Mallarmé." *Humanisme Actif,* 1 (1968), 105-110.

943. Blake, Elizabeth Stanton. "Some Aspects of Phonemic Reinforcement in the 'Poésies' of Mallarmé." *Dissertation Abstracts,* 28 (1967-68), 1812A.

944. Caluwé, Jacques de. "Propos sur Mallarmé." *Revue des Langues Vivantes,* 34 (1968), 93-102.

Concerns exegesis of *Autre Eventail de Mademoiselle Mallarmé.*

945. Chadwick, C. "Du nouveau sur *Prose pour des Esseintes.*" *Revue d'Histoire Littéraire de la France,* 68 (1968), 87-88.

946. Chisholm, A. R. "The Role of Consciousness in the Poetry of Mallarmé and Valéry." *Comparative Literature Studies,* 4 (1968), 81-89.

Compares the concept of "consciousness" in M.'s and Valéry's poetry: "While Valéry, like Mallarmé, is preoccupied with consciousness, his approach to it is more objective, one might say more scientific."

947. Cohn, R. G. "The Assault on Symbolism." *Comparative Literature Studies,* 5 (1968), 69-75.

Refutes Yvor Winters' unfavorable criticism of M. (see 400).
Shows how Winters "has misread Mallarmé, one of his prime
whipping boys."

948. Corsaro, Antonio. *Astrattismo nella poesia francese del seicento
e altri studi*. Palermo: S. F. Flaccovio, 1968. 382p.

Contains three studies on M.: "Mondrian e Mallarmé," "Il
linguaggio," and "Ritmi astratti diacronici in 15 poesie."

949. Dumas, Olivier. "Mallarmé, Platon et *La Prose pour des
Esseintes*: exégèse." *Revue de l'Université de Bruxelles*, 20
(1967-68), 122-146.

950. Durand, André. "Un Sonnet inédit de Mallarmé?" *Revue de
Belles-Lettres*, 93, No. 3 (1968), 51-54.

Indicates that the sonnet "Parce que de la viande..." is not
an *inédit* as is stated in the *Œuvres complètes*, since it was
published in the *Anthologie Hospitalière et Latinesque* in 1913.

951. Gaède, Edouard. "Le problème du langage chez Mallarmé."
Revue d'Histoire Littéraire de la France, 68 (1968), 45-65.

Investigates "la problématique du langage... en tant qu'elle
s'est imposée à la réflexion de Mallarmé lui-même, et en tant
qu'elle se manifeste explicitement dans ses écrits aux divers
stades de son évolution."

952. King, William W. "Baudelaire and Mallarmé: Metaphysics
or Aesthetics?" *Journal of Aesthetics and Art Criticism*, 26
(1967-68), 115-123.

A comparison of Baudelaire's and M.'s aesthetic philosophies.
States that the basic distinction between the two poets "is in
their metaphysics rather than in their poetics. The referents
of M.'s symbols are other symbols: the referents for Baudelaire's
are immediate correspondences to the Absolute."

953. Lentricchia, Frank. "Four Types of Nineteenth-Century Poetic." *Journal of Aesthetics and Art Criticism*, Spring 1968,
pp. 351-366.

Considers M. in a brief section entitled "Symbolist Theory:
Magical and Constructive Imagination." Sees M.'s greatest contribution to Symbolist theory as "his effort to establish the
poem as a contextual entity with substantive status in a language purified, or emptied, of all external reference."

954. McLendon, Will L. "A New Reading of Mallarmé's *Pitre châtié*." *South Central Bulletin*, 28, No. 3 (1968), 75.

> Abstract. See 1038.

955. Michaud, Guy. "La personnalité de Mallarmé." *Synthèses*, 23 No. 260 (1968), 71-75.

> An interpretation of M.'s personality from an astrological viewpoint.

956. Orlando, F. "Le due facce dei simboli in un poema in prosa di Mallarmé." *Strumenti Critici*, 2 (1968), 378-412.

> Discussion of *Frisson d'hiver*.

957. Paxton, Norman. *The Development of Mallarmé's Prose Style*. Geneva: Droz, 1968. 176p.

> A detailed analysis of M.'s prose works which investigates "those stylistic changes which mark the successive stages in the evolution of Mallarmé's prose, considering it ... as a chronologically developing language to be examined at different periods of its development." Appendix presents the original texts of M.'s articles which appeared in the *National Observer* and the *Revue Blanche*.
>
> a) J. Bonnefont, *Etudes Littéraires*, 2 (1969), 122-125.
> b) C. Chadwick, *Revue Belge de Philologie et d'Histoire*, 48 (1970), 590.
> c) A. R. Chisholm, *AUMLA*, 34 (1970), 345-346.
> d) A. Fongaro, *Studi Francesi*, 14 (1970), 181-182.
> e) A. H. Greet, *French Review*, 45 (1971-72), 254.
> f) H. A. Grubbs, *Modern Language Journal*, 53 (1969), 363.
> g) E. Souffrin, *French Studies*, 25 (1971), 224-225.
> h) D. Steland, *Erasmus*, 23 (1971), 988-991.

958. Podraza-Kwiatkowska, Maria. "Mlodopolski entuzjasta Mallarmégo Wobronie Antoniego Langego-krytyka." *Ruch Literacki*, No. 5 (1968), pp. 283-289.

959. Polieri, Jacques. "Le Livre de Mallarmé: A Mise en Scène." *Drama Review*, 12, No. 3 (1968), 179-182.

> See 1068.

960. Popo, E. "Mallarmé en de musiek." *De Vlaamse Gids*, 52 (1968), 33-37.

961. Robichez, Jacques. "*La Gloire*: remarques sur un poème en prose de Mallarmé." *Annales de l'Université de Paris*, 38 (1968), 27-32.

962. Schmidt-Garre, Helmut. "Dichtung, die Musik sein vollte." *Hochland*, 60 (1967-68), 624-635.

Concerns Wagner and M.

963. *Synthèses*, 22, Nos. 258-259 (1967-68), 17-118.

Issue containing eighteen previously unpublished articles concerning M. (collected by E. Noulet): Stefano Agosti, "Technique et connaissance dans la poésie de Mallarmé"; Lloyd James Austin, " 'L'Après-midi d'un Faune': essai d'explication"; Vito Carofiglio, " 'Pur': mot-clé et mot témoin chez Mallarmé"; Alberto Castoldi, "L'esthétique de l' 'écriture corporelle' dans l'œuvre de Mallarmé" (discusses M.'s conception of the dance); A. R. Chisholm, "Mon absent tombeau" (notes on the first quatrain of "Victorieusement fui le suicide beau..."); Gardner Davies, "Petit Air II"; Jacques Duchesne-Guillemin, "Sur la 'prose' " (commentary on *Prose pour des Esseintes*); Antoine Fongaro, " 'Des guirlandes célèbres' " (discussion of the second quatrain of "Quand l'ombre menaça..."); Robert Goffin, "Rétrospectives"; Joseph Guglielmi, "Actualités de Mallarmé" (a contemporary interpretation of M.); Albert Henry, "Valéry a-t-il emprunté à Mallarmé son vocabulaire poétique?"; Maurice-Jean Lefebve, "La mise en abyme mallarméenne et la preuve par X" (interpretation of "Ses purs ongles..."); Luigi de Nardis, "L' 'intérieur' mallarméen: un problème de philosophie de l'ameublement"; E. Noulet, "Le ton dans la poésie de Mallarmé" (see 1065); Francesco Piselli, "...Pour un système mallarméen (aperçu)"; Jean Pommier, " 'Ou que le gaz récent...' " (concerning interpretation of *Le Tombeau de Charles Baudelaire*); A. Raybaud, "Mallarmé, inventeur de la théâtralité?"; Francois Van Laere, "Le hasard éliminé: l'ordonnance d'un livre de vers..." (a discussion of several editions of M.'s *Poésies*); Simone Verdin, "L'action restreinte" (concerning M.'s personal philosophy).

964. Verdin, Simone. "*Prose pour des Esseintes*, exégèse." *Revue de l'Université de Bruxelles*, 20 (1967-68), 122-146.

1969

965. Agosti, Stefano. *Il cigno di Mallarmé*. Rome: Silva Editore, 1969, 115p.

> A detailed explication of "Le vierge, le vivace et le bel aujourd'-hui ..." taking into consideration its thematic relationship to M.'s other poems.
>
> a) M. Porro, *Strumenti Critici*, 15 (1971), 277-280.

966. Austin, L. J. "Mallarmé et le réel." In *Modern Miscellany Presented to Eugène Vinaver by Pupils, Colleagues and Friends*. Edited by T. E. Lawrenson, F. E. Sutcliffe, and G. F. A. Gadoffre. Manchester: Manchester University Press, 1969. xiii, 314p.

> An essay considering M.'s conception of reality and his attitude toward it.

967. ———. "New Light on Brennan and Mallarmé." *Australian Journal of French Studies*, 6 (1969), 154-162.

> Concerns M.'s influence on the Australian poet.

968. Block, Haskell M. "Mallarmé the Alchemist." *Australian Journal of French Studies*, 6 (1969), 163-179.

> Discusses M.'s relationship to the alchemical tradition, especially concerning his conception of the "Grand Œuvre."

969. Bruns, Gerald L. "Mallarmé: The Transcendence of Language and the Aesthetics of the Book." *Journal of Typographic Research*, 3 (1969), 219-240.

> Discusses M.'s unusual use of typography in *Un Coup de dés* through which "the world of print comes to occupy that magical universe in which poetry finds the mystery of its being."

970. Campos, C. L. "Symbolism and Mallarmé." In *French Literature and Its Background*. Edited by John Cruickshank. Vol. 5: *The Late Nineteenth Century*. London: Oxford University Press, 1969. viii, 229p.

> A general essay concerning M. and his poetry in which author maintains that the search for an objective comprehension of

M.'s poetry is futile: "The strangeness of Mallarmé's poems, the measure of their power, has not lessened over the past eighty years.... The greatest mistake is to hope that time and historico-scientific modes of inquiry will elucidate these defiant human structures...."

971. Chaillet, Jean. *Etudes de grammaire et de style.* Vol. 2. Paris: Bordas, 1969. 400p.

Includes a detailed explication of "Le vierge, le vivace et le bel aujourd'hui...."

972. Chisholm, A. R. "Mallarmé's 'Poétique très nouvelle.'" *Australian Journal of French Studies,* 6 (1969), 147-153.

Discusses M.'s *ars poetica.*

973. ———. "Two Exegetical Studies" (Mallarmé, Rimbaud)." *Esprit Créateur,* 9 (1969), 28-36.

Exegesis of *Billet à Whistler.*

974. Citron, Pierre. "Sur le sonnet en -yx de Mallarmé." *Revue d'Histoire Littéraire de la France,* 69 (1969), 113-116.

Explication of "Ses purs ongles...."

975. Cohn, Robert Greer. "Laforgue and Mallarmé." In *Laforgue: Essays on a Poet's Life and Work.* Edited by Warren Ramsey. Preface by Harry T. Moore. Carbondale and Edwardsville: Southern Illinois University Press, 1969. xxx, 194p.

A comparative study of M. and Laforgue indicating similar themes in their poetry.

976. ———. "Wherefore *Igitur?*" *Romanic Review,* 60 (1969), 174-177.

Investigates various possible sources for the name "Igitur."

977. Davies, G. "The 'Finale' of *Les Noces d'Hérodiade.*" *Australian Journal of French Studies,* 6 (1969), 216-252.

See 701.

978. Dragonetti, Roger. "La littérature et la lettre: introduction au 'Sonnet en -yx' de Mallarmé." *Lingua e Stile*, 4 (1969), 205-222.

> Discussion of "Ses purs ongles...."

979. Dumas, Olivier. "Mallarmé: un poème sur l''art de fumer un cigare.'" *Revue des Sciences Humaines*, Nos. 133-136 (1969), pp. 83-91.

> Concerns "Toute l'âme résumée...."

980. Faye, Jean-Pierre. "Mallarmé: l'écriture, la mode." In *La Mode, l'invention*. Paris: Editions du Seuil, 1969. 226p.

> Concerns *La Dernière Mode* and its place within M.'s total literary production.

981. Freeman, Thomas Parry. "El uso del sueño en la poesía de Benn y de Mallarmé." *Folia Humanistica*, 7 (1969), 709-719, 807-820.

> A study comparing the use of dreams as a poetic theme in the works of the German poet Gottfried Benn and M., using Charles Peirce's philosophy as a critical basis.

982. Frey, John Andrew. *Motif Symbolism in the Disciples of Mallarmé*. Washington, D. C.: Catholic University of America Press, 1969. xix, 158p.

> A published dissertation (presented in 1957) which investigates the influence of M.'s "motif symbolism" on minor Symbolist poets. Frey defines "motif symbolism" as "a function by which two images of equal value enjoy an interior correspondence, and are so joined as to make the tonality possible only because of their interpenetration and unity."
>
> a) L. J. Austin, *Revue de Littérature Comparée*, 33 (1959), 604.
> b) L. C. Brumig, *Romanic Review*, 50 (1959), 228-229.
> c) R. Champigny, *Modern Language Notes*, 73 (1958), 393-395.
> d) H. Laitenberger, *Zeitschrift für Französische Sprache und Literatur*, 72 (1962), 225-230.
> e) A. G. Lehmann, *French Studies*, 12 (1958), 280-282.
> f) B. A. Morrissette, *Symposium*, 12 (1958), 239-243.

983. Gadoffre, Gilbert. "Mallarmé anarchiste." *Western Canadian Studies in Modern Languages and Literatures*, 1 (1969), 40-43.

> Briefly considers anarchistic elements in M.'s personal philosophy: "Fortement installé sur des positions idéalistes, il nargue le monde extérieur avec autant d'impudence que ses amis activistes narguaient l'Etat bourgeois, parfaitement conscient des pouvoirs destructeurs de sa pensée."

984. Gill, Austin. "An Allegory of Love: Mallarmé's *L'Assaut*." *Australian Journal of French Studies*, 6 (1969), 306-316.

> Discussion of *Le Château de l'Espérance* (whose first title was *L'Assaut*), which the author believes "belongs not to Mallarmé's songs of innocence but to his songs of experience" and is incorrectly classified with the "Poèmes d'enfance et de jeunesse."

985. Girolamo, Nicola di. *Cultura e conscienza critica nell' "Hérodiade" di Mallarmé*. Bologna: Casa Editrice Pàtron, 1969. 313p.

> A complete study of *Hérodiade* concerning its genesis, stages in composition, and importance as a poetic expression of M.'s aesthetic philosophy.
>
> a) W. Hirdt, *Studi Francesi*, 15 (1971), 379-380.
> b) J. Onimus, *Revue des Sciences Humaines*, 36 (1971), 487.

986. Guiraud, P. "L'*Azur* de Mallarmé." In *Essais de stylistique*. Paris: Klincksieck, 1969. 283p.

987. Hatzfeld, H. " 'Sonnet': A la nue accablante...." In *Initiation à l'explication de textes français*. Munich: Hueber, 1969. 191p.

988. Jones, Rhys S. "Mallarmé and Valéry: Imitation or Continuation?" In *Gallica: Essays Presented to Heywood Thomas by Colleagues, Pupils and Friends*. Cardiff: University of Wales Press, 1969. 271p.

> Investigates M.'s influence on Valéry.

989. Laitenberger, Hugo. "Mallarmés Gedicht *Le Tombeau de Charles Baudelaire.*" *Neusprachliche Mitteilungen aus Wissenschaft und Praxis,* 22 (1969), 79-89.

990. Lawler, James R. *The Language of French Symbolism.* Princeton: Princeton University Press, 1969. xi, 270p.

> A study of Mallarmé, Rimbaud, Claudel, Valéry, and Apollinaire. In the first chapter, "Mallarmé and the 'Monstre d'or,'" Lawler examines a significant motif found in *Toast funèbre*: the *monstre d'or,* which he believes "may well be taken not merely as a plastic image but, more especially as a symbol of poetry itself."

991. Lund, Hans Peter. *L'Itinéraire de Mallarmé.* Copenhagen: Akademisk Forlag, 1969. 206p. (*Revue Romane,* Special Issue No. 3, 1969.)

> Explication of M.'s works taken in chronological order of composition tracing the "suite d'une évolution, sinon d'une révolution, de l'attitude existentielle de Mallarmé poète... la manière que Mallarmé a de concevoir la vie." Also contains a useful chronological table of M.'s literary production from 1854 to 1898.
>
> a) M. Olsen, *Revue Romane,* 1 (1970), 138-141.

992. ————. "Les Noces d'Hérodiade, mystère — et résumé de l'œuvre mallarméenne." *Revue Romane,* 4 (1969), 28-50.

> An analysis of this work.

993. Mallarmé, Stéphane. *Correspondance: 1886-1889.* Edited by Henri Mondor and Lloyd James Austin. Paris: Gallimard, 1969. 446p.

> Annotated edition of M.'s correspondence from 2 Jan. 1886 to 20 Dec. 1889. Contains supplemental letters for the periods covered in the previous volumes (700, 855).

994. ————. *Divagations.* Preface by Jacques Schérer and Marcel Bleustein-Blanchet. Paris: Librairie Saint-Germain-des-Prés, 1969. 128p.

995. Mercier, Alain. *Les Sources ésotériques et occultes de la poésie symboliste (1870-1914).* Vol. I: *Le Symbolisme français.* Paris: Editions A. G. Nizet, 1969. 286p.

In a section on M., Mercier studies the difficult problem of the poet's association with the esoteric tradition. Instead of attempting to prove that M. was a practicing "adept," the author follows "avec attention ses idées et ses sources d'inspiration qui recoupent souvent — sur le plan poétique évidemment — les conceptions de l'ésotérisme traditionnel.

996. Missac, Pierre. "Stéphane Mallarmé et Walter Benjamin." *Revue de Littérature Comparée,* 43 (1969), 233-247.

Discusses M.'s influence on Benjamin.

997. Müller, Armand. *De Rabelais à Paul Valéry: les grands écrivains devant le christianisme.* Preface by Pierre Moreau. Paris: R. Foulon et Cie, Imprimeurs, 1969. v, 277p.

In a brief chapter, considers M.'s attitude toward religion, specifically Catholicism. Concludes that M. "s'arrête à l'angoisse et à la chute, et il refuse Dieu, quitte à conserver l'absolu."

998. Naumann, Walter. "Deutung eines Gedichts von Mallarmé." In *Französische Literatur von Beaumarchais bis Camus: Interpretationen.* Edited by Dieter Steland. Hamburg: Fischer Bücherei, 1969. 350p.

Interpretation of "A la nue accablante tu...."

999. Piselli, Francesco. *Mallarmé e l'estetica.* Milan: U. Mursia, 1969. 299p.

A study of M.'s aesthetic philosophy considering in detail its genesis, transitional period, and maturation.

1000. Posani, Giampiero. "Mallarmé: la morte di Hèrodiade e di dio." *Saggi e Ricerche di Letteratura Francese,* 10.

Exegesis of *Ouverture ancienne d'Hérodiade.*

1001. Rottenberg, Pierre. "Une lecture d'*Igitur.*" *Tel Quel,* No. 37 (1969), pp. 74-94.

1002. Rousselot, Jean. *Mort ou survie du langage.* Paris: Sodi, 1969. 277p.

Contains "L'impasse de Mallarmé."

1003.   Sagnes, Guy. *L'Ennui dans la littérature française de Flaubert à Laforgue (1848-1884).* Paris: Librairie Armand Colin, 1969. 513p.

> Contains a section on M.'s *ennui* and its original form of expression in his poetry. Concludes that "Mallarmé a intellectualisé l'ennui."

1004.   Scales, Derek P. *Aldous Huxley and French literature.* Sydney: Sydney University Press, 1969. 94p.

> Pp. 48-50 discuss M.'s influence upon Huxley.

1005.   St. Aubyn, Frederic Chase. *Stéphane Mallarmé.* New York: Twayne Publishers, Inc., 1969. 175p.

> A good introductory text. Because of its necessarily limited format, this volume is not a comprehensive study of M. and his works, but offers analysis of many poems, including *Igitur* and *Un Coup de dés*, as well as a useful *précis* of the development of M.'s poetic concepts, a chronology, and a basic critical bibliography.
> a) H. M. Block, *French Review*, 45 (1971), 255-256.
> b) H. A. Grubbs, *Modern Language Journal*, 54 (1970), 142-143.

1006.   Sartre, Jean-Paul. "Mallarmé (1842-1898)." *Quarterly Review of Literature*, 16 (1969), 488-495.

> English translation of the Preface to the Gallimard edition of M.'s *Poésies* (885). An existentialist interpretation.

1007.   Serstevens, Albert t'. *Escales parmi les livres.* Paris: Nouvelles Editions Latines, 1969. 239p.

> Contains a chapter on M.

1008.   Shroder, Maurice Z. "The Satyr and the Faun: A Definition of Romanticism." *Symposium*, 23 (1969), 346-353.

> Compares the Faun of *L'Après-midi d'un faune* and the Satyr of Hugo's *Le Satyre* and discusses their significance as literary symbols: "...if we juxtapose the songs they sing, we find that the Satyr and the Faun conduct an imaginary dialogue on the nature of art, the relation of art to reality, and the artist's approach to the world." (Cf. 919.)

1009. Smith, Albert B. "Gautier and Mallarmé: An Unnoticed Parallel." *Romance Notes,* 10 (1968-69), 249-252.

> Compares Gautier's *Arria Marcella* (1852) and M.'s "Mes bouquins refermés sur le nom de Paphos. . . ."

1010. Strmeñ, Karol. "Stéphane Mallarmé sedem básní." *Slovenské Pohľady,* 85 (1969), 92-100.

1011. Swift, Bernard. "Mallarmé and the Novel." In *Modern Miscellany Presented to Eugène Vinaver by Pupils, Colleagues and Friends.* Edited by T. E. Lawrenson, F. E. Sutcliffe, and G. F. A. Gadoffre. Manchester: Manchester University Press, 1969. xiii, 314p.

> Indicates M.'s opinions on the novel, which were generally unfavorable: "Mallarmé considered the novel to be an overtly figurative art form, the objects being normally contemporary, and language and style constituting simply the substance of figuration."

1012. Theisen, Josef. "Endzeit des Buches? Betrachtungen zu Mallarmés Livre." *Neueren Sprachen,* 18 (1969), 365-372.

> Concerns M.'s conception of "the Book" and its philosophical significance.

1013. Vidrine, D. R. "The Theme of Sterility in the Poetry of Mallarmé: Its Development and Evolution." *Dissertation Abstracts,* 29 (1968-69), 618A-619A.

1014. Welch, Liliane. "Mallarmé: A New Concept of Poetry." *Dalhousie Review,* 48 (1968-69), 523-529.

> A reconsideration of M.'s writings in order to "prepare the way for some insight into a new concept of poetry for us today."

1015. Williams, Thomas A. "Negation and Affirmation in Mallarmé." *Romance Notes,* 10 (1968-69), 247-248.

> Williams uses Rudolph Otto's *The Idea of the Holy* as a basis for understanding M.'s paradoxical pairings of negation and affirmation in his poetry.

1970

1016. Abastado, Claude. *Expérience et théorie de la création poé-tique chez Mallarmé.* Paris: Lettres Modernes, 1970. 64p.

> Discusses M.'s creative theory and practice: "Plus systemátique qu'Edgar Poe, plus hardi que Baudelaire, plus patient que Rimbaud, Mallarmé posa le problème de l'ecriture dans toute son ampleur et sa rigueur.... Abordant l'acte créateur sous l'angle linguistique, il tenta de trouver la formule algébrique du poème."

1017. Austin, L. J. "Mallarmé et le mythe d'Orphée." *Cahiers de l'Association Internationale des Etudes Françaises,* 22 (1970), 169-180, 300-302.

> Considers M.'s relationship to the Orphic tradition in poetry.

1018. Bachelard, Gaston. *Le Droit de rêver.* Paris: P.U.F., 1970. 250p.

> Contains "La dialectique dynamique de la rêverie mallarméen-ne." States that "un thème mallarméen n'est pas un mystère de l'idée; c'est un miracle de mouvement."

1019. Barbier, Carl Paul, editor. *Documents Stéphane Mallarmé.* Vol. 2. Paris: Librairie Nizet, 1970. 284p.

> See 939.

1020. Benamou, Michel. "Recent French Poetics and the Spirit of Mallarmé." *Contemporary Literature,* 11 (1970), 217-225.

> Concerns contemporary criticism's continuing interest in M. and his literary theories.

1021. Block, Haskell M. "Interpreting Symbolist Poetry." *Comparative Literature Studies,* 7 (1970), 489-503.

> A review-article concerning 900.

1022. Bouvet, Alphonse. "Rhétorique, grammaire et poésie." *Annali dell'Instituto Universitario Orientale di Napoli* (Sezione Romanza), 12 (1970), 35-42.

Explicatory notes concerning "Le vierge, le vivace et le bel aujourd'hui. . . ."

1023. Burnshaw, Stanley. "Many Meanings and One?" *Sewanee Review*, 78 (1970), 383-389.

Review-article concerning 846.

1024. Chisholm, A. R. "Two Notes on Mallarmé." *Essays in French Literature*, No. 7 (1970), 33-37.

Concerns *Feuillet d'Album* and the first seven lines of *Le Tombeau d'Edgar Poe*.

1025. Clive, H. P. "Oscar Wilde's First Meeting with Mallarmé." *French Studies*, 24 (1970), 145-149.

Questions Eileen Souffrin's dating of Wilde's visit with M. (see 707). Indicates 3 Nov. 1891 as the correct date.

1026. Cohn, Robert Greer. "Keats and Mallarmé." *Comparative Literature Studies*, 7 (1970), 193-203.

Suggests probable influences on M. from Keats's works, notably *Sleep and Poetry* and *Endymion*.

1027. ———. "Proust and Mallarmé." *French Studies*, 24 (1970), 262-275.

Investigates "the concrete artistic relationship" between Proust and M.

1028. Contini, Gianfranco. *Varianti e altra linguistica: una raccolta di saggi (1938-1968)*. Turin: Giulio Einaudi Editore, 1970. viii, 686p.

Contains "Sulla trasformazione dell' 'Après-midi d'un faune,' " a study of this poem and its progressive stages of composition.

1029. Derrida, Jacques. "La double séance." *Tel Quel*, No. 41 (1970), pp. 3-43; No. 42 (1970), pp. 3-45.

Discusses M.'s theory and practice of literature.

1030. Epstein, Edna Selan. "*Hérodiade*: la dialectique de l'identité humaine et de la création poétique." *Revue des Sciences Humaines*, Nos. 137-140 (1970), pp. 579-592.

Discussion of *Les Noces d'Hérodiade*.

1031. Fullwood, Daphne. "The Influence on W. B. Yeats of Some French Poets (Mallarmé, Verlaine, Claudel)." *Southern Review* (Baton Rouge), 6 (1970), 356-379.

Concerning the influence of M., mentions particularly *Hérodiade*.

1032. Grassi, Ernesto. "Der Tod Gottes: Zu einer These von Mallarmé." In *Das Altertum und jedes neue Gute für Wolfgang Schadewaldt zum 15. März 1970*. Edited by Konrad Gaiser. Stuttgart: Verlag W. Kohlhammer, 1970. 560p.

A study of M.'s personal philosophy (pp. 195-214).

1033. Haas, Doris. *Fluch aus der Wirklichkeit: Thematik und sprachliche Gestaltung in Werk Stéphane Mallarmés*. Bonn: Romanische Seminar der Universität Bonn, 1970. 166p.

A philosophical study concerning M.'s conception of reality and his various attempts to escape from reality in his poetry indicated by certain recurring themes (reminiscence, dream, absence, death, nothingness) and by his frequent use of periphrasis, which the author calls "flight from linguistic reality."

1034. Kirsop, Wallace. " 'The Greatest Renewal, the Greatest Revelation': Brennan's Commentary on Mallarmé." *Meanjin*, 29 (1970), 303-311.

Concerns Brennan's personal observations and commentaries on M. collected and published in the Chisholm and Quinn edition of *The Prose of Christopher Brennan* (Angus & Robertson, 1962).

1035. La Rochefoucauld, Edmée de. *Courts métrages*. Paris: Grasset, 1970. 212p.

Contains a chapter on M.

1036. Lawler, James R. "Saint Mallarmé." *Yale French Studies,* No. 44 (1970), pp. 185-198.

Discusses M.'s influence on Valéry.

1037. Lousigrand, Jean. *De Lucrèce à Camus: littérature et philosophie comme réflexion sur l'homme.* Paris: Didier, 1970. 328p.

Contains "L'angoisse de l'artiste: Mallarmé."

1038. McLendon, Will L. "A New Reading of Mallarmé's *Pitre châtié.*" *Symposium,* 24 (1970), 36-43.

1039. Mehlman, Jeffrey. "Entre psychanalyse et psychocritique." *Poétique,* No. 3 (1970), pp. 365-385.

Includes a discussion of Mauron's psychocritical studies of M.

1040. Neumann, Gerhard. "Di 'Absolute' Metapher: Ein Abgrezungsversuch am Beispiel Stéphane Mallarmés und Paul Celans." *Poetica* 3 (1970), 188-225.

A stylistic study on M.'s use of metaphor. Includes a discussion of *Autre Eventail de Mademoiselle Mallarmé.*

1041. Paz, Octavio. "Stéphane Mallarmé: 'Sonnet en yx.' " *Delos,* No. 4 (1970), pp. 15-28.

Discussion of "Ses purs ongles. . . ."

1042. Pestalozzi, Karl. "Mallarmé: *Autre Éventail de Mademoiselle Mallarmé.*" In *Die Entstehung des lyrischen Ich: Studien zum Motiv der Erhebung in der Lyrik.* Berlin: de Gruyter, 1970. xiii, 364p.

1043. Porter, Laurence M. "Vigny's Influence on Mallarmé's Early Poetry." *Romance Notes,* 11 (1969-70), 536-538.

Notes influence of Vigny's poems, such as *Le Bain, La Fille de Jephté,* and *Dolorida,* upon M.'s *juvenilia.*

1044. Usinger, Fritz. *Dichtung als Information: von der Morphologie zur Kosmologie.* Mainz: Hase und Koehler, 1970. 294p.

Contains "Das Geheimnis der Dichtung Mallarmé's" (pp. 227-235).

1045. Verdin, Simone. "La triple voie." *Cahiers Internationaux de Symbolisme*, Nos. 19-20 (1970), pp. 63-76.

Include a discussion of rhythmical structures, particularly "spirals," in M.'s works.

1046. Wais, Kurt, editor. *Interpretationen französischer Gedichte*. Darmstadt: Wissenschaftliche Buchgesellschaft, 1970. xxii, 415p.

Contains interpretations of *Le Tombeau de Charles Baudelaire* (by Jean Pommier), *L'Après-midi d'un faune* (by Antoine Adam), and *Brise Marine* (by Hellmuth Petriconi).

1047. Walzer, P. O. *La Révolution des Sept*. Neuchâtel: A la Baconnière, 1970. 68p.

Study of Lautréamont, M., Rimbaud, Corbière, Cros, Nouveau, and Laforgue as participants in the "poetic revolution" of the late nineteenth century.

1048. Williams, Thomas A. *Mallarmé and the Language of Mysticism*. Athens: University of Georgia Press, 1970. xi, 99p.

Interprets M. and his work in terms of the mystic tradition in Western thought, considering not only Christian mysticism, but the esoteric philosophies of the Cabala and Hermetic alchemy as well as the thinking of modern students of mysticism, such as Aldous Huxley, William James, and C. G. Jung. Includes exegesis of M.'s most difficult writings from this point of view (*L'Après-midi d'un faune*, *Igitur*, *Hérodiade*, and *Un Coup de dés*).
a) R. G. Cohn, *Romanic Review*, 63 (1972), 313.
b) ———, *Revue d'Histoire Littéraire de la France*, 73 (1973), 920.
c) H. A. Grubbs, *French Review*, 45 (1971-72), 256.
d) D. J. Mossop, *French Studies*, 27 (1973), 91-92.
e) L. Somville, *Etudes Littéraires*, 4 (1971), 242-244.

1049. ———. "Mallarmé's *Un Coup de dés* as Myth." *South Atlantic Bulletin*, 35 (1970), 24-25.

Abstract of a paper, read during the 1969 meeting of SAMLA, in which author demonstrates that "the larger structure and content of *Un Coup de dés* is the same as that of the most ancient and most widespread cosmogonic and eschatological myth."

1050. Zuckerkandl, Frédéric. "L''absent' chez Mallarmé." *Synthèses,* 25, No. 285 (1970), 20-25.

> Investigates M.'s use of "absence" as a poetic theme and discusses its symbolic significance.

1971

1051. Barbier, Carl Paul, editor. *Documents Stéphane Mallarmé.* Vol. 3. Paris: Librairie Nizet, 1971. 367p.

> See 939, 1019.

1052. Brie, Hartmut. "Mallarmés Verhältnis zur Wortstruktur und seine Technik des Negationsprozesses." *Neueren Sprachen,* 20 (1971), 380-384.

> Discusses M.'s personal philosophy and its relationship to his poetic method.

1053. Cannon, Margaret Hart. "The Sole Survivor: A Romantic Motif." *Dissertation Abstracts,* 31 (1971), 6004A-6005A.

> Contains a chapter concerning the "Maître" of *Un Coup de dés.*

1054. Chadwick, Charles. *Symbolism.* London: Methuen and Co., Ltd., 1971. viii, 71p.

> In a brief chapter, "Mallarmé and the infinite," states concisely M.'s aesthetic principles and offers commentary on "Ses purs ongles ...," "La Chevelure," and *Un Coup de dés.*

1055. Cohn, Robert Greer. "Mallarmé and the Greeks." In *The Persistent Voice: Essays on Hellenism in French Literature Since the 18th Century in Honor of Professor Henri M. Peyre.* Edited by Walter G. Langlois. New York: New York University Press, 1971. 217p.

> Investigates "interesting vestiges of the Hellenic tradition" found throughout M.'s works, including his earliest poetry and prose, critical writings, *Les Dieux antiques,* and *Les Mots anglais.*

1056. Edwin, John Francis. "Mallarmé and Claudel: An Intellectual Encounter." *Dissertation Abstracts*, 32 (1971), 426A.

1057. Gill, Austin. *Mallarmé's Poem "La chevelure vol d'une flamme...."* Glasgow: University of Glasgow Press, 1971. 27p.

    a) A. R. Chisholm, *AUMLA*, 38 (1972), 245.

1058. Howarth, W. D., and C. L. Walton. *Explications: The Technique of French Literary Appreciation.* London: Oxford University Press, 1971. xlvii, 270p.

    Contains an explication of "Victorieusement fui le suicide beau...."

1059. Joseph, Lawrence A. "Coco Barroil et la 'Prose pour Cazalis' de Mallarmé." *Revue des Sciences Humaines*, Nos. 141-144 (1971), pp. 545-556.

    A discussion of the above poem found in the "Vers de circonstance." Identifies "Coco Barroil" as Fernand Barroil (1846-1922), a friend of Cazalis.

1060. Judrin, Roger. "Stéphane Mallarmé." *Nouvelle Revue Française*, No. 220 (1971), pp. 67-77.

    General commentary on M. (written for the *Encyclopedia Universalis*).

1061. Kromer, Gretchen. "The Redoutable PTYX." *Modern Language Notes*, 86 (1971), 563-572.

    A detailed discussion treating the derivation and meaning of the word *ptyx* found in "Ses purs ongles...."

1062. Linkhorn, Renée. "Les Fenêtres: Propos sur trois poèmes." *French Review*, 44 (1970-71), 513-522.

    Compares the three poems with this title by M., Baudelaire, and Apollinaire.

1063. Magny, Claude-Edmonde. *Littérature et critique.* Paris: Payot, 1971. 453p.

    Contains "Le Ramage et le plumage," a general discussion of M.'s aesthetics and personal philosophy.

1064. Mossop, D. J. *Pure Poetry: Studies in French Poetic Theory and Practice, 1745 to 1945*. Oxford: Clarendon Press, 1971. xviii, 264p.

> Contains a study of M.'s theory, giving careful consideration to its evolution. Concludes that "despite the aesthetic common factor, the kind of pure poetry to which Mallarmé was led by his search for metaphysical purity was substantially different from that which he wrote earlier in his career.... Emotion is certainly present in this pure poetry but is subordinated to the intellectual abstraction, and is by the same token less personal."

1065. Noulet, Emilie. *Le Ton poétique*. Paris: Librairie José Corti, 1971. 269p.

> Contains a brief chapter on M. analyzing the phonetic aspects of "Toute l'âme résumée...," but concludes that M. became, toward the end of his poetic career, more interested in the visual, typographic aspects of poetry: "Il inventa cette extraordinaire utilisation typographique à laquelle nous sommes habitués maintenant grâce à lui, mais qui reste une hardiesse littéraire."

1066. Oxenhandler, Neal. "The Quest for Pure Consciousness in Husserl and Mallarmé." In *The Quest for Imagination: Essays in Twentieth-Century Criticism*. Edited by O. B. Hardison, Jr. Cleveland: Press of the Case Western Reserve University, 1971. xiv, 286p.

> A comparative study of Edmund Husserl and M. "as adventurers of spirit who at once define the limits of our condition for us and choose as their destiny the pushing back of those limits toward the horizon."

1067. Pelletier, Anne-Marie. "Langage et fonction poétique: application à la syntaxe de la poésie de Mallarmé." Dissertation. Paris, 1971.

1068. Polieri, Jacques. *Scénographie, sémiographie*. Paris: Denoël-Gonthier, 1971. 248p.

> Includes a discussion, accompanied by detailed drawings and diagrams, of a possible scenographic realization of M.'s "Book."

1069. Richardson, Barbara A. "Mallarmé's *Prose pour des Esseintes*." *Romance Notes*, 12 (1970-71), 87-92.

1070. Schleicher, Helmut. "Die Struktur der 'Tombeaux' von Mallarmé." Dissertation. Cologne, 1971.

1071. Smith, Harold Jeffrey. "Mallarmé's Dramatic Lyric." *Dissertation Abstracts*, 31 (1970-71), 1813A-1814A.

1072. Smith, Madeleine Marion. "Mallarmé's 'Grimoire': The Formative Phase of a Poet's Life with Special Reference to Baudelaire." *Dissertation Abstracts*, 31 (1970-71), 1295A.

1073. Strauss, Walter A. *Descent and Return: The Orphic Theme in Modern Literature.* Cambridge: Harvard University Press, 1971. viii, 287p.

> In an extensive chapter entitled "Mallarmé: Orpheus and the Néant," discusses M.'s place within the Orphic tradition in poetry and explicates much of M.'s poetry in terms of the modern conception of the Orphic myth. Believes that M's philosophical "process of annihilation and nihilation... are new categories, applied to the idea of the Orphic descent that is now not so much an attempt to recover Eurydice as it is to recover a new sense of being, through which poetic vision and the power of song and the integrity of being are redeemed."

1074. Tiedemann-Bartels, Hella. *Versuch über das artistische Gedicht.* Munich: Rogner und Berhard, 1971. 159p.

> A study of the poetry of Charles Baudelaire, Stefan George, and M. Offers an analysis of the "Ouverture ancienne" of *Hérodiade* taking into special consideration the emendations of the manuscript.

1075. Verdin, Simone. "Mallarmé et Joyce, somptuosités vitales et magnifique veille de la pensée." *Courrier du Centre International d'Etudes Poétiques*, No. 84 (1971), pp. 17-28.

> A comparative study. States that "révolutionnaires écrivains les plus scrupuleux de la signification, Mallarmé et Joyce opèrent avec la même foi fanatique en la forme."

1076. ———. "*Un Coup de dés*, l'orgue et la danse." *Courrier du Centre International d'Etudes Poétiques*, No. 84 (1971), pp. 3-15.

> Exegesis.

1077. Verhoeff, J. P. "Anciens et modernes devant la *Prose pour des Esseintes*: un examen critique de quelques interprétations." *Revue d'Histoire Littéraire de la France*, 71 (1971), 226-246.

> A critical appraisal of interpretations by Austin, Chadwick, Poulet, Richard, and several others. Poulet's interpretation occupies a central place in the discussion.

III. INDEX OF AUTHORS, EDITORS OF CRITICAL EDITIONS, AND TRANSLATORS

(References are to entry numbers)

IV. SUBJECT INDEX

(References are to entry numbers)